The Porch

The Porch

Meditations on the Edge of Nature

Charlie Hailey

The University of Chicago Press

Chicago and London

The University of Chicago Press, Chicago 60637
The University of Chicago Press, Ltd., London
© 2021 by The University of Chicago
Published 2021
Printed in the United States of America

30 29 28 27 26 25 24 23 22 21   1 2 3 4 5

ISBN-13: 978-0-226-76995-0 (cloth)
ISBN-13: 978-0-226-77001-7 (e-book)
DOI: https://doi.org/10.7208/chicago/9780226770017.001.0001

Library of Congress Cataloging-in-Publication Data

Names: Hailey, Charlie, 1970– author.
Title: The porch : meditations on the edge of nature / Charlie Hailey.
Description: Chicago : University of Chicago Press, 2021. | Includes
    bibliographical references and index.
Identifiers: LCCN 2020036203 | ISBN 9780226769950 (cloth) | ISBN
    9780226770017 (ebook)
Subjects: LCSH: Porches.
Classification: LCC NA7125 .H35 2021 | DDC 721/.84—dc23
LC record available at https://lccn.loc.gov/2020036203

♾ This paper meets the requirements of ANSI/NISO Z39.48-1992
(Permanence of Paper).

In memory of my father

Contents

1

PORCH

A manatee's breath drifts across the porch screen. It is a sound so delicate yet insistent that I stop breathing. I count time in the rings of smoothed water that drift with the river's current toward the ocean. I listen for the next breath but this manatee is moving fast, and its footprints blend back into the burnished roll and flicker of the river that holds its own breath between tides. The manatees are on the move this January day as Florida warms after a cold snap. What we call fire weather is what most other parts of the country think of as winter, but manatees know the subtle changes of the lower subtropics. They feel the air through water, like we feel it in porches.

That was the fourth manatee I've heard in the past hour. The extraordinary can become routine, but it never gets old. Set back from the river, we don't always see them, except when we catch a black snout sending out its wake like a skidding duck or a piece of driftwood plowing the current, and except that time when a mother came into our lagoon with her calves—the littlest looked like a puppy. There's another one, louder, closer, but on a porch earshot isn't necessarily eyeshot. It rained last night, and the cedars drip like metronomes. A kingfisher calls, far enough away to mix with the gentle lapping of breeze and river on limestone. It is quiet today, but it feels like anything can happen. I hear my own breath again, waiting.

This porch where I write will soon be underwater. For seven decades it rode hurricanes and winter storms. In another seven, the sea will cover the boards where three layers of flaking paint sandpaper my bare feet. We do not complain about this reality, neither the porch's vulnerability nor the paint's inconstancy. In a position both privileged and ill-advised, I sit here by choice, aware of what's coming and what's at stake, saturated by a knowledge of this place and its climate—one that is constantly and dramatically changing. Here, on the porch, theory meets practice. There's the idea of a changing climate, and then there's actually witnessing its effect. Here on a porch, the unseen is inescapable, like the manatee. And the mullet who just splashed in the brackish water taut with low tide. I didn't see the fish, but I heard the dazed flump of reentry into a river saltier than it was last year, and now watch the ripples widen from this joyful leap.

In our time here, the porch's floor has been inundated once, and nearly a second time. A fragile wrack line still clings to the porch's concrete pile, just below the wood framing of its floor. The flecks of cedar needles, tiny bits of shell and soil, left there from this fall's hurricane, seem trivial compared to what happened up north in Mexico Beach, but it's all part of the same thing, this living on the coast, which is really living *in* the coast, deeply embedded in the littoral. Not fixed in place, but held adrift between tides, floating. Like all the things that

Hurricane Hermine and her seven-foot storm surge set afloat in our porch and its cabin, four years ago.

When we took the boat out to the cabin the next day, the tannin-stained water was still lapping onto the porch. When my son and I stepped up onto the porch, we walked into a washing machine that had just finished its cycle, one set for heavy soil and turgid water moving this way and that. Even though no doors were ajar or windows broken, it was like someone had ransacked the place, leaving it turned in on itself. Like nature was trying to find us, trying to send a message.

When I walk out on the porch now, I instinctively check the water for signs of change. I watch and hold my breath. I am teaching myself to sit on a porch. I am learning to read what's around me. Checking for sign, I scan the water. Floating.

This is a book about the porch. It is a book about a specific porch, this one. It is also about the idea of porch. But since porches are inseparable from their environment, this is also a book about place. This porch is on a river along the coast of the Gulf of Mexico. A modest piece of architecture in a remarkable estuary. If you float the Homosassa River, you might see it off your starboard side just beyond markers 62 and 63, where the inlet of the lagoon pries open stone and forest. Here, water far exceeds solid ground. Insects love that saturated earth, so the porch is screened. It has eight columns and a sloped floor. It fronts onto a river, not a street. No mail comes here, but the power company reads the meter from a skiff once a month. This porch and its idiosyncrasies have been here for more than seventy years, but they might not last another seven.

This old porch holds clues for the near future. It is anachronistic and exceedingly contemporary at once. This book celebrates the porch, but it does not advocate a return to the past. It draws on porch's deep histories, but it is not a history of porches. Nor does it serve as a scientific treatise on climate change. It is a call to action but a reflective one, built on the humanity and nature of porches. Porches witnessed climatic change long before we were aware of climate change as a crisis. They occupy a timeline that folds back on itself, caught between past, present, and future.

An architect, I am fascinated with how porches are built, how they function, and what their built form means. Building a porch taps into the timeless, elemental lessons of archetypes like Marc-Antoine Laugier's hut, Henry David Thoreau's cabin, and Gottfried Semper's origins of architecture in mound, hearth, enclosure, and roof. A porch must also negotiate equally fundamental *edges* of architecture, where experience tempers essence and building yields to nature.

I think there are four core elements to thinking about a porch, each carrying porch's essence and paradox: tilt, air, screen, and blue. *Tilt* works from the basic premise that slope yields balance. *Air* mixes freshness with conditioning and public with private. *Screen* maintains openness with enclosure. *Blue* makes the invisible visible and finds intersections of the actual and the imagined. These four elements demonstrate the fundamental nature of the porch to our humanity, as they also build a case for the porch as an indispensable site to feel, understand, and address climate and its changes. As a whole, they tell a story of dwelling and home, resilience and acclimation.

These elements do not build an ideal porch, but one that

is instead quite messy. Like the edges of a porch, the boundaries between them are porous, just like screens admit air and a tilted floor reflects the blue paint of a ceiling. Like a conversation on the porch, each element's stories intertwine, and follow tangents that eventually circle back home. Put another way, the Homosassa porch is a central voice that invites others to join the telling. It gathers their stories, recollecting the past, capturing the present, and looking to the future. It is my hope that the porch built here, with its four elements, demonstrates how other porches can serve as muse, structure, and method for tuning us to a rapidly changing climate.

Porches embrace exposure, but a porch along a river near the coast is particularly vulnerable, so this is also a book about openness to climate, people, wildlife, and ideas. Porches heighten senses and instill a sense of wonder. The gratification they bring—the joys of sitting, watching, waiting, talking, creating—requires change. A porch is an extraordinary vehicle for becoming sensitive to variations, large and small, and to reflect deeply on them. A porch welds experience to idea like nowhere else.

A porch is a bellwether, and the chimes that hang from the robin's egg blue ceiling above my head are rattling with more than just the cooling breeze. But even in this sobering context, the porch is a place of contentment, and its inherent capacity to adjust to change provides an indispensable site for us to engage the climate we have made, here on catastrophe's threshold.

*
* *

The porch and its cabin were built in 1950, one of the first on the Homosassa River. Here, amid the river's latticed marriage with the gulf, the fishing is good, so good that Winslow Homer, Grover Cleveland, Thomas Edison, and John Jacob Astor all came looking for redfish, trout, and tarpon. Howard T. Odum, pioneer of systems ecology, also came here to study the river's head springs and its "marine invasion" of fish and crabs. At the time the cabin was being built, there were thirty-four different fish, sixteen of them marine species, in the springs. The redfish, trout, and tarpon were joined by sharks, sting rays, catfish, needlefish, killifish, sheepshead, snook, mangrove snapper, schoolmasters, pinfish, remora, jack crevalle, and blue crab. The snook's presence there in particular was a mystery—a "curious problem." The snook's traditional range was farther south. They had not been caught in the river and had not been observed running to or from its mouth. What were they doing here?

Chasing salinity, as it turns out. They and the other species plied nine miles of brackish river water all the way to the head springs, in such numbers that engineers were known to stop their trains to cast a line into the "fish bowl." Odum called it a "very peculiar environment" because the rich bounty foretold the slow, emergent but insistent, saltwater intrusion than now transforms more than just the fisheries. The spring's salinity and constant temperature—seventy-two degrees, even in winter—were portents of what the rest of the river would become.

Yesterday, within sight of the porch, along a muddy cove where the tidal marsh melts into the river, I caught a twenty-three-inch snook. They're now almost as common here as catfish, and twenty-three inches doesn't rate much mention.

Later, on the porch, listening for manatees, I think the river has become the outdoor laboratory envisioned by those mid-century marine biologists. The habitat they saw as "notoriously rigorous" with "shocking and formidable conditions" now describes not just the estuary itself, but the radical change at work in it.

Today, Homosassa's fishing reputation remains, though it is quiet by Florida standards. The river can fill with activity on weekends and during scallop season in the summer. Seventy miles west of Disney, this region is an actually magical place. At the lower swing of Florida's Big Bend, it's known as the Springs Coast, and the Homosassa is one of four rivers made from first magnitude freshwater springs. Manatees shuttle between the gulf's variations and the springs' constant seventy-two degrees. The waterway is a highway of temperature change.

Our cabin's official address is 13459 The Homosassa River. No roads reach the cabin, and the river is our street. On the coast, mainland residents can see an early indicator of sea level rise when a flooded road prevents access to their houses. But our porch, boat access only, is already one step closer to what the rise portends. We have already stranded ourselves.

Land and water are relative terms here. Where one starts and the other stops changes every day, every hour, every minute. If pressed, we could say the cabin is halfway between land and water, halfway between the mainland and the gulf. Our car is two and a half miles away, the same distance that our pontoon travels to reach the open water, along the Homosassa's winding channel. I call it a channel because the Coast Guard marks it with buoys and a few fixed posts. But the metal shafts rust through at their water lines, the floating drums drag with flood tides and storms, and oysters build new shoals on wayward crab traps, haunting the channels as ghost traps. The marked channel is unreliable, and the Homosassa can be treacherous, even for boaters who know it, like the sheriff, who once bumped the bottom twice in a low winter tide at the Hell Gate narrows, where my son and I were gathering boat propellers. The town of Homosassa used to close that pass at night with actual gates. From our porch, we hear skegs, props, and even the whole lower units of motors grind across oyster bars and limestone. When the shrimp boats gear down, they are passing those narrow gates of hell.

Homosassa isn't Venice, the cabin is no palazzo, and our pontoon—except when we pole it over mud flats in winter—has no kinship with gondolas, but we feel a connection to a place where daily life's reliance on water has put it at risk. Those islands are subsiding as the water rises, tourists ride outsized vessels whose wake threatens fragile shores, and, like Venetians entering their palazzos from rear canals, we turn the pontoon off the Homosassa and head up a creek to the back dock that is our entrance. That dock connects to a raised wooden walk that takes us up to the back door. When high waters bring the sea across the ground and under our cabin, it is *acqua alta* and I think of the elevated walkways put out across Venice.

A wooden sign above the back door greets you: Welcome Aboard. This cabin is floating, and if it were a ship, the porch would be at its prow, looking out on the river. Sometimes in a storm, the porch feels more like a crow's nest, rising, falling, tilting on high seas. The cabin sits back from the river enough that boaters catch only fleeting views. Cedars and oaks arch over a small lagoon that connects with the river through a break in the limestone bank. Behind the lagoon's dock, the gray paint of the board and batten matches the patina of the aluminum roof. The screened porch covers the width of the original cabin, and an open deck to its side fronts an addition from the 1980s. The shadow-dark screens of the porch push the cabin even deeper into the trees, plunged into a forest girded by water.

Rain plays the metal roof like a drum, and the gutters feed two cisterns that weigh fifteen thousand pounds when full. Sometimes I think about that weight pressing down on the island, a lot of ballast for an already loaded vessel. But sitting on the porch during a rainstorm, it's easy to think about other things. Rain on metal is a gift of opposites, both restful and rousing. I imagine it as the sound of ancient Greek drums, the ones that look like tambourines but are closed on both sides. Two-sided drums, their skins are close together like the aluminum stretched over the cabin's original metal roof, rusting underneath. When it rains, the air in between sizzles and resonates.

Sitting on the porch under a bacchic beat, I think about how tympanum—*tympanon* in Greek—used to mean drum but is now an ear's membrane and, in architecture, a recessed panel in a church portal. A porch to the church's nave, it is a place where sculptures echo the footfalls of parishioners. Stepping and stooping and stumbling. Drops of rain on a porch roof. Today when I opened the screen door and stepped out from the porch onto the deck, I looked up to the gutter and saw the leaf of a wild staghorn fern growing out of the rich soil of oak leaves, cedar needles, and raccoon droppings that had collected. Its green frond waved to the cloudless sky.

The porch brings a bit of order to the entropy of this landscape that is flooding, eroding, and sinking. Its islands are lacework. Its sinks and rivulets are scoured by rain, tide, and storm. The land looks the same from above at five feet or five thousand. A piece of broken limestone from along the river is a topographic map—a carved and crumbling chart of the whole region, built on rocky sponge geologists call drowned karst, defined by the way brackish water engorges and habitually floods this porous limestone. Our cabin swims in it. But the porch is a rectangle, a finite geometric figure on a fractal coastline. It measures exactly 118 inches deep and 236 inches wide. A ratio of one to two, about ten feet by twenty feet. The porch is two perfect squares clinging to the side of what had been a one-room cabin, which is also a square, twenty feet by twenty feet. That degree of precision is surprising out where foundations sink, walls list, rust dances, and mildew blossoms. I had to check those numbers twice.

The Homosassa porch is simply wood and nails. The framing of the walls is exposed. To sit on the porch is to occupy a fish's skeleton, looking out. Ten posts are ten ribs backboned with a low wall at knee height. Ceiling and floor are plywood skins stretched across a spare, gaunt structure, more cartilage than bone. Between post, rail, and plate is the inner lining of the low wall's board and batten skin. Shadows fill the gaps between wide boards battened on the other side.

The back of the porch is the cabin's outer wall, another skin ribbed with battens. In places, thick sap of heart pine bleeds out of the boards. The battens are strips of cedar, furry like the bark of the trees all around the cabin. Where the rough-cut wood is more closely shorn, it has the sandpaper texture of a shark. The pine wall boards vary in width, but the rest of the lumber has standard dimensions—one by two for the battens, four by four for the posts, two by four for the rails and plates that ride the outer edge of the floor.

The simple construction is a reminder that you're outside. The open frame might feel unfinished. Its play between in and out might be read as trickery, a Klein bottle of impossible space. But from inside the porch, its outer mien is one of wholeness and honesty. The porch confesses its making, and it resides truthfully between inside and outside. Its most recent coat of paint is a gray that has aged like a stain, melting into the wood and its grain. The floor is scuffed. Otherwise what you see is trim and tidy. Shipshape. Below deck is a different story.

Slipping beneath the porch, I am an underwater diver. My side and back scuff along a seabed built thousands of years ago, and I face the problem of telling time in a land where the ground is thin and where the upheavals of wind and rain, storms and floods disturb layers and confuse chronologies. Everything subsides, and stratigraphy ruptures. How do you measure time in saturated earth? What if your watch piece is an estuarial porch?

Underneath, I am also a student of myth, a rogue metaphysician. The framing of the porch floor is a mix of rough-cut and dressed lumber, wide two-inch-thick boards and the atrophied, thinner boards of the latter twentieth century. Two by sixes are sistered next to thick heart-pine joists. Randomly notched boards have been added as bridging between joists; some have the signatures of rafters—level cuts and birds mouths. So I think the porch is Theseus' ship. And, for that matter, it's like any old ship that has been maintained.

In this reading, the porch grew in stages. Where it meets

the cabin, the sheathing boards slide below the floor's frame. Painted red, they are white where battens were removed for other construction. It is possible that the porch was added to a one-room cabin. The frame of the floor also hints that the porch might have been a deck without a roof, or it might have been open, without screening. Thick beams run out from the cabin to meet the front beam; its outer face, now hidden behind board and batten siding, is painted with the original red.

How much of the first porch is left? Which parts have been rebuilt from salvaged boards, from lumber delivered on spring tides? This is an exercise in keeping a piece of architecture afloat, substituting, replacing, and shoring. Is this the original porch? That's the question that Aristotle asked of Theseus' ship. I know from other parts of the cabin that maintenance is a salvage operation—a commonplace here on the coast. The ebb and flow of the river offers exchanges. It pries away boards, but it also offers pieces of buildings from upriver and downriver, even from out at sea. I make this flotsam fit into an idiosyncratic program of repairs. Yes, this is the same porch. In fact, because of these disparate parts, it is the essence of porch.

On my way out from under the porch, I study the foundations. The concrete of the footings has been poured across the limestone ground, into its crevices and holes. It fills the spaces where water once sculpted porous stone. A little way up the coast, cement plants harvest and crush this same stone for concrete like this. The foundations under the porch and the older part of the cabin have a smooth reassuring finish, even if they are a little thin. They appear solid compared to those under the newer side. Those foundations spall and crack as the rebar rusts and expands, because whoever laid them up mixed brackish water from the creek with the cement. The ship of the porch rides on cement, lime, and steel, but also on seawater.

There's something else that haunts me. I sit on the porch, and my eye is seven feet above this afternoon's slackening tide, halfway through its cycle. No official measurements were taken here, but locals know Hermine brought a seven-foot storm surge one midnight three years ago. Luckily, it blew in on a strong low tide, and the water marks on the wall panels inside the cabin string a line eighteen inches below my eye. In calm weather like today, that seven feet feels comfortable, even safe. But if a storm like that (barely a category 1, out of five) coincided with today's average mid-tide, then I would be at eye level with the surging water.

Hermine wasn't a direct hit. But there was one in 1950, the year the cabin was built. The first week in September, the hurricane named Easy slammed into the coast twice, what's called a cyclonic loop. Its category 3, one-hundred-twenty-mile-an-hour winds either delayed construction of the cabin or baptized it in more than forty inches of rain that still ranks as the state's highest twenty-four-hour total. The porch and its cabin are already questionable exercises of human will in a constantly changing land, and I have to wonder if the original owners second-guessed their project in the middle of the tempest's two-pronged attack.

But when I learned the origin of the cabin's lagoon, I wasn't so sure. We had speculated that its serene waters originated from a spring, rising between cracks in the limestone, flowing into the river and only recently silting with mud and sand. This coast is stippled with springs and rounded sinks where freshwater wells up. Wouldn't it be great, we thought, to dredge the lagoon and revive the spring? But this lagoon was made by dynamite. Looking at its burnished surface reeling quietly with high winter clouds, it is hard to imagine the blast from sticks of TNT pressed into the honeycombed stone. Our first clue should have been the boulder balancing precariously on the water's edge, but our idealized vision overshadowed any suspicions until the second owner's son paddled into that lagoon one day and recounted its origin story.

On the porch, I've learned not to make assumptions about what unfolds around me—like the approaching sounds of boats and people, or the shifting winds that may or may not bring a midday shower, or our chance meeting with the second owner's son. I do assume that whoever built this cabin and its porch laid the dynamite *before* starting to build. Not just because it would make sense to protect new foundations from shockwaves, and walls and roofs from flying debris, but because the cabin fits the lagoon. There is a subtlety to the cabin's placement in the land, albeit a sensitivity tempered by the violence of the blast. And the porch is at its epicenter, a calm eye amid the wildness of the place and the audacity of living here.

Intention placed this porch. As the first cabin on the island, its builder could freely choose its position—on slightly higher ground over here, near deeper water access there, or under the shade of oaks closer to the hammock of mature trees. But here it is, in a low spot, on its limestone substrate, more pitted than elsewhere. Sit long enough on the porch, study the lines of sight, watch the solstice sun rise at the porch's corner, peer into the clear lens of the lagoon, notice how the air moves throughout the day, marvel at the reflections overhead, and this porch shows that it wants to be here. It looks across the river, up a long creek. On the same axis, behind you, a smaller creek winds through the marsh. This porch pins cabin and lagoon to these vistas; it tethers you to this place.

That lagoon and this porch were planned. Like Claude Monet's pool of lilies, the lagoon is worthy of painting. I have spent hours watching how light changes, shimmers, and corduroys across the tannin-stained fluid. When he planned his garden, Monet laid out a bridge and other vantages on the pool's wonders. I walk to the edge of the porch, and the lagoon is a canvas of floating seagrass, Spanish moss, idling mullet, and dancing water bugs. The lagoon prepares the porch for the river. It is a foreground to the river's middle ground of currents, stipples, and gestures. The far shore and the receding creeks are its background. It is an impressionist's laboratory out here in the gulf where most forgo painting for fishing and hunting (except for Winslow Homer, who did all three). This porch and its cabin might seem anomalous in their careful placement, but to spend time here is to become intimately aware of what this place offers. Whoever made this porch and its cabin knew where to build. And Monet's pool can also be a lagoon that records a coastal microcosm of nature as well as more expansive lessons and insights, as its waters rise and fall and continue to rise.

⁑

A house has its own air. It may hold air like a sealed Ball jar or, if it's one of the old houses I've lived in, breathe air like a torn shirt or split jeans. Airtight or leaky, the walls of a house still protect from weather and the changeable conditions of open air. A porch holds nature's air, and going out on a porch has traditionally offered changes in climate and perspective.

When you step out on a porch now, you board a vessel on a sea of change. As you sit there, time brings shifts in temperature and breezes, the ebb and flow of sounds, drifts of smell, an upwelling of vision. But today, firmly lodged in the Anthropocene where human activity governs, a porch brings other changes as well. Whether you realize it or not, you and your porch are moving. Open to the environment, your porch shifts climatically, while its conditioned house essentially stays put.

I remember reading in *Granta* that the average English garden was effectively moving sixty-six feet south every day, as it warmed. Four and a half miles a year. That was in 2003 when reports fretted about the prospect of a single Celsius degree rise in global temperature. Now we regularly talk about two or three times that—a pace that sets the Northern Hemisphere's porches racing southward. They leave their air-conditioned houses in a wake of energy consumption and hermetic isolation.

Today the Homosassa porch moves south a hundred feet every day. Since we bought the cabin seven years ago, we have effectively moved to Tampa fifty miles away. Current estimates for the next decade send the porch farther south, past Florida's Venice and on to Naples. When the porch arrives at that latitude, north Florida will have become south Florida.

But our porch is also heading west. This part of the Gulf of Mexico is exceedingly flat, and a local rule of thumb says that water depth changes a foot for every mile of distance. Assessments of the rise in the gulf's levels vary, but a conservative estimate of one inch every two years would mean a foot every twenty-four, and would place our porch—towing its cabin with it, since sea level rise happens whether the air conditioner is on or not—in open waters in another seventy years. As dramatic as that might seem, it feels slower than the porch's plunge southward. But when you factor in spring tides and storm surges, we would do well to have half that time.

On its voyage south and west to the tropics and out to sea, our porch passes mangroves and Brazil pepper trees heading north. Red mangroves are moving farther and farther up the coast. They ride the warmer temperatures, making land as fast as it is receding. They don't mind the saltier water, and they have adapted to the sea's rise and fall. As the mangroves move north, they also head east, slowly and methodically inland. Clinging to the river's edge, the mangroves are silent witnesses and respectful ushers as native coastal trees also move inland, away from the salt of rising seas. Their retreat is hurried along by the invasive pepper trees that thrive in the warming temperatures and shove aside red cedars and live oaks that are still alive but declining.

On its westward voyage, the porch also encounters rampikes, trees that have died as saltwater replaces freshwater. Each turn of the river toward the gulf opens a longer vista, bringing more rampikes into view. After Hell Gate, countless palm trunks prick the horizon, a forest of telephone poles. Hammocks of cedars and a few oaks cluster among the palms like so many mourners. Others are solitary, roaming the horizons of marsh grass and mangroves. Their skeletal remains, mostly cedars, some of them ancient, already look like driftwood long staked in the ground.

Moving back and forth between salty gulf and freshwater spring, it becomes clear that the porch occupies the cusp of this transition, this rampike wave, this roll of pepper trees and mangroves, a brackish tipping point between land and sea. The porch floats like driftwood in a slackened tide. Porches wait, and this one, loosely anchored to the limestone of its ancient coral bed, pauses with chain pulled tight, and its ropes straining, as the flukes of its foundations still try to dig in.

And so the porch charts its course. It is a moving vessel on a floodtide of change, yet it tarries in one place. It waits as change approaches. Sit out here for a little while, and you will feel the weather turn. Sit out here for a little longer, and climate change will come to you.

On a porch, you travel without leaving home.

To get my sea legs, I watch a stand of rampikes across the river. Staring. Mesmerized by their silvering patina. Drunk on slowness. Four cedar trees and one palm. They lean east, away from the gulf, hinting at landward winds siphoned up along the river. I somehow feel the smoothness of their trunks polished by the wind. I also feel the roughness on their leeward side where the sun splits and draws their grain. The palm rises above the rest of the stand, a gentle camber through the gnarl and twist of the cedars. They twist mutely in a wash of rain and sun, saturated and dry, dark when soaked and blinding white when dry. On the porch, I read the future in their pose and the weather in their visage.

An osprey lands on top of her familiar palm trunk. Her high-pitched call tells her mate the fish are here. Finger mullet run across the flooded rock, through the mirror image of the rampike stand. She waits patiently, and her presence might have the dread of a raven's warning, for the origin of *rampike* turns on that bird, and the dead trees foretell a shaky future.

But there is timelessness in her repose. It holds the beauty of this river and the joy of watching and seeing. Her being there tethers the present to the past. Connects the place to its history, and the river to its legacy of resources and the communities they supported. Her presence links nature to culture.

The osprey's palm rises from a midden of oyster shells harvested a thousand years ago when the river's population far exceeded what it is now. Though worn down by current and storms, these middens still line the river as bluffs, islands, and subtle hammocks. Another osprey once surveyed a land of canoes, cooking fires, smudge pots, and villages at every river bend. Our cabin is built where Indigenous people camped. I think of the porch as a guest in one of these camps. If only we could sit for a while with our hosts. For now, the porch's sills and tables have become a visitor's museum, a reliquary of sorts, with shards of burnt pottery, arrowheads, and chert tools.

Mangrove snappers flick the water. Juveniles, less than ten inches long, they will soon head south to grow up in even warmer waters. The osprey lifts from her perch and dives. I watch the rampikes left in her wake. I see the figures Winslow Homer painted outside Gloucester Harbor in 1876. An adult and three children lean with their sailboat in the chop under blue-green air filled with clouds, their edges white with exposed canvas. The bent palm is their mast. The wind in their sleeves is why Homer packed watercolors when he fished and painted the Homosassa River. The tilt of their bodies is Homer's connection to the elements of nature.

Three decades after his Gloucester painting, Homer began vacationing in Homosassa. He cast his line toward the shore where these rampikes would have been seedlings. Now the cedars hold a century of change. I can feel the warmth of the sun just looking at it light their trunks. I also feel the sun warming the backs of the figures on the boat. It is like Homer's process, and it is why evidence of the painter's adjustments in figure, tone, watercolor, and climate lie just below the final layer of paint. He traced over and over as he tuned closer and closer to what he was seeing. Painting and fishing, Homer acclimated himself. The accumulation of paint is evidence of that acclimation.

The glaze of water over the port side of the Gloucester boat is the type of thing that inspired Homer to fish and to paint. It is also what stirred him to wrap a porch around the second floor of his studio in Maine. That porch hangs off the side of the original stable building like an ancient barnacle, like the catwalk of a lighthouse. There he could watch Saco Bay and the Atlantic's turbid blue.

What those figures on the boat feel, their finely tuned pitch of serenity, gaze, and rapport, is why I'm sitting on this porch. What Homer saw is why I'm writing, watching, listening, talking on this porch. Homer called his Gloucester painting *A Fair Wind*. Over time, as its popularity grew, people called it *Breezing Up*. Maybe because it captured the day's pragmatic outlook or signaled a country's optimism after war, or maybe because it simply caught a fine breeze. Like a porch.

The osprey rises again to her perch. Wind brushes her feathers and ruffles the skinny water below the palm. The river folds and then smooths under the draft, and it feels like hours but it is only a few breaths later when my pages curl in the breeze. I get up to examine the piece of driftwood that stands on the dusty sill. Its sharpened end pushes into the screen. Its grain is like the roiling water of a floodtide as it presses through a narrow cut in the river we call the Pearly Gates. The stream of manatees has slowed, and I move from the side of the porch that is less traveled, more room-like with its couch, chairs, and tables, to the side with doors, also like a room but worn with footfalls—"heel-gnawed" as Faulkner would say—and dusted with sand from sandals, towels, and drying dogs.

Am I inside or outside? A turkey buzzard's shadow drifts and lifts across the screen and floor. Feathers rasping as they release the air of flight, the bird balances on top of another headless palm, close by, between lagoon and porch. I open the screen door and look up.

*
**

A lizard tarzans from cedar trunk to porch screen. For a moment, his dark form swims the heavy air, and my first sketch of the day tethers him to the frame of the screen where he will spend the morning catching gnats. This sketch is like many I have made on the porch, following the contours and silhouettes of what I see. It is called a wandering line drawing for the way your eye meanders along edges. Your goal is a continuous line, so that you diverge, or "wander," from one edge to the next, where they intersect, without lifting your pen.

I usually start with a vertical line along a porch column, then move across the sill to a cedar trunk, on the lagoon's shore and the exposed bouquet of an oyster colony, up another tree or limb, then farther out to the far shore. I drag the line along bristled grass, smooth wavelets, bobbing flotsam, and waving treetops. I am tracing the contours of porch, land, and water, and I remind myself to slow down, to measure my breath with the pace of the line, as my hand follows my eye.

The continuous line doesn't just link; it tunes. Sketching—and thinking—like this reminds me that the porch is not just a space; it is also a method for tuning person and place. And that process is a delicate, sometimes extremely fragile, exercise in fine-tuning, with an intimacy only porches can offer in the immensity of the world.

It's late March and a northeast wind has blown the low tide lower. In almost a decade of watching, I don't think I've seen it this low. The river feels drained. Its limestone banks are pitch dark rims above burnished water. Even lower are small bluffs of muck and broken shells, exposed. Here are stories of erosion and sediments, messy histories of other sea level changes. Amid the ironies at work where land and water meet, the marsh is rising along with the sea. From the porch I can scan the rich compost for movement as I begin another sketch.

A fiddler crab waves his right claw. It is so much larger than his left that his efforts of balance seem miraculous. Is he motioning to me? *Come over here.* He directs a symphony of other fiddlers brandishing outsized claws—white half-notes across black mud—in near-perfect unison. Moving to her own bobbing rhythm, a plover bounces along from rock to mud, and clouds of prehistoric insects—known menacingly as machilids, or more stylishly as collembola—scurry with the ebb and flow of bird and crab. Sound resonates from the lagoon as if from a bowl.

It's a good time to look for clams and fiddler crabs, and a raccoon walks stiff-legged, careful but weary. She stops and raises a paw that is really a hand, nose to the air. I lift my pen. She has been excavating all morning, and wears estuary mud on her skinny legs like knee socks. She reaches deep into a hole up to her neck. I can read the concentration in her eye as she feels for shells and claws, grasping at movement, pulling, quickly splashing a crab into the water, then twisting it into her mouth. I have woken early, and she has stayed up late, and now we meet. She is an opportunist, and I am a witness. Both of us are edge-dwellers, treading contours, drafting what is at once banal and magical. Since before daylight, she has worked this widening fringe left in the neap tide's wake. My pen still hovers over the page when I realize she has already traced what I set out to draw. She retreats into a clump of ferns as the sun moves higher.

These are fragile drawings that connect the porch to its place, collapsing what is near and what is far. They evaporate distance. Sketching is like stepping through a marsh, wandering through a house opened for spring, running your finger along cedar bark or rough-cut pine, pressing your cheek against the screen's cool mesh, pacing a porch's length, stirring your toes in the lagoon's tepid broth. All at once I am here on the porch and there in nature, sitting in a tree's dappled shade, or swimming in the tide's pull.

I grew up in a house without a porch. That might be why I've gone in search of porches as an adult. It's also not quite true, because the suburban house where I lived for eighteen years had a covered front stoop and a back patio. Both of these, I realize now, share qualities with porches. The stoop faced south, and its uncovered brick plinth was a sun-warmed perch to rest, read mail, or wait for a delivery. It was also just wide and deep enough to host a group of carolers or a small throng of trick-or-treaters. On the back of the house was the patio where I sat with friends, fed box turtles, and once watched a tornado lift the glass top from a table. That patio measured the seasons. Rolling out its canvas awning signaled summer and the end of school, and pulling it down meant shorter and crisper fall days.

What then is a porch? The standard definition is a covered room outside a building's entrance. Most would probably agree that the Homosassa porch fits this definition. But that porch also opens deeper meanings and paradoxes, just as porch's common definition raises as many questions as it answers. What constitutes coverage? How big is a room, and is there an ideal depth for the porch? When does inside become outside? What do porches tell us about departure as well as arrival? With questions like these, we summon past porches and literary porches and also welcome in porch's siblings like the patio and stoop.

The air that wraps a building's edges, whether or not technically a porch, carries potential: the benefits of public life, the thrills of nature, the atmosphere of weather, the exhilaration of coming and going, the calm of simply sitting down, the warmth of family and friends, and the restfulness of solitude. Porch is that place where inside and outside mix, where architecture's edges encounter climate, where hosts meet guests, and where we all might acclimate.

When I sketch with a pen, ink bleeds through the page where I pause to think. Which is to say that these sketches measure time like a porch—holding time and suspending it, like the airborne lizard. Just as porches mesh near and far, they also connect old and new, slow and fast. They are thresholds between then and now and between today and tomorrow.

Porches have been eulogized since they began falling

away from air-conditioned houses after World War II. But they remain. Some would say they are more popular than ever. Statistics from the construction industry show a porch renaissance in the past two decades. Granted, some of these porches are too narrow for a chair, a swing, or even a bench. They reside on a house's front where balusters, rails, and flag holders build an image of the porch, a symbol of the past like picket fences. Such porches mix nostalgia with commodity. What they lack in space, they make up for in the yearning for Norman Rockwell's porches and in higher property values. Too small for sitting, they may still protect their houses from weather, but they are just outsized mailboxes for Amazon deliveries, susceptible to porch pirates. Porch is also overused as a metaphor, but that's not new either. Today, porch identifies all kinds of outdoor communal spaces in cities and "front porch" communities online, just as centuries ago it was used to describe entryways to books—like this one.

Porches have a necessary immediacy. They need to be experienced now. Porches might be draped in nostalgia, built with traditional materials like wood, or styled as classical porticoes, but they effortlessly make room for modern life's contradictions, even as they slow things down and help people connect. They are deliberate, like that raccoon. They readily capture and hold what millennials call "moments." They are the original social media devices, and the real-time of their screens complements what we call "screentime." And now porches navigate an indeterminate future. Though timeless, porches are temporally charged, fluctuating, urgent.

Porch comes from Latin *porta*, which means gate. On a porch, you occupy the doorway; you become the gate. *Porta* also means passage, entrance, door, and port, so that porch shuttles meaning as it also harbors climates and adapts architecture to its environment. It accommodates movement between the sacred and the profane in churches as willingly as it lodges guests and cooling breezes for a house. It offers rest, breathes fresh air, tells stories, shivers and sweats, plays music, eavesdrops, cries, laughs, and watches the sun rise and then go down.

When I look at my sketches, I can read the weather in the lines. I feel the cold in the twitching lineaments drawn with rigid fingers. The smear of ink is sweat on a hot day, when I was too immersed in drawing and thinking and watching—and just being—to turn on the ceiling fan. There is something about writing on a porch that works for me, and I don't mind the inclement weather, even bundled up in crisp air or when shards of lightning flash across the page. Lucidity comes with fresh air, which can also bring discomfort. That's certainly not for everyone, but there is a porch for each of us. Not only that, we can't live without porches and what they tell us.

Long thin lines are quick movements to capture something fleeting, like a passing boat or the lizard who swings across the screen. A jolt of thunder still pulses in the quick jerk of a line's course. On a porch, we lend ourselves to the world, and the world lends itself to us. When we sit down on a porch, we give up certain things. We cede control over our environment, but in return we gain what we can't find anywhere else. On the porch, I seek to understand how what we build makes this possible.

My sketches discover as they go. Their wandering lines map the tangle of what I see and what I think I see, of what I'm feeling and experiencing, and what I'm imagining. This sketching, like sitting on the porch, tunes me to a place of wonder where I can watch, listen, and intimately witness change.

⁑

The shirtless philosopher types on a porch in Miami Beach, while kids climb over his chair, on his table, on his back. Precariously balanced, they hug him, kiss him, and tap at the Underwood's keys. John Dewey laughs and savors the attention, reaching to hold the children, as he also hits a few more keys. He works in the chaos of experience, unsettled but rolling with the moment's joy and amity. Dewey wrote on porches cast in the maelstrom of life and nature, and here in the home video from 1943, a cloudless sky—the deep blue after a storm has blown through—pierces his chair's rattan webbing and spins behind the playground that is this porch. Only at the end, when we see that the philosopher sits next to the ocean, his back to the beach, does the vignette become anchored.

With a porch for an office, interruptions are likely. But the porch is also a place for interiority where you, like Dewey, might retreat into your mind yet remain outdoors, physically connected to the environment. Porches put you where you might not otherwise be. At the frontier of your house, in the public eye, outside during a thunderstorm. Along edges, porches hold stability and precariousness, a mix that defines experience. They make room for what Dewey called "the actual work" that goes into the "true nature of experience." Such endeavors temper comfort with risk. A porch mixes domestic stability with the uncertainties of movement and the changeable nature of what's outside. It cedes some control to its surroundings as it relies on its house for support.

Porches provide us access to the full range and dimension

of experience. In Key West, Dewey wrote on the porch where he witnessed Franklin Delano Roosevelt's trips to and from the Naval Air Station during World War II, and on the back porch where he leaned over a hexagonal card table among banana trees and birds of paradise. In Nova Scotia, the philosopher pulled his desk outside onto the open porch next to Sawler Lake. In one iconic photograph, Dewey sits on the edge of his rustic birch chair, in only sandals, socks, and shorts. He leans forward to adjust paper in his typewriter that barely fits on the table, a reference book perched over one corner. The dog at his feet looks through the trees toward the lake, where two fishermen float. The dark wide trunk of a tree contrasts Dewey's head and white hair, as if to anchor a thought, glinting off his spectacles, to ground and sky. The photographer Edmund Norwood sought out the everyday lives of his subjects, and this scene is one of full disclosure. Here is Dewey, shirtless, human, made small by the chair sized for a giant and crafted from raw tree trunks. Here also is Dewey the mystic and the seer, a penitent in the wilderness. We feel the sun on his back, the distance toward the far shore, and even that thought he grasps at in the grooved platen knob.

I think I can see what Dewey is thinking. And now I think I have a better understanding of the relation between the known and the unknown. Here is Dewey writing about the two sides of existence: "The visible is set in the invisible; and in the end what is unseen decides what happens in the seen; the tangible rests precariously upon the untouched and ungrasped." I like to think that Dewey composed this on a porch, since that is what happens on porches—they set what we see within what we don't. The results are as exhilarating as they are peaceful, as frightening as they are satisfying. When we go out, we enter the unknown, and a porch allows us to pause where the two meet, the visible nesting inside the invisible.

This mix of stability and uncertainty is, says Dewey, the very origin of philosophy. So the porch houses a kind of philosophy that can swing between the poles of being and becoming. A porch is a work in progress. It is a fertile meeting place that brings together conventional shelter, laboratory, and retreat. It's where Aristotle and Kant might meet up with Heraclitus and Bergson and hash things out. It hosts the full range of experience.

Porches offer lessons in paradox and contradiction. They celebrate the in between, as they teach us the value of thresholds. In and out, private and public, arrival and departure, social and natural, here and there, near and far, sight and sound, introversion and extroversion, stable and precarious. On a porch, we live paradox, working between opposites, thinking about what we see, trying to measure what we sense, and as Dewey says, "penetrating the true nature of experience." Tuning in. Acclimating.

To acclimate infuses habit with change, mixes protection with exposure. Risk with security. Making us comfortable as we move in and out of our so-called comfort zone. Tuning us to our surroundings, near and far. Toward what we know, and what we don't.

⁑

Early spring sunlight squints through treetops across the river. Spear ends of the cordgrass catch the light, and mist puffs on the water like something is burning. This morning I walked out on the porch to warm up. Usually, it's the other way around. Porches are generally, sometimes nostalgically, thought of as places to cool off in gentle breezes, under the languid spin of ceiling fans. But on this early morning in late March, the cabin still harbors the night's chill. A red sun greets me as reflections dance overhead. It warms my face, and the couch has a burrowed heat like someone has just left the cushions. I grasp the porch air like a stone that still holds the rays of a passing sun.

The porch has five screens along its front. And this morning each one disappears in the low sun; each lifts to begin the day's performances. Five stories. Straight ahead, a plover, shoulders drawn tight, dances on the limestone that knuckles out of the water where lagoon meets river. At the lagoon's edge, a spooked needlefish sends out a wake much larger than itself, and far to the right, deep in the trees but close to the porch, two lizards wrestle and thrash before falling to the rattle of oak leaves on thin soil. Tiptoeing over the wrack of yesterday's high tide, a night heron takes silent leave, so quietly that I question whether he was there at all. Brown pelicans fly low under the lifting mist on their way to the marina's pilings. They touch the velvet of the river.

One story cuts across all the others. This was our first trip to the cabin in a few months. We arrived in darkness, so we hadn't seen the changes that January's record cold had cast across the buttonwoods along the river's edges. Natives to Florida, buttonwoods crave the sun. They prefer the beaches, yards, and even the parking lots far south on the peninsula. But these specimens have followed that sun here, where the lowest temperatures drop well below freezing. Each one is ordinary yet heroically steadfast: "not showy," "not particularly outstanding," but "a tough tree!" the USDA fact sheets tell me.

It is a pioneer without being invasive. It tolerates pollution, drought, and storm surge. It has been used to smoke fish and meat. It can furnish railroad ties and boats. Its bark treats bleeding and colic. Its name derives from the scales of its bark and from its flower heads, densely packed liked buttons. It is a reclamation plant that stabilizes earth. It prefers coastlines over rivers. Yet here it is, a hundred miles from home, clinging to the Homosassa's limestone. The buttonwood is botanically unexceptional but climatically extraordinary.

When the polar vortex blew through, the river's latent heat protected the buttonwoods' base, swaddling them in warmer air. From the porch, I can see the low rake of morning sun light up a ribbon of green that tracks along the shoreline, three feet above the water, about the same height as our porch railing above the floor. Above this line and all the way to the top, sheaves of brown deadwood rattle in the breeze. The lush green band of leaves furnishes a living wainscot around the river's room. Now the porch, where I slowly wake up, enlists its own lens of air, water-warmed and sun-warmed.

To acclimate is to adjust to change. That's the scientific definition primarily used in meteorology and biology, but this meaning also extends to social, political, and cultural situations. Humans, animals, even plants modify their systems to survive. Technically speaking, acclimation is a temporary adjustment to gradual changes in the environment, particularly weather and climate. The buttonwood clings to the edge of the river with the resolve of a castaway. Its roots grasp the shoreline's rock like arms hooked over flotsam, and it has survived winters huddled in only marginally warmer river air. It grows here—it even flourishes—because it has acclimated to a precarious situation and its sometimes radical changes. That buttonwood has learned, for the moment, to survive on the rock where land and water and air meet.

Acclimation is less permanent than adaptation. It is shorter-lived and reversible. In our contemporary moment where change is the norm, that makes it potent. Acclimation's tenuous nature is also its strength, pointing toward an agility, a ready responsiveness to changes in climate. If the buttonwood is a castaway, it survives upside down with its lower third breathing and soaking in energy perilously close to the water, while the rest succumbs to colder air. Porches do the same. They breathe fresh air, temper chill and swelter, shed rainwater, and let storms blow through. This morning when I stepped out into the porch's warmed air, I sought one of those temporary adjustments.

Acclimation is how porches delicately tune person and place. They offer access to changes in temperature and air, differences between inside and outside. I left a cold house to find warmth. I also admitted myself to the plotlines of nature, an ongoing drama where the porch is a box seat that presses out onto a stage where everyone and everything is an actor. And porches also tune person to person. Later this morning, our conversations will echo across the river. Our sounds will mix with the sounds of other families as they shout over idling motors or talk quietly around fishing poles and bait buckets. A porch invites conversation as it also bridges host and guest. A porch offers a repertoire for tuning: sitting, resting, sleeping, watching, talking, eavesdropping, greeting, coming, going, ruminating, creating. Porches are scenes of acclimation.

Climate is embedded in the word *acclimation*, but not too deeply. The prefix *ac* emphasizes—with an even harsher *c*—this core idea. It sets climate in motion, as it also moves us—

readers, porch-sitters, living beings—*toward* climate. In acclimate, climate becomes a verb. It is an action as it is also a call to action. Acclimate asks us to consider a future where climate is not just change but also crisis. All of this gives the sense that to acclimate is more than mere adjustment. It is a process of tuning, of making minor adaptations but with an increased awareness of what is going on around us. And an increased sense of urgency as those changes accelerate.

Acclimation is a reciprocal process that asks something from each side, from each person and from each place, from each animate actor. On a porch, we meet nature halfway, and it gives back. That chilly morning, I watched a gnatcatcher carefully pick cedar twigs from the porch screen. The rings around her eyes were white spectacles as if to capture the tiniest no-see'ums that have lifted like vapors from the damp ground now that clouds have covered the sun, or as if to study the minute details of nest-building, or to get a better look at me, on the other side of the mesh. It is humbling to be acknowledged like this. On a porch, I feel joy and weight.

The gnatcatcher leaves for her nest, and the air lowers. I turn on the porch light as the clouds deepen. Whether it describes a social or natural atmosphere, climate can be an abstract concept, but porches link experiences to ideas. Porches are barometric, helping us measure change. Like the weight of air or its latent warmth. All day I thought about how the line in the buttonwood made visible the subtle climatic differences that make the porch so comfortable. Later, on our boat, I will see how this line between green and brown oscillates higher and lower with changes in sun and salinity.

The delicate tuning I experienced on the porch will extend to include thinking about the implications of the record cold here, about how changes in climate also tell the story of climate change, about how the smallest differences have far-reaching effects. How that simple line in the buttonwood tethers the porch to much broader changes. How porches provide evidence that our extended environment is changing. How acclimate shares a prefix with acknowledge.

A porch is a place to weigh the world.

2

TILT

. . . the steadfast tilted deck of the earth . . .

After the hurricane, the cabin's floors started to pitch and roll. The scour of water hastened the settling of foundations, and the flood's uplift raised the ends of beams and floors and walls with them. Before, it had been only the porch that felt like the deck of a ship, but now the wooden sign that says "Welcome Aboard" has taken on a new meaning. It dates to the cabin's early years, and I wonder if the original owners were just carrying through with the nautical theme, or if they anticipated the sea's threat. Perhaps they were already questioning the house's seaworthiness. On board the porch, with your back to the house, you sense the downward turn—not yet a plunge—over the base of green, into the lagoon's trough, and onto the next crest of the river. If this front porch is the cabin's bow, the porch floor is its pitch.

Most porch floors are not level. Some slope precipitously—even rashly. Others slide ever so subtly, whether by design, by chance, or in error. And part of a porch's cant may build on the original intention and be a function of time and weathering because of the sometimes tenuous connection a porch has to its house, or because its foundations have not been set with sufficient care or engineering. When it does have a pitch, a porch floor typically slants down and away from its house. The simple reason is weather. Like roofs, porch floors are exposed to the elements, so they must shed rain. That is the practical explanation, but the effect is much richer and more complex. Its pitch tethers porch to body and brings poetry to the porch's basic utility. A porch's slope sets you on edge, usually in a good way. Like Dewey's thesis that experience includes the precarious as well as the stable, a gently tilting porch makes room for instability. Walking across a porch's floor, you experience incline and imbalance. Moving down the slope, you might lurch forward slightly. Stepping across the slope, you might feel like one leg is a little longer than the other. Unsteadiness becomes a porch's very ground. It is a gentle reminder of your body and its connection to what James Agee called the "tilted deck of the earth."

I have spent a lot of time on the front porch of Marjorie Kinnan Rawlings' house in Cross Creek, Florida. Many years ago, when I first ventured out onto it, I ignored the park ranger's warning to watch my step and reeled forward. Not because the slant of the floor was steep—it's only a bit more than a quarter inch per foot, but because its gentle tilt brings with it a much less subtle change of location and position. That experience is inscribed in the language of porch arrivals: I walked *out* and *onto* the porch. Leaving a house for a porch brings a sense of release with its relative openness, diversion with its brightness and its views, and delight with its joy of arrival. If I had entered that porch from the screen door at its front, as a historically accurate visitor or as a state park tourist, rather than as a guest of the ranger, I would have moved uphill, giving my body more time to adjust to the slope, while adjusting to my position as a guest. Either way, the slope reminds the body of its need for balance, as it moves out onto something different, a place where change, movement, and transitions occur. Porches keep you on your toes. And just as porches land us along a building's edges, they also remind us that we are in a vulnerable, even fragile, place.

⁂

The two men lay stretched out on the front porch. Listening. I have always imagined that their eyes were closed, although they remained open in thought. It wouldn't matter either way because the night air around the sharecropper's cabin was so dark—"heavy dark," as Agee writes. You had to hear distance rather than see it. This is the last scene in *Let Us Now Praise Famous Men*, as James Agee and Walker Evans listen to the back-and-forth calls of two foxes, which mirror the conversations they've had with each other and with their hosts, many of them on porches, as they learned about the daily lives of three sharecropper families in Alabama. The relay between foxes and men is also the exchange they have had as writer and photographer with the people and their place—what Agee will call a "structure of special exaltation."

On the porch, Agee and Evans lay between the depth of the world and the family asleep inside the cabin. The world includes foxes, love, history, mortality, and joy; and the cabin holds the Gudgers—George, Annie Mae, Maggie Louise, George Junior, Burt Westly, and Valley Few. Awash with thoughts, desires, sand, dirt, and watermelon seeds, everything they have gathered and all the residues of daily life, it is the porch that connects the house with its surroundings, both material and ephemeral, visible and invisible—"What is taking place here, and it happens daily in this silence, is intimately transacted between this home and eternal space." The tilt of the porch angles up as a slash that binds the house/world transaction.

Agee and Evans' book begins and ends on the porch. Named "On the porch: 3," this section concludes both the book and a series of three vignettes that knit the project together, welcoming the reader back to the porch at intervals. I've returned to this book and these sections many times over the years of thinking about porches, about writing, and about living. This time what struck me was the tilt. The book's front matter has cast the persons and places, and the final scene plays out on what Agee describes as an enormous stage.

That stage is the world and it is also the porch. Its tilt sets in motion this "most significant" story and its "unfathomable" music. One cause of the tilt is the unexpected entrance of the foxes, as if from the wings of a theater, an appearance Agee and Evans can access only because they listen from the porch. So, the foxes share the stage with the two men laying on the porch, and the tilt is the vulnerability of the world's equilibrium, but also its joy. If the latter emerges from porch's "lucky situation," then the former is a "scab" where the porch protects "essential human frailty" against the enormity that Agee and Evans experience in silence. The tilt is a minute yet wholly significant change—and here Agee taps the sublime—"upon the surface of a tenderly laboring sea."

I stop reading and bend toward the little table where the book lays open. I realize that I have seen the porch's slope in the bore of the sea pushing upriver. And then in the roll of the river when its current takes over again with the slant of a slackening tide. I had always thought of water bodies, particularly the ocean, as flat. Decades ago, when I built a wooden boardwalk to cross the dunes farther up the gulf, we leveled its beams along the sea's horizon line. But closer in, from the porch, I can see water's slope, its labors both tender and cruel. And I ride that very inclination, swaying slightly, whether from insight or vertigo or both. The book's broken binding has kept its pages in place on the little table until one lifts slightly and beckons me to keep reading.

Agee and Evans filled their book with tilts. In the silence of the porch, they "feel the very tilt of the head" of the calling fox. Evans' photographs make visible other tilts: the listing porch of a store, the relaxed incline of an older man in a rocking chair outside a dance hall, the slanting beam of a sharecropper porch seen from the side, chairs—occupied or not—tilting against the porch's back wall, the angle of a man's crossed legs under the ornate woodwork of an elevated front porch, the inclination of shadows into the porch of a post office crowded with men, the cant—just off a vertical axis—of a young tree's trunk that supports gourd birdhouses. This last image in the book is an emblem of the "steadfast tilt" of the porch. It is a stage suspended on the axis of the world.

Agee casts his "on the porch" sections as parentheticals that tilt across and into the rest of the narrative. They bind the work together, and throughout *Let Us Now Praise Famous Men*, we learn that we can occupy only the edges of mystery, its perimeters. Such vulnerability on the margins of knowledge and experience, needs shelter, the kind of conditional shelter only a porch can offer. As idea and architecture, it welcomes the eccentric position of Agee and Evans. It makes room not just for the body but also for the book's narrative. Agee writes: "If I were not here; and I am an alien; a bodyless eye; this would never have existence in human perception." The actual porch and the book's written porches make this possible.

In a footnote we learn that these vignettes, now cast as connectors and thresholds, were the seed of the project and intended as its core all along: "I may as well explain that *On the Porch* was written to stand in as the beginning of a much longer book, in which the whole subject would be disposed of in one volume. It is here intended still in part as a preface or opening, but also as a frame and as an undertone and as the set stage and center of action, in relation to which all other parts of this volume are intended as flashbacks, foretastes, illuminations and contradictions." Lead-ins, immediate presents, touchstones, referents, tilts—these porch scenes are portals and frames. As porches are. They also furnish the center stage through which the entire narrative arcs. As porches do.

The oak boards of the porch where the men sleep support two beds: a Chevrolet's back seat and a wicker divan's thin cushion. Agee prefers this makeshift pallet of quilted cotton for its similarity to what the children sleep on and its proximity to what he cherishes as "the finality and immediacy of floors." A steadfastness against certain unsteadiness. Agee describes how each porch bed requires balance of its sleeper because the deck is sloped and the car seat's springs incline from tall to short. As always he is precise and exhaustive with possible solutions: recentering your weight, compromising between high and low, long and short, curling up on your side, stacking books under low ends, sleeping on your belly, toes to the deck, packing a towel under the side of your head. As always, he writes incisively of experience: "Our bodies learned to adjust themselves to holding a tension of balance while they were unconscious."

Enacted on the porch, this kind of balance gives a tenuous but firm equilibrium to their rest but also the narrative as a whole. Being on the porch presents an intimate, bodily connection to the porch and, by extension, to the world.

*
**

Last night I slept on my porch. I can't say that I feel all that rested, yet I have the elusive but palpable sense that I accomplished something, as at the end of a day when you kept busy, doing things, going from here to there, but not having much tangible to show for it. And still there is a deepening satisfaction with that time. I look back on it with a combination of sympathy and longing, as the slow recollection of the night catches up with me, in the same way that an idled boat's wake catches up to its hull, or the way a house's distant rooms hold the smells of cooking earlier in the day. These thoughts tread on the romantic notion of sleeping on porches. Such an idyll includes light breezes, freshets of air, spring-like scents, gentle sounds of insects, lapping water—a real-time sleep-aid soundtrack, only real, and gathering all the senses. That's all there, but the visceral experience of sleeping essentially outdoors brings with it instinct, and the inescapable presence of nature, animals, even other people. You're outside the domestic Faraday cage of your house, and the signals you get are not in your control.

My headboard is the outside wall of the house. Boards and battens splinter and scratch against the pillowcase. A single mattress, dragged from inside, hammocks into its metal bed-frame. Blankets scroll together more like a sleeping bag than proper bedding. They form a cocoon that I shift in and out of throughout the night, too warm and then too cool in the late December air that doesn't drop below sixty degrees. But these adjustments aren't just a function of a winter evening with above-average temperatures.

Sleeping on a porch is like camping in a tent and sleeping bag, where you feel the changes around you. No walls delay the creep of temperature, thin veils of canvas or screen only slightly repel the press of insects and winds, sounds ebb and flow like a radio signal fading in and out. The porch in winter can be cold. Very cold in other parts of the country. Bill Bryson relished the tranquility of his grandparents' sleeping porch, but he also recalled the chill of winter nights there. Preparation required layers of clothes and everything from blankets to tarpaulins, from overcoats to pieces of carpet. It was like "sleeping under a dead horse," and a slight shift in position would dissipate the thin layer of warmth around your body. Whether under heavy blankets or without any covers, you lie back, cradled in the changes, subtle and extreme, all around you. Sleeping out becomes all about falling asleep.

Actual sleep rarely visits a porch. It is all about the process—sleeping, not sleep—drifting off and slowly waking up. A porch mixes night and day, just like it blends inside and outside; each waxes and wanes into the next, never quite achieving fullness. A porch is not always attuned to the rhythms of sleep because sleeping there brings with it alertness. Instincts abound, and it's not so much survival but curiosity.

On this side of sleep, senses heightened, my feet inches

from the screen, I listen. Everyday sounds take on bigger implications: an acorn falling on the metal roof is a gunshot, the rattle of a palm frond against its trunk is the midnight scrape of a door opening, the murmur of wavelets is a conspiratorial conversation, the scour of a spooked trout becomes the slide of a large alligator. I lose track of the hour. Crickets, frogs, toads, fish, night herons play at melody but it's nothing I've heard before. Maybe John Cage has composed the land's soundscape, playing, rolling, lulling, rising, falling, but then a new note here, there, and silence. This happens every time—the familiar becomes wonderfully new. Drifting off I see the thinnest cuticle of moon just risen over the tree line. I imagine its waning crescent leans back, falling as its body swings upward. Then it's gone behind the hoary caul of invisible clouds.

I wake up in what must be the middle of the night to water sounds. The lagoon has become a paddling pool, and all the kids' friends are over. But it's more primordial than playful. Fins press water into air. Tails slap, slosh, and drip. Mouths gulp, and mullets smack. Bent tails snap, as waves hiccup in rock clefts. The amount of activity is thrilling. The porch is a stethoscope to the lagoon's core. What's hidden during the day pulses loudly in darkness.

When I wake up again, dew lays on my exposed skin like a thin gauze, a film of moisture that rolls across the river in a cloud lit by the mainland light's false dawn. Sky, horizons, river merge into a whitening mass. I doze off and when I come to, the dew has lifted in the coldest part of the morning. The crickets sound tired, our water pump is cycling, and Venus has joined Mercury in the not yet lightening sky. This is when the stone-crab boats rip through the incoming tide. Their motors might break the illusions of natural cadence, but they also map the river. Engines run rich, and I hear their strain in the idle zone where road access ends, then the diesel roar through Salt River's cross-current and the gearing down at the narrow pass before Tiger Tail Bay, where full throttle will sound like an interstate semi until the deep resonance rattles the floor as their boats cross the pools we simply call "the hole." The boat captains have told us it is seventy-five feet to the bottom; we have sounded thirty-five. It is still the deepest spot we know, short of going twenty miles offshore.

The crab boat hardly slows at the narrow wicket of the Pearly Gates, between markers 62 and 63, and it might be running thirty knots, all piercing Q-lamps and tumescent floods, then the rumble of another downshift at Hell Gate, before the wide open but slow doppler across Gustaf Bay and onward to the gulf. I lose its sound in one more idle zone before I hear it again, faintly, as the pulse of its motor opens up to a horizon of crabs and traps. In the slosh of its wake, a shrimp boat follows, slower. Its searchlight catches the foam that lathers the river.

Crabbers wake me at first light. "I don't know why but I always want to throw him in. . . ." Like the traps sinking into tannin water, baited for blue crabs, the crabber's voice tapers off into lapping tides and distance. Throw who in? I strain to hear more, but catch only the smell of rotting fish and chicken scraps from their skiff's chum. This is the crew we saw yesterday on our way out. We waved and they nodded and lifted a hand from the tiller. We get along with the crabbers like most neighbors out here. You do your thing; I'll do mine. They harvest crabs, and we harvest their wayward traps and buoys. Ghost traps stack up next to our back porch. I think they sometimes tie up at our back dock, taking a break from pulling, baiting, and setting. Once we collected what must have been not a ghost trap but a perfectly good one. It was gone the next day.

More awake now, I study our collection of crab trap buoys in the corner. We unspooled some from the dense tangle of mangroves and retrieved others from spiny depths of spartina, but I wonder if we should set them all afloat. The sunrise ruddles like fired clay, and in the half light, it's easy to confuse tree trunks with porch columns. Later today, in that golden hour of light before dusk, the porch's structure, deep in shadow, will frame a strip of moving pictures. The night light that was Tampa's distant glow has faded. Venus still pierces the eastern sky.

It's the brightest sunrise I've seen, and our labrador is a bright red ball on the couch. There's a ribbon of gray blue just above the tree line so that the scarlet is a compressed band along the horizon. A mourning dove calls. Is there always a dove in the morning? What I recall most clearly is the sound of the pelicans as they flew up the river, their shadows floating through the porch. Filling it, wide as a passing cloud. Their wings were polishing a window. Passing closer, they shook out a bedsheet crisped with sunlight, one just taken down from the line.

The closest pelican clots the sun, and I realize today is the winter solstice. Low sunlight grazes the southeast corner of the porch. I feel the ecliptic, that turn of the earth that makes seasons as it also draws currents that make the drafts the pelicans ride across the morning. It is that tilt of the earth that a porch grasps so beautifully and tenuously. Like the wing of a pelican that taps the river in a subtle tip side to side. I have slept with the tilt of the floor, my head two inches higher than my toes, just enough to see over the rail and into the world. Just enough to see the wing prints drift downriver.

*
**

Three inches. That's the difference in elevation between the porch's houseward edge and its outer knee wall. Three inches slope toward the lagoon, toward the river, toward sea level. That's both a little and a lot. It's a modest change over the ten-foot depth of the porch. It's a massive change within the porch's estuarial context. Along this part of the gulf where land slopes about a foot per mile, minute changes in sea level have enormous impacts, but such change washes discreetly across mudflats, mangrove forests, and drowned karst. The porch slope magnifies this effect tenfold. Sea level rise means that water at the outer edge of the porch when we bought the cabin would now be up to its inner wall, lapping at the front door. Just as a porch slope's vertical change can be difficult to gauge and harder to see, so are climate change in general and sea level rise in particular. But if this porch were to slope up directly from the water's edge, a porch-sitter would witness the sea move nearly two feet closer to the living room's floor each year. Two feet closer to inundation. Even this gradual slope can play host to catastrophic change.

The purpose of a porch's slope is to send water the other direction, away from the house. Building codes don't specify the slope, but trade recommendations range from an eighth to a quarter of an inch per foot. The Homosassa and Cross Creek porches have steeper pitches, closer to a third of an inch per foot. The steeper a pitch, the faster it will shed the deluge, important in Florida where it rains hard and a lot. Some would say it rains like it did in the Bible, and Rawlings, in

The Yearling, has Penny observe one such rainstorm: "This must be the way the Lord made the blasted ocean." Then the porch must slowly dry out in humid air. Steeper is better, up to the threshold of comfort. Some building contractors balk at building in a slope because it doesn't look or feel right. It deliberately casts imperfection into a finished product.

Whether builders like it or not, a slope is essential for the closed surface of plywood or tongue-and-groove flooring. The need for a slope lessens if there are gaps between boards. If it is meant to be a screened porch and you leave these gaps, don't forget to add screen below the floor, or insects—mosquitoes, cockroaches, spiders—will rise up into your porch like last year's flood. Even palmetto bugs will squeeze their fattened bodies through when it's a dry season and they're looking for water.

The slope of the porch on the Homosassa cabin is enough to make you feel slightly off balance at first, but not enough to make it uncomfortable if you sit crosswise for a little while. Off-kilter, the porch floor reminds me of the search for level ground when camping. A gentle slope is close enough, and our bodies adjust. And when you face the direction of the slope, it tips you toward what you're looking at. That tilt is just enough to see a little more of the ground in front. It's as if you've grown a few extra inches. The slope leans you toward the ground, the water, the river, and the constant tidal shifts. It tips you on your toes, pausing just before the moment you might tumble forward. It is a low-slung bird's-eye view. You're not so much looking over the lagoon to the river, as you're looking down into it, with the river as a backdrop. And so the lagoon becomes a vitrine for what it reflects and what it holds. Clouds, manatees, buzzards, anhingas, patches of blue, pelicans, crabs, mullet, and clouds of mud. Drifting seagrass, floating mangrove seeds, waving Spanish moss, and flickering palm fronds. The near ground becomes nearer.

*
**

When I sleep out on the porch, history is my bunkmate. I am testing Agee's tension of balance, as I'm also gauging the benefits of fresh air and following a long tradition of sleeping on porches. This legacy includes those who have sought cooler air in summer months and crisp air in winter. It includes patients in and out of sanatoria, Californians alongside turn-of-the-century bungalows, Marjorie Kinnan Rawlings on her daybed in Cross Creek, as well as fictional middle-class Midwesterners like George Babbitt oversleeping on his porch in Sinclair Lewis' classic, and Zora Neale Hurston's retreat for Arvay in *Seraph on the Suwanee*. It also includes presidents.

In the summer of 1918, Woodrow Wilson climbed out of a third-floor window of the White House and entered a sleeping porch on the roof of the southern portico. He was exhausted by war and isolation. The screened embrace of the "sleeping shelter," as its designer called it, must have been comforting. It also must have offered the fresh air that Wilson's physician prescribed and that his first wife, Ellen, had sought before she died of tuberculosis a few years earlier.

I set out looking for this porch based on a single intriguing photograph from the Library of Congress. A thinly framed enclosure with a stretched canvas roof is anchored by guy wires to the White House roof and its heavy balustrade. It is more tent than permanent room. The portico curves behind the transparent screen, and the mansard roof of the State, War, and Navy Building looms in the background. This pho-

tograph is ostensibly a government document with a practical purpose, inventorying a piece of architecture. It also allows its subject to take flight. A canopy of maples on the left seems to hold this treehouse aloft. As the White House roof fades along the photograph's grainy edges, the sleeping shelter finds its footing in an array of curves and angles. It catches the wind like the flag above the Navy Building. A smoky horizon is askew. It collapses distance as it lifts across the Potomac. This workaday image is a practical tool of documentation, but like a porch, it is also freighted in sentimentality. With delicate efficiency, it suggests a momentary release from the pressures of leadership. With fleeting simplicity, it hints at the provisional, like the last days of summer that signal a return to work and responsibility. It's a camping trip on the roof of a national symbol, and I can't imagine a president sleeping there today.

The label on this photograph attributes the porch to William Taft. The twenty-seventh president was an advocate of fresh air, which he called "nature's sweet restorer," and his experience as Governor General in the Philippines left him longing, particularly during Washington's summers, for the cooling effects of his rattan bedstead there. His physician, William Osler, promoted outdoor living in any climate, and after his presidency Taft wrote the introduction to Irving Fisher's seminal *How to Live*. That book highlighted national and individual health responsibilities as it also underscored the benefits of an open-air lifestyle, which Fisher saw as no "fad" but an unavoidable healthful imperative. Taft's introduction similarly makes the case for healthy living based on modern science. He argues that public health is the statesman's primary responsibility, and he equates individual and family health with the core duties of a citizen's patriotism.

Taft suffered from sleep apnea, and the reluctant leader often sought to elude the mental and physical confines of his position. He escaped to the White House's edges—its roofs and balconies and porches—as he also set out on long drives in the countryside. The president was seen pacing the south portico's roof on the night of his silver wedding anniversary in 1911. During Taft's term, the *Washington Post* reported on "the deplorable fact that there are only seven bedrooms in the White House. Those addicted to the sleeping-porch fad may have their cots put on the portico." Taft may have slept in the White House's porticoes, but the sleeping shelter in the photograph—to my disappointment—was not his but Wilson's.

On May 22, 1918, the capital's temperature climbed to eighty-five degrees. Allied airmen were on the southern front, and a draftsman in the office of Colonel C. S. Ridley drew the details for the sleeping shelter on top of the White House. Ninety-two years later, I found Wilson's sleeping shelter, filed away at the bottom of a metal drawer, buried under technical engineering documents, lodged in the National Archives' suburban outpost in College Park. It's a remarkable drawing, pencil and ink on light vellum. Careful lines show the shelter's location. The hatched solidity of the White House walls contrast with the single thin lines of the shelter's screen and the narrow fragility of its posts. In the section drawings, a "moveable flight of stairs" provides access to the window openings. The perspective sketch in the upper right corner floats like a lightly tethered kite in DC's humid breezes.

When I sleep on the porch in Homosassa, I feel like I'm suspended across an "intimate immensity." It is an intensely private, almost cocoon-like space, but one that opens to the breadth of the world. I wonder what the president felt as he climbed those moveable stairs to ride the bright air of the sleeping shelter. At the end of that year, Wilson would leave for Paris to begin negotiating peace. There he was at the conclusion of a war, at the beginning of a terminal illness worsened by a stroke the following year. And yet here he is, for the moment, resting on the roof of a national symbol.

The drawing notes that the shelter's floor is "to be laid on top of present tile roof according to conditions on the job." Like so many porches, this project was contingent. Its execution relied on factors that were out of its leader's control, beyond the control of the army that designed and built it. In the photograph, the shelter is in the middle of the portico roof, away from the third floor. I do not know if this change from the drawing was caused by "conditions on the job" or a modification after Wilson's time. This porch on the roof tilts the

White House toward the ephemeral. It loosens the solid and the closed, as it remains firm and protected.

Archival research is akin to fishing. On the porch and in the creek behind the cabin, I have spent hours scanning the water for signs of fish. I cast and retrieve, but mostly watch all that is happening around me. I learn more about the environment the longer I sit. Like the signature of a tailing redfish across the expansive marsh, that photograph of the shelter attributed to Taft hinted at a whole ecology of documents in the National Archives. Before I finally caught the sleeping shelter drawing, a fortnight of research took me through Taft's quest for fresh air and stories of how other presidents inhabited the periphery of the White House. Fishing and researching, I have learned a lot about edges. And delving deeply into transitory, yet vital, places like porches has taught me how the liminal can be pivotal to knowledge and how the ephemeral can be fundamental to human experience.

I am convinced that the porches of the White House were added to connect presidents with their distant homes. After British troops set fire to the White House in 1814, the president's house could be rethought, and James Monroe soon added the south portico. Seven years after architect James Hoban completed its reconstruction, President Monroe could step out of the White House and look south toward his birthplace in Westmoreland County, Virginia. In 1829, construction began on the north portico. Though ostensibly designed to receive visitors, this porch also looked toward the sitting president's home. If it had been completed before he left office, John Quincy Adams would have stood under its roof and looked northward toward his home in Quincy, Massachusetts.

Porches are readymade devices for connecting with what's right around us, but a porch's steady gaze can also hold the longing for distant places. Theodore Roosevelt laid wooden boards on the roof of the White House so he could survey the "hardy life of the open" beyond Washington. Harry Truman added a balcony on the southern façade to expand his private living quarters. Opposed by the public, the press, and the Fine Arts Commission, this relatively minor addition was controversial because of its visibility. The president claimed Thomas Jefferson had always had this modification in mind, and he went ahead. The Truman Balcony, nested in the south portico's grandeur, is a porch within a porch, a private outdoor room within an exceedingly public space.

If that edge failed to afford enough privacy, the roof could. Behind the south portico's balusters, renovations could go largely undetected. And so the sleeping shelter began a series of additions that trace how a leader's private needs are accommodated in what might be the most public house in the world. The sleeping shelter remained on its roof frontier, out of the public eye, for nearly a decade. Tents and screens that endure can crystallize into something more permanent; nine years after its guy wires were pulled taut, Calvin Coolidge replaced the original screened shelter with the Sky Parlor. Franklin Delano Roosevelt later called this glassed-in room the "sun porch." He saw it as a bright escape where he could have quiet conversations. He was likely having lunch there with his family while Agee and Evans were sitting and talking with sharecropper families on the porches of central Alabama.

In his second term, Truman transformed the Sky Parlor into a more extensive Solarium, with a promenade around it. There, in dress shirt and bow tie, Dwight Eisenhower could relax and fire up the grill for hamburgers, steaks, and quail. The Solarium hosted Caroline Kennedy's kindergarten classes, and Ronald Reagan convalesced there after being shot. This is also where Richard Nixon told his family he was stepping down. The sleeping shelter had spawned an enduring roof architecture.

Soon afterward, speech balloons started lifting from the south portico in Garry Trudeau's *Doonesbury* cartoons, imagining conversations between presidents and advisors. They rise like fireworks cracking with internal drama, rhetoric, and questions, like voices leaking through a sleeping porch's screen. They sometimes read like annotations to the architectural details of balustrade, chimney, and roof. The disembodied words are an entry point; they seem to come from just the other side of the heavy balustrade atop the portico, as if the president and his advisors are crouching there. It is as if the White House still speaks through the ghost of the sleeping shelter.

*
**

When you're building a porch, the floor comes early. Porch floors can be wood, concrete, or simply dirt. After you've cast or laid the foundations and set the posts, you can frame the floor. Here in the south, most porches are framed in wood and raised to let air pass under the floor, drying the earth and cooling the house's microclimate. Raised porches keep their wood—and their occupants—away from insects, whether they feed on cellulose or flesh. The overall effect is that the porch floor creates a new ground, a deck that hovers over the earth. Like sloping ground, its own tilted contour allies it with the never perfectly level planes of nature. The porch floor grasps the stability of the house as it also embodies its own uneven topography.

Some porch floors are raw and others are painted. All porch floors contend with weather and wear that other surfaces in the house manage to avoid. The Homosassa cabin's porch has three layers of paint: gray, chocolate brown, and red. Each coat fractures along the plywood grain, racing like streaks of rainwater toward the front. The slow march of feet and furniture across the porch is seven decades of birdwatchers, daytime nappers, wet dogs, and porch-sitters. Which is to say that a porch floor also measures time. In the porch floor's paint we can divine one cycle of the house. A new coat of paint marks a time when the cabin reached a limit of weathering. It might also signal a change in tenants—three coats of paint, three owners.

Amateur but aspiring chromochronologists that we are, it's not hard to see that the first coat, more than sixty years ago, was red, a meat red, the color of stained cedar or a weathered red barn. We had seen hints of this color below split battens but didn't know its provenance until we looked closely at the porch floor. This red cabin in the woods in the middle of the last century had a single color for walls and floors, as if it had been dipped in tomato soup and left to dry. The brown is more of a mystery. It's not clear if it's a stopgap between red and gray, or if it was also a house-wide color. The gray is where we are now, a neutral shade warmed by the colors underneath. This porch floor is a work of art, a Pollock in reverse, chipped and ruined, eroded and partially erased. I can't bring myself to paint it, although doing so would complement this historical process. Its own years of use would eventually reveal the cycles below.

A few years ago, when I paid regular visits to the porch in Cross Creek, I arrived one morning to find the ranger preparing to clean the floor. That summer had been one of the wettest on record. Coming after years of drought, I wondered if this gauzy dampness was what Rawlings would have felt, what her porch writing atmosphere would have been. She liked to travel and hunt during the winter, and despite the heat, she wrote in the summer when it was quieter and there were fewer visitors. Not only writing and sweating, but writing and wringing, and slogging through saturated air and soil. The ranger said this was the worst mildew bloom she had seen. But such conditions seemed common in Rawlings' time. I had seen the old pictures of the guest wing's board and battens darkened with mold. When tourism slows in the deafening heat, the Cross Creek house is closed for annual renovations, repairs, and maintenance. The ranger added bleach to the bucket of water as Rawlings would have done, and started mopping.

On the porch, I wrote: *The smell of fresh paint has replaced the tea olive blossoms. The front steps were repainted last night, and I must avoid them when I leave today. Cleared of furniture, the porch turns its hide like a dog waiting to be brushed. It feels smaller. Its floor has been lightly sanded to a silver sheen that is a century's patina unburdened by sealers or finishes. Naked, it affirms the patience of wood, resigned to Florida's soup, but supple in its rolling boil. Soon to be bleached—more tradition's conceit than necessity, it will gray again under the eastern sun. On the south end, the daybed's frame rests comfortably, shifted away from* the walls, and the houseward end leans toward the east like a flower to the sun. A footstool and asparagus fern are to the right of the screen door. The porch's slope facilitates cleaning and overall maintenance. There aren't any scuppers, and bleach water simply drains out the entry, its screen door held open with a wisp of wire. But there's a deeper significance to a floor that is cleaned the same way it fends off weather. A porch's tilt links daily life to environmental reality. On a sloped porch, we learn to practice resilience.

A porch's slope also maps climate into geography. To build a porch floor is to approximate the earth's surface. Before we knew the earth was round, we understood its inclined relation to the sun. Changes in latitude meant changes in solar angle and temperature, and so climate changed with position. Our word for climate comes from *klima*, which is Greek for slope. When Parmenides first divided the known world into different climate zones, he called them *klima*, effectively translating the rounded surface of the globe into sloped segments of land and water. In their journeys north or south, ancient mariners navigated these *klima*, as we—aboard our tilted porches, riding their slopes—must navigate worlds where position now changes because of climate.

⁑

I have thought a lot about the ideal depth of a porch. Familiarity breeds partiality, and I am convinced that the Homosassa porch is just right. Two inches shy of ten feet, it makes a comfortable room where we can sit around a table to play games, pull out a bedframe along its gentle slope, or sit back against the house at a comfortable distance from blowing rain. As an architect, I could cite design standards that try to quantify porch dimensions. Four feet can hold a rocking chair. A more generous depth for sitting and moving around is six feet. More than eight feet and the porch starts to compete with the house, like the exuberant porches—one of them twenty-feet deep—that anchor but also engulf the Gamble House, an iconic turn-of-the-century California bungalow by architects Greene and Greene. Sometimes, porch swings measure their porches. In Key West, a place that is home to more porches than anywhere else I have seen, they are shallow or deep, depending on whether the swing faces to the front or hangs crosswise.

I have found other depths similar to that of the Homosassa porch. At Cross Creek, Rawlings extended her house's original porch, which she derided for its thinness as a mere "excrescence." The expansion was funded by proceeds from *The Yearling*, which narrated its own share of porches. That new porch, the one where I have spent hours sitting, is one hundred seventeen inches deep, just an inch less than the cabin's porch. Rawlings used every inch to write at her round pine table with its palm trunk base. Further down the porch, whose length is three times its depth, she hosted Christmas dinners and sat and talked with visiting writers and neighbors. At the southern end, near the carport, the last third held a daybed. The porch's depth allowed for multiple uses along its length, like a series of small open-air rooms strung across an open plan.

⁎⁎

Lightning to the east, and the clouds are paper lanterns. Pulses of wind dive over the treeline and sprint across the river, bending palm fronds, then making cedar branches wave. The porch screen sifts the wind. Cedar needles and small bits of Spanish moss fall away, and a sifted breeze reaches bare arms, legs, faces. It feels warm, then much colder. Our faces strobe with more lightning. The screens don't filter out the metallic smell of the storm. It's just after sunset, dusky enough for fireflies. This storm will soon chase us inside, but first it will blow harder, sheets of rain will curtain across the river, hard drops will press into the lagoon and staccato the porch roof, softer droplets will aerosolize through the screen, and finally the world will turn on its side and rain will find the back of the porch.

There's nothing quite like experiencing a storm on a porch. It is exhilaration on the edges of catastrophe. There are also lessons here—how the floor sheds stormwater, how a porch absorbs the power of a storm. I saw this suppleness when I helped repair a house that went through the eye of Hurricane Andrew in south Florida. The house was severely damaged, but its two end porches were left intact even though they cantilevered precariously from the second floor. Winds near two hundred miles per hour ripped away their screens but blew on through. Building codes acknowledge this resilience when they exempt porches from the protection of hurricane shutters. There are two ideas here: the porch is an expendable part of the house or it is inherently prepared for storms. Maybe both are true, but the latter tells a lot about the strengths that can be found in a porch's weakness. How a porch resists a storm is that it lets the storm inside. Rain moves in and out, and wind moves through. Porches are models of resilience.

✲✲

Porch floors bounce. Ours bounces quite a bit because thin joists—two by six inches—aren't really meant to span ten feet—usually more like eight or nine. Some deflection is all right, though not this much. But it is not unusual for porches to stretch the limits of materials, extending our experiences along with them. What that bounce sacrifices in safety, it makes up for in comfort, like the extra cushion of a running shoe. It can be disconcerting to walk across the floor and feel the bob of a boat's deck, but it must have been worse. On my most recent trip under the porch, where I also uncovered a fishing rod in the flotsam of last week's king tide, I studied the boards that were added to shore up the spans. Midway along the central beam, a chunk of pressure-treated wood—thick, like the blocking from someone else's porch somewhere upriver—tries to bear the porch's weight directly into sodden ground. It twists with a dancer's pirouette. Another stopgap has repurposed an old rafter to support the joists halfway across their impetuous run from the center beam to the edge. Wedges and shims mark further attempts to level the porch's eccentricities. And the rafter's tail falls short of the front beam, floating like a ship's prow before a seawall. The other ten-foot span, where I am writing, still hangs unsupported. Getting accustomed to the porch's bounce is like finding your sea legs.

Porch floors flex and tilt. Sometimes, a building's imperfections are the perfect adaptations to conditions that inevitably change, just as tilt requires bending before bouncing back. I think about all the lightning we have witnessed on the porch. As each storm approached, we wondered when to go inside, feeling safe and reckless at the same time. A porch's resilience leverages that risk of exposure. Like finding moments of balance in a spinning, off-kilter world. On the porch, it becomes apparent that the world's imbalance—its ecliptic angle—is the balance of the seasons. On the porch, Agee reflects on how the earth "leans through a very slightly eccentric course." In some ways, Agee and Evans' chronic leveling of their makeshift beds on the porch is also their reckoning, as they stretch out and talk. Cormac McCarthy called this the "warp of the world." Their tilt means that porches are gyroscopic spaces constantly seeking balance as they pivot on the earth.

Porches assume a soaking. They balance wet and dry. The Homosassa cabin's porch is rustic, and there are no scuppers to drain water through the low knee walls. There are no outlets for the rain that comes in, but the water somehow finds its way out. It looks for gaps between the wall plate and the plywood floor, for holes between batten and board, for that wedge of air under the screen door. Water exits, just as it must fall after a hurricane's surge. I have witnessed the sluice of a rainstorm but not the flood of a hurricane, only its aftermath. I imagine it as a kind of architectural alchemy in which air slowly becomes water, and the porch holds that water like air for a time, a frozen moment, hesitating as if this might be its new medium. And then, just as you acclimate to this new world, it changes. Water back to air.

And so a porch's tilt recollects core attributes of resilience: sobriety, levity, and buoyancy. The slope of a porch is its clearheaded response to the need to shed water. Porches keep us humble; they are reminders of vulnerability, youthfulness, and smallness. A three-inch slope is a small but significant tithe amid human fantasies of perfection. Agee pointed out that those "delusions of . . . strength and wisdom" make it difficult for us "to carry in our minds in any literalness the fact of our small size and our youth." The tilt of porches is also the light-heartedness that lets us shrug off setbacks like so much wind and rain. They might even be a tilt-a-whirl for the senses on the edge of your house. When you walk along its slope or when you sit crosswise, it gives a sense that you're slightly off balance, and you might be on a boat that hasn't been centered or in a vessel where someone has just scrambled to its edge and leaned over the gunwale to see a manatee or a dolphin. And although porches float on air and not water, there is a kind of buoyancy to porches that makes them resilient. Something buoyant requires constant leveling. Which is why porches are like boats, and why porch floors aren't level.

3

AIR

A funnel weaver crouches where the corner boards gap. Her web is an inverted tent in front of her burrow. Its filaments shine in the afternoon sun. Before I painted the ceiling the color of a robin's egg, these spiders used to lay out their satin balconies all across the porch's air. Now we mostly find their webs in window frames, under soffits, and along the other edges of the house. It must be the coolness of late fall that has brought this sojourner back onto the porch for warmth. Her burrow is above the column at the front, safely below the puzzling blue of the ceiling. How do you build with air on what already appears to be sky?

Their bite is harmless, but their bodies are large as paperclips, with long twist ties for legs, and they jump. Though we keep our distance from them and their wolf spider relatives, I can't avoid their webs, and I marvel at how they siphon insects; how their guy wires, thick and thin, trace invisible contours; and how flues of silk seem to bend air. They remind me that a house, much less a porch, is a tenuous endeavor. Their funnel webs are ephemeral porches to their inner retreats, and I can't forget that Thoreau wrote that the "house is still but a sort of porch at the entrance of a burrow." They remind me that a porch is built from the air that wraps a house and overlaps with nature and this funnel weaver ether.

I haven't discovered a technical term for the air that surrounds a house. Maybe "porch" already names it. Or maybe it doesn't need to be named, only played. As children in North Carolina, Earl and Horace Scruggs stepped through this air when they practiced their timing for a bluegrass song. Strumming banjos, the brothers set out from their porch in opposite directions around the house and hoped to meet exactly where they had started. Their notes must have made their own weather. Crackling, pinging, hammering, chopping, dreaming, waking. Around the edge of the house, just above the skin of the earth, Earl learned how sound carries in foothill air, what humidity does to a banjo's stretched head, where music comes from.

Rudolf Geiger called the air that hovers just above the earth nothing more than "the air layer close to the ground." Rudolf's older brother invented the instrument that detects radiation, but Rudolf himself focused on another kind of disturbed air—the air from your feet to just above your head, where ground conditions interfere with atmospheric readings. Earth's friction, temperature fluctuations, topographic inconstancies, water, grass, stone, and dirt all create what Geiger called "special conditions." Meteorologists try to avoid this messy air with its "chance influences" when they set their instruments two meters high. Perhaps they seek what W. H. Auden calls the "untilled air" that precedes human presence. But Geiger believed this air that prevails in the "boundary layer of earth and atmosphere" harbors the microclimates that help us understand the macroclimate.

Geiger studied all sorts of microclimates where those special conditions occurred: gardens, potato fields, smoking forests, tree shadows, felled clearings, alpine slopes, snow-melts, riverbanks, even automobiles. Geiger referred to them as "habitat climates." The air of those places bears all of habitation's complexities, all the muddle of living. This is the air where porches mix the atmospheric with the cultural, the natural, and the social. When a porch takes up residence in a house's atmospheric skin, it localizes climate, it brings living to climate, and climate becomes a way of life.

If Geiger taught me that air is where things happen, then Peter Sloterdijk connects air to thought and consciousness. Like a porch to its house, air resides at the limits of perception. It links what we can't always see with what we might struggle to comprehend and articulate, and the porch makes room for it. Sloterdijk characterizes air as "a medium that allowed humans to realize the fact that they're always already immersed in something almost imperceptible and yet very real, and that this pace of immersion dominates the changing sites of the soul down to its most intimate modifications." With its air, a porch expands climate from the atmospheric to the cultural and the social and to the intellectual. In that sense, the porch is an architecture of the noosphere, the so-called thinking layer of the earth. It is where we sort through phenomena and where we can think deeply about the climate around us. In a porch's air, we contemplate connections between dwelling and atmosphere. We ruminate on what "habitat climate" means.

Air is material as well as medium, and a porch holds both. It holds atmosphere and narrative, the climatic and the cultural. And it mixes them to the point they can't always be parsed. In a Eudora Welty story, the air of a porch can be saturated with emotion as well as water. With such pathetic fallacy, air carries the opening and shutting eyes of a house, and the sleeping porch in her story "The Winds" holds the "strange fluid lightning" that fills air now wondrously "soundless of thunder." More than personification, air is a full-on character that walks in its "stupor" across the fields of adolescence.

Air sets the porch's plot in motion. It welcomes surety and chance, the expected and the unexpected, guests and rain, strangers and lightning. It holds things and moisture, but also words and stories, dreams and thoughts, as clear as the scent of a tea olive that wafts through porch screens, yet as ephemeral as those gossamer threads of the funnel weaver.

A mosquito must have followed me onto the porch. Earlier, it buzzed in my ear, and now it bounces against the funnel web. Its vibrations bring the spider out of her burrow, and, suspended on air, she watches her visitor fly away.

The most guests we've had on the porch is seven. We are four, and it was clear on that stormy day in July that our porch's capacity is eleven. Which also turns out to be the limit of our hospitality. We had gone out early that morning to scallop the shallow flats near channel marker 4. On this kind of morning, cloudless and calm, water's transparency becomes vertiginous. A low morning sun lit eelgrass and corals with a seraphic glow. Vitreous. This clarity further thins the bay's flats. Ten feet appears ten inches, and it takes your breath when you leave the channel and look down on hard bottom and fish and turtles, bracing for the moment you run aground.

A late morning squall chased us back to the river's mouth, and from there our pontoon inched forward through the kind of rain that hurts. Sheets of cold, impossible in midsummer warmth, blurred vision, and numbed skin. Lightning flashed on a rental boat running full throttle out of the channel, on the wrong side of the green marker that signals the limestone reef hidden just below the water's surface. Locals call it the "Devil's knuckle." Even without the veils of rain, you still wouldn't see it unless you read how the water's grainy fabric bunches up over the shoal. The storm drowned our calls, and we felt the impact even as its grind was lost in another clap of thunder.

We tied off to the marker, and my son and I swam over to the reef. The motor's skeg was firmly lodged in the bones of ancient coral, soft enough to accept the steel fin and hard enough to hold on. When all seven on deck moved to the front of the boat, the stern lifted and we spun the pontoon free. With no time to look at the damage as the storm's winds picked up, we towed them back to our cabin. They will wait out the storm on our porch as guests—and thinking back on it, I'm reminded of the ancient Greeks. Our visitors were tourists caught in a storm. We could tell they just wanted to get home. Their trip wasn't epic, but their visit recalls how porches hosted Odysseus, who was no stranger to storms or shipwrecks on his own journey home.

After the hero escapes Calypso on a handmade raft, an angry Poseidon brews a storm that casts Odysseus ashore on the island of Scheria. He is discovered by the Princess Nausicaa, who takes him to her father, Alcinous. The King welcomes the unknown guest with speeches and banquets and at night offers a bed on the porch: "white-armed Arete told her maids to place a bedstead beneath the portico, and to lay on it beautiful purple blankets, and to spread above them coverlets, and on these to put fleecy cloaks for clothing. . . . and welcome it seemed to him to lie down to sleep. So there he slept, the much-enduring noble Odysseus, on the corded bedstead under the echoing portico. But Alcinous lay down in the inmost chamber of his lofty house."

King Alcinous and Queen Arete follow the rules of ancient Greek hospitality. *Xenia* calls for hosts to open their houses to visitors, whether friends or strangers, and the porch offers a place of shelter for them, under a roof but outside a house's interior chambers. The porch provides a space for what philosophers have called the "right of the visit," which is distinct from the right of residence. The porch isn't considered any less comfortable than the rest of the palace. Homer's descriptions of lavish bedding and deep echoes across a generous room attest to that. In modern houses, where climate is controlled in the main interior of a house, peripheral living areas like porches remain open to the elements and, by extension, open to visitors. So, the unconditioned porch fits well with unconditional hospitality.

These rights and traditions were strong enough that they were practiced even when hosts and guests were traveling, and even between enemies. Near the end of Homer's *Iliad*, Priam sneaks into the Achaean camp and finds the tent of Achilles to retrieve the body of his son Hector. Even though Achilles killed Hector and dragged his body for twelve days, the Greek warrior dutifully receives the Trojan king and makes a bed for him on the porch of his substantial tent. Homer has Priam's bedstead furnished with the same accessories— coverlets, "purple blankets," and "fleecy cloaks"—that would greet a guest on a palace's porch. It is a temporary porch fit for a king—or anyone else. Yet Priam still sleeps among enemies, and his guide Hermes wakes him in the night to sneak him out of the camp along with Hector's body. Just as the porch is a place of hospitality for adversaries, strangers, and friends alike, it also hosts visits from messenger gods.

Stories of ships and travelers remind me of the houseboat that used to be moored in our back creek. Talking with previous owners solved the mystery of a shore-power outlet at the back dock and a single piling coiled with thick ropes. Their faded photograph shows a thirty-foot vessel with open-air decks fore and aft and thin railings around the roof. I still marvel that they must have piloted it up and down the shallow creek. It mostly stayed in port, tied to the piling, its three pontoons beached on the muck at low tide, waiting to host guests. To sleep on this boat was a hospitality on par with the ancient Greek porch; it had the roominess of another cabin, and its upper deck offered sleep sheltered by the Milky Way's glow.

There is a rough equivalency between the docked boat and the decked-out porch. Each bonds host and guest along tethered strands of coming and going, whether suspended in water or floating on air. But when King Nestor hosted Telemachus, the thought of the son of Odysseus sleeping on the deck of his ship launches the indignant Argonaut into an effusive speech that anchors hospitality not just in the host's duty, but even more so in the capacity to make a guest feel at home. Nestor offers his porch as an integral part of his palace—a room wrapped on three sides with ornately frescoed walls where guests sleep under warm "cloaks and fair blankets" below a roof lifted high on two stout columns. This well-appointed porch is the size of a small house, and its airy grandiosity also has plenty of room for the household's bachelors so that Nestor's unwed son Peisistratus can join Telemachus, each on his own "corded bedstead under the echoing portico."

At the core of Nestor's palace is the megaron, the Mycenaean building form with a great hall fronted by a vestibule and an open porch. Our modest cabin is no palace—it could easily join Telemachus on Nestor's porch, but the two share an elemental architecture. Nested in each is the original composition of a single room with a hearth inside and a porch on the front. The clarity of their squared volumes and the simplicity of their layout chart the passage between outside and inside and between public and private worlds. The open porch fronts an inner refuge as it also extends outward for air and guests. In its simplest form, the megaron's side walls project beyond the front just enough to flank the porch. They look like arms stretching outward for a hug. They also remind me of a beetle's mandibles. A while ago, when a stag beetle wandered onto the porch, I thought about how he grasps the air in front of him with those serrated jaws. Here, whether out in front of an ancient megaron or a scooting beetle, are the origins of a porch—an essential reaching. Porches embrace air and guests.

⁑

The air of a porch welcomes the sun. Traditionally facing east and south, the Homeric porch, like our own, greets the rising sun and tracks its journey skyward, and I wonder if Telemachus, waking to the classic "rosy-fingered" dawn of Homer's narrative, felt the same thrill as we do when a ruddy sun edges the corner column on a late summer morning. But it doesn't just receive light and warmth for its sleeping visitors; it grasps and hangs on. It flares with the sun. The prefix of the Greek word Homer uses for porch connects it to fire—the way it kindles, lights up, burns, and blazes. And I suspect the Greek porch harbored both sun and fire—archeologists have found hearths on megaron porches—and I can picture the soft warmth of torches there.

Those torches are an ancient equivalent of the porch light, which is one way a porch makes a home for its guests. Pools of light spill out between a porch's columns, or a screened porch becomes a billowing lantern for those outside. A light on the porch signals that you are home, or at least you might be. It has a double meaning as welcome and warning, but generally a porch light is an invitation that makes anyone who sees it a potential guest. Scientists at MIT recently called a laser beacon meant to attract the attention of extraterrestrial beings a "porch light," as if it might be a universal sign of life and hospitality.

A porch light attracts closer life forms as well. Vladimir Nabokov ardently turned on the lights of porches and verandas to draw in the moths he collected. The veranda of a Utah ski lodge was for him a kind of hunting blind, and he stayed up all night gathering specimens. During the day, Nabokov would have watched for butterflies from other porches and verandas, like the one on the Black Sea where he spent a week in June unwittingly talking with a convalescing Franz Kafka. In his autobiography, Nabokov melds two porches—the ones where he caught moths and the ones that serve as thresholds to memories. On the Proustian evocations of ether's smell, he says that the "stuff would always cause the porch of the past to light up and attract" the "blundering beauty" of moths.

In Nabokov's telling, porches drift lightly and float kaleidoscopically. They meet air like a butterfly's wings at dusk.

The Russian writer recalled sitting at the age of fourteen on the family veranda with a book in hand as his mother, trance-like, lay out glossy cards on a table in the summer night and the "thick, velvet heliotrope-soaked chasm into which the veranda glided." From the Homosassa porch, I have seen sphinx, hawk, and saltmarsh moths. In daylight, there are zebra longwings, cloudless sulphurs, and monarchs—have they crossed the gulf from Mexico? Last year, a mangrove skipper rested on the screen for a day, slowly stretching black wings, as late November sun glinted on iridescent blue.

When I return to the cabin from paddling the river at night, a single lamp on the porch guides me. Its burning incandescence is the paling fire of a lantern tethered to the lagoon that is filled with stars.

Our guests had to wait out the storm. Freed from the shoal, but now marooned on an island with strangers. Though its screens dampened air's bluster, they shivered as they arrived on the porch. Lightning and thunder and excitement had tempered formalities, but it still felt strange because we don't have many visitors. For expediency, we tied up their boat at the neighbor's dock, and they came to the porch from the front, not the back, where we dock our boat. Power for the cabin also enters at the back. A single, precarious electrical line dips and swings across the marsh, and a pole dug into the limestone drops a thin cable to the cabin. The line is a New Jersey businessman's legacy. He needed power for his restaurant at the mouth of the river, and a deal was formulated in the 1980s that he could have his electricity as long as cabin owners along the way could tap into this power source, a luxury for such rustic and remote living. One day we jumped at the sound of two electric company employees who came looking for our electric meter. They had docked their boat out back and tromped through the cedars and pepper trees, swearing and carping at the jungle.

Wait long enough and the world comes to you. Porches are waiting rooms where boredom and chance intersect. When I first sit down on the porch, I stare across the river at the vignette I am so familiar with. The opening of the lagoon frames the stand of silver rampikes and the hatch marks of cordgrass between river and forest hammock. It is a picture, reassuring in its slow change, exhilarating in its flickers of life, but also provoking, as the import of those changes becomes apparent. A gray fringe steadily grows along the muzzle of the receding forest. Young mangroves rise out of the crowded grass, like schoolkids eager to be recognized. Low tide reveals ragged edges of oyster colonies that sharpen the limestone bank. Even a rushing floodtide stretches time. This view is a canvas that hangs in suspension. It is also a living canvas, and I wait for something to happen.

Today, the air on the porch is still. Uncannily still. It is stretched taut, and nothing can move. The day began with the wail of airboats pulsing across distant marsh. Passing neighbors waved through the noise of their mud motors. A cooling breeze brings a gentle swing to the plaster sculpture hanging from the porch post. Last summer we made plaster casts on a beach of oyster shells down the river. White with time, their smooth inner porcelain reminded us they had been shucked centuries earlier. This midden near the river's mouth holds so many thousands of shells that it makes its own island, eroding a bit more with each boat's wake and each tide. Water reaches deeper into layers of time, and oak trees tilt and fall from the riverbank and its cliff of shells. I wonder if our casts are less about sculpting something and more about trying to stem this erosion. Their crunch reminded us that we walked more on air than shell. These plaster casts, with their homemade coquina, hardened clouds of shell, seaweed, and driftwood, now barnacle our porch like a new kind of oyster colony.

Yesterday, green fronds brushing palm trunks were the sound of manatee breaths, brown fronds were cardboard dragged across pavement. Sun glazed the backs of pelicans flying upriver to the fish market, where the night's catch was being cleaned. I was mesmerized by the cobra swing of a green pelican's body, hypnotizing then striking fish in the shallows. The earnest flight of a cormorant swept downriver. But today it is quiet, has been for what seems like hours. Water lightly wakes its shore, and even the gentle shush of wind is gone. I wait and everything waits. Waiting on a porch has an atavistic tenseness. Waiting that extends millennia. In equal measure, I am at ease and uneasy on a porch where boredom mixes with expectation, contentedness with anxiousness. The stillness of the air bears a deep sense of belonging, tinged with alienation. Being here is relaxing but it brings heightened senses. I see it in my dogs who peer over the porch's rail. Their noses move and twitch with the expressiveness of a human face. I see the tableau, but they know all the actors: otters, raccoons, manatees, dolphins, mice, squirrels, a distant bobcat or black bear or a deer. I must wait for them to show, sign the air or water with movement.

Then I see it, a glint of sharpened light. Across the river where the grass meets the water. First it is something on fire.

Then it is a tailing fish, a big one, where the snook ran last year. It bobs up and down, more flotsam over where we find buckets, buoys, bottles. Now it is a beacon, a mirror signaling. Something ineffable. A heliograph, small but so bright that it holds the sun. I watch and wait, expecting the river to extinguish it, swallow its light, but it intensifies. I climb down from the porch and paddle over. A single leaf, bent midway down its blade, dips in and out of the water. A single movement across immobilized air. In a guide to Florida grasses I will learn that this is the flag leaf, the last leaf before the spartina grass flowers. Far inland, wheat farmers know this means to prepare for harvest. The message for me is how to read details of the estuary and its marsh cycles. Now, I wait for those wetted blades that mark time.

We don't wait for visitors on the porch because we don't really expect them. The most surprised we've been was when two kayakers hailed us from the lagoon. One was the son of the cabin's previous owners, wanting to show a friend where he spent time growing up. He told us stories of camping with his grandfather in the hammocks and middens across the river, beyond the waving grass, far up the creek's veins. He explained the winch on the cedar tree that overhangs the front dock: when the lagoon silted up after a storm they would pull the boat around, tie its bow to the winch's cable, throttle forward, and blow the sediment into the river. Homemade dredging.

He remembers sitting on the porch's glider rocker and watching the light change in the palms across the river. He said this place made him who he is. He thinks it began even before he was born when his parents lived here full-time. His father commuted to a nearby town to work as an emergency room doctor, and his mother, even toward the end of her pregnancy, kayaked all over the marsh. He remembered the snuffle of armadillos in the saltbush and watching raccoons from atop the houseboat in the back creek. He remembered the kerosene heater that smelled like burning dust and the deep turpentine smell of the heartwood pine that frames the cabin. He was fascinated with how palms never grow straight. Before paddling away, he said that this place inspired him to become an ecologist, and he plans to study the mangroves that are now common this far north along the coast. It had been almost twenty years since his last visit, back when mangrove seedlings barely made it through the winter.

Those guests reminded me of the notes that came with the cabin. Later, I sat on the porch and flipped through the sheaf of lined notepaper, simply titled "Some Things You Need to Know." In the upper right corner, cursive script says October 7, 1997, dating it to our visitor's grandparents. I had forgotten how much information was in there, and how much we really didn't know, but also how much we had learned on our own, by doing—testing and improvising—but also by thinking—waiting and watching. That four-page document is packed with practical information, laced with stories. Water systems, sewage disposal, property markers, utilities, weather, wildlife, fireplace, drinking water, and the docking cove. This last section echoes our visitor's account, while it also alludes to different perspectives: "The 'No Name Storm' several years ago caused more silting in the cove. There is no legal way to get it out. Regular in and out helps keep the entrance open. It helps when the tide is low and outgoing, to put the bow of your boat against the dock and put the engine (carefully) in forward. This drives silt out into the river. Local river people can tell you how to solve the problem more efficiently but . . ." The writer trails off like sound dissolves in air. That ellipsis tells a story. . . .

**

When our shipwrecked guests arrived, we invited them onto the porch, put coffee on, passed around a pile of towels, and watched the storm. The cabin's front porch looks out onto an avenue of boats, and when the weather is good on weekends or holidays, the river is a pageant of sea-doos, skiffs, pontoons, and larger yachts. When there is an early afternoon storm in the gulf like today, that parade reverses in a mad race of spray and shouts and temerity back up the river to shelter. Usually, we are avid spectators but this time we had joined the spectacle.

We watch people and boats on the water as if they are pedestrians and cars on a road. A favorite porch game is to guess the type of boat by its sound—the cycling of its motor, the way its hull strikes the water, the number and cadence of its voices. If we had heard our stranded guests on their way out this morning, their pontoon would have sounded like all the other rentals—gutted motor straining full throttle, wash bubbling and gurgling in the motor well, pontoons sloshing across the wake of other boats, happy tourists laughing and yelling over the engine.

In this game, the shrimp boats are the easiest, particularly in the morning before most other boats are out. Each has its signature—Miss Squeaky sets out a bright Q-lamp to probe the waking air, Just Be Claws is the newest boat and has the quietest motor, Captain Herb gears down to shoot the gaps when the river channel narrows, and Ugly Duck plays talk radio as you feel the seismic hum of its motors in your chest. Next easiest are the crabbers. One of the boats—I think it's the crew that puts out the buoys painted like strawberries—runs a forty-horsepower two-stroke. The motor's twang and its thrust and idle are distinct, but it's the smell of fish chum that gives them away. It clings to the porch screen like the seaweed on a crab trap's wire mesh. Jet skis are all motor, pontoons burble, and the hulls of bay boats resonate with the river's depth.

Sometimes, watching the world from the porch is like looking through the gap of a door left ajar. Stories come from these slivers of air. Flannery O'Connor watched town life from the porch in Milledgeville, and then farm life from her Andalusia porch. In each place, she described watching the world as if through a "crack in the door." Where the lagoon opens into the river, we catch glimpses of the boats we have been listening to. They reel between arching cedars, and the stories unfold, some fast, others slower. In this window of air, we have seen a mother change her baby's diaper on top of the brine tanks of a passing shrimp boat, and recently I watched a husband and wife rescue an injured sea turtle more than half the size of their skiff. One summer, returning scallopers took turns peeing off the back of their boat, in full view of the river. Eco-tourists nearly tipped their guide's pontoon, idling at the lagoon's mouth, when they clamored to one side for a better view of dolphins making their daily feeding run up the river. I could hear the guide narrate this river safari: "They are super-fast. I thought they might follow our wake. . . . Sometimes they raise their noses and bodies out of the water in a challenge." Wildlife frequently upstages human drama; the other day I watched those same dolphins coordinate a hurricane swirl of mud and water around a school of fish. Trapped along the far bank, the mullet leaped into their mouths. I am told that this mud ring feeding is specific to the bottlenose in this part of the gulf.

A place for watching and longing, the porch transports us without our having to leave. Writers have long used porches as devices to move plot, reflect character, harbor drama, and connect readers to setting. The porch is a stage that we watch, but also a place where we join characters on their watch. We are there, too, looking out, straining our eyes down a dusty street, waiting. We are with them, watching. When I read *The Ballad of the Sad Café*, I am right there with five others on Miss Amelia's porch as a figure moves slowly toward her store. A human? An animal? A calf? Or is this "somebody's young'un"? Definitely a stranger. Closer, the hunchback emerges from dim moonlight into the porch's yellow light. It is the porch where he acts out feigned grief publicly and where, at the end, fully identified as Cousin Lymon, he paints half the porch bright green. A longtime porch-sitter on her veranda that overlooked the Hudson River, writer Carson McCullers knew about watching places and people from porches. She knew that porches look inward as they also look out. Later, the townspeople will look from the porch back into Amelia's office as the hunchback's nefarious plans unfold.

The porch hides as it reveals because its door is half open and half closed. It can be read as an invitation to enter, while it is also a caution. In McCullers' story, Amelia's porch is on her property but not what she considers her premises. She allows her guests to drink on the porch, just as drinking on a front porch has been legally defined as not drinking in public, although it is often in full view. Such a place offers a vantage point that exists in a kind of social limbo, a place where the extrovert and the introvert each finds a home, where eavesdroppers and thieves, voyeurs and exhibitionists, socialites and loners all might feel comfortable. A porch hovers between seeing and being seen.

Watching the world from a porch also challenges sight. Filaments of light gently split the boards along the low wall at the front of my porch. There is one sliver, wider than the others, that I imagine to be a bore sample through air. It is just wide enough that I can read the wedelia's emerald glow, the pickle green swing of palmettos, and the lagoon's slate surface. That light is where the winter wood and summer wood of grain have parted, and sap still bleeds. That sliver of air reminds me that there are many ways of seeing.

The young woman shakes with cold in the rocking chair. Even as the storm casts warm gusts through the screen, her shudders move through the layers of blankets we normally keep in reserve for winter. Our son piles on more when he notices her lips have turned blue. They never did tell us their names, but we came to know them with the stories they told. The older bearded man—the patriarch everyone else looked to before they spoke—had planned the trip along with his two teenage sons, who sat shirtless to his left and right, as if this display of muscles and tenacity might impress their father. They had lived in Ocklawaha, then Pasco County, and now Beverly Hills—the Citrus County version. The man wanted to show the Gulf Coast to his best friend, who was visiting from Illinois with his wife and two kids, a boy and a girl.

Our children play board games with the kids and then start a puzzle on the coffee table. The man, who we now realize has been drinking all morning, talks about his years in the swamps of central Florida. On a porch, pathetic fallacy isn't just a reflection of weather and mood. It works more directly as it guides conversations and the rise and fall of plotlines, and for an hour and a half we will listen to his stories as the storm matches the cadence of his voice. Much later, with the storm and the storyteller finally spent, the sun and our senses will return.

Some of his stories are standard Florida—a northerner's relocation south and a partial retirement that requires an assortment of stopgap jobs. Others are specific to this region and its mix of fresh and salt water. He loves boats and spends every opportunity out in swamps and lakes, and his misreading of the channel marker confirms that those inland bodies of water likely don't have such navigational aids. The rest sound like today's story—tales of boating mishaps, dislodged plugs, ragged props, and lost anchors. And now the new story of the storm and the reef. Such narratives have been the currency of guests since ancient times.

Air carries stories, which alight on the edges of buildings like pollen on screens. And when Homer invokes the echoing colonnade of Greek porches, those ancient spaces resonate not just with sound but also with myth. I don't think I understood how ancient Greeks lived so closely with these stories until I walked around the Erechtheum, the temple on the Acropolis dedicated to Athena and Poseidon. Growing up in Nashville, known as the Athens of the South, introduced me to classical architecture, and in the replica of the Parthenon there, I could imagine walking through the porches of antiquity. They conveyed monumentality and the proportions and rhythms that Greek architects deployed with such skill, but for me they didn't yet hold myth. When I worked for a summer in Athens, the Erechtheum taught me how Greek architecture tied itself intimately to its site and how legends and stories shaped the edges of classical buildings. The Erechtheum's porches helped the temple hug its uneven slope, captured the stories that saturated ancient air, and embraced the sacred grounds that bore their marks and traces. It is an idiosyncratic building and its porches traded formal symmetry for what I think of as narrative symmetries. Those porches balanced myth with the realities of stone.

Most days after work, I would climb the steps from the agora to the Propylaea, which acts as a porch for the whole Acropolis site. It frames a clear view to the Parthenon, but the Erechtheum, though smaller, demands equal attention. The maidens, or caryatids, of the south porch eliminated the distance—both temporal and physical—between us. Their bright figures, in front of deep shadow and each face slightly different, anchored and humanized the temple. To their left, a single column of the east porch made a slender shaft of air with the far corner, and they seemed to stand guard of the west porch to their right, protecting its broken pediment and shattered columns from further ruin. Farther back, the north porch pinioned the temple to terraced stone. Over a near horizon of rubble, between its tall columns, are blue sky and the limestone cap of Mount Lycabettus in the distance.

The porches of the Erechtheum tell the story of the contest for Athens. The city's first king, Cecrops, part human and part snake, sought a patron deity. From among the gods, Athena and Poseidon competed for this honor, and each presented a gift to the city. The god of the sea struck his trident into the ground, and an extraordinary fountain flowed. The Athenians were struck by its beauty, but soon found that its waters were salty like the sea, of little use despite its splendors. With much less drama, the goddess of wisdom buried a seed that soon sprouted. It rapidly grew into an olive tree that provided shade, wood, and olives. Athena won the competition, and the Erechtheum housed not only a golden lamp that burned all year and a wooden sculpture of the goddess, but also the stories of this contest and other legends at the core of Athenian identity.

To walk around the Erechtheum is to retrace these foundational myths. There, on one of the north porch's floor stones, are the marks of Poseidon's trident. Three deep scratches pierce the marble as if it were once softened clay. Another scar in the floor is a semicircular hole that is said by some to have emitted the sounds, smells, vapors, and mysteries of the sea. A hole in the roof about the size of a door opens up another version of this story. Some believe that Zeus, father of Athena, signaled the end of the contest for Athens with a bolt of lightning. In the sculpted scene of the Parthenon's west pediment sculpture, Athena and Poseidon seem to react to an event out of the scene's frame. In 1903, excavators believed they had discovered the lightning's point of impact, a mark known as Enelysia. And so the porch makes room for both myths—the impact of a trident and the path and strike of a lightning bolt.

Another porch is said to have protected the olive tree

planted by Athena. Scrambling up the steep slope to the west side of the Erechtheum, I find a tree planted much more recently amid the ruins. From the Propylaea, the west porch had appeared to grow out of this olive's dark leaves. Archeologists have found evidence that the same kind of tree once grew in the pronaos, the entry porch to the temple's interior. An olive tree grown in a porch. And not just any porch but one that literally "shoulders" two other porches, north and south.

Porches barnacle air, and the Erechtheum grew by accretion. As its layout shifted over time, the air around it continued to be charged with meaning. The hot winds blowing over the stones of the Acropolis speak with the ring of a trident on stone, the crack of lightning and rumble of thunder, and the rustle of leaves in a sacred tree. Porches grow around such stories like oysters on rock saturated by myth. Turning from Athena's tree toward the southwest corner reveals the porch of the maidens. Its figures, patiently bearing the weight of the roof, gaze placidly toward the Parthenon. The caryatids are reminders of the very origins of Athens. It was here, before the porch was built, that Athenians fed honey cakes to a snake, the patron beast of Cecrops and an oracle for the city's fortune. It is said that a deep foreboding fell over the city when the snake didn't accept the cakes.

As I walk around the Erechtheum, tripping over stones, sketching, taking photographs, I read accounts from Pausanias who was "much amazed" at the mysteries of this temple. I am likewise enthralled by these porches and the stories they hold. The Greek traveler tells how the maidens are also reminders of the Arrephoroi, two acolytes of Athena who lived on the Acropolis and once a year carried an enigmatic basket the goddess had given them. I move from porch to porch. Like

an acolyte myself, I am immersed in each story's riddles and, like an archeologist, I try to decipher this temple's complex history through its porches.

Dodging other tourists, I turn east and Pausanias' story continues to spin: "the maidens descend by the natural underground passage . . . across the precincts . . . of Aphrodite. They leave down below what they carry and receive something else which they bring back covered up." My fellow traveler's circumspection only deepens the mystery. Among the slender columns of the east porch was an altar to Dione, for some the mother of Aphrodite. Ancient Athenians, navigating their own walks across the Acropolis, would have made the connection between this story told on the east porch and the procession of the Arrephoroi, visible in the caryatids. They carry the porch's roof like those secret baskets, and the porch in turn bears its mysteries. The difficulty of the archeologist is actually the capacity of the porch to accommodate the many layers and plotlines of myth. Porches readily shift for the story, as they can just as easily adjust to land and contour and view.

Back in front of the caryatid porch, I think about how the draped figures have been replaced with replicas but still reveal the weathering of pollution, wind, and rain. I wish I could hear more of their stories. Mute witnesses to time, they have watched Lord Elgin make off with one of their group to England, they have seen the destruction of war, and now their porch is a backdrop for the selfies and photographs of throngs of tourists. I try to imagine being there at the end of the Panathenaic Procession, ancient Athens' most important event, which stitches the city together like the *peplos* that the Arrephoroi wove throughout the year. We all look up at the porch, high on its podium, and behind the screen of the caryatids, they have just presented the garment to Athena's wooden statue inside the Erechtheum. Earlier during the procession, far from the Acropolis, we could see the north porch of the Erechtheum along the outcrop's rocky crest. More prominent than any other building, it marked our destination. And leaving the agora on our procession and beginning the steep walk up, there it was again, the north porch, peeking above the trees and rock.

Myths connected citizens to the founding of their city, and porches, like those of the Erechtheum, made those fleeting events visible and timeless. They made tangible spaces for the stories. Toward the end of that summer in Athens, I was walking through Monastiraki at dusk. Looking up from the Tower of the Winds, I could see the north porch illuminated, a gold lantern in the purpling sky.

Porches are places built of air, and they link climate to myth. If the interior of a building captures and displaces air, then porches weave it. Air becomes as much a building material as wood, metal, or marble. That air ripples with stories. It is infused and circled like a timber's sap rings that narrate the seasons across springwood's dark grain and summerwood's lighter shades. The Erechtheum's porches led me back to John Ruskin, and I sit on the cabin's porch on the front edge of a spring storm, reading *The Queen of the Air*, where Ruskin sets out to study Greek myths of clouds and storms. It's an obscure book, but one that cuts to the core of myth and air and, in my mind, the story of porches. In the preface, Ruskin marvels at how the "Greek conception of an ethereal element pervading space" forecast modern physics. Ruskin writes on the first of May in 1869 (and I'm reading his preface exactly one hundred and fifty years later), only months after John Tyndall delivered his paper that first gave scientific proof for why the sky is blue. Tyndall sings of the "elastic medium" that "fills all space" and of the heady "vibrations" of those "aether particles" that make the "heavenly azure."

Ruskin makes the case for Athena as the "queen of air." He retells stories of her as he outlines the ways that she serves as air's agent. Fresh air is the "spirit of life" that Athena brings to Penelope as she waits for Odysseus' return. It is the breath that gives soldiers strength in battle. His florid prose in full swing like the breeze that now tugs at the book's pages, Ruskin writes: "Whenever you throw your window wide open in the morning, ..."—I don't think Ruskin wrote on porches, but I imagine him throwing open his study window: ". . . you let in Athena, as wisdom and fresh air in the same instant, and whenever you draw a pure, long, full breath of right heaven, you take Athena into your heart, through your blood." Athena, queen of air, also feeds the leaves of trees, not just those of the olive but of the forests, and brings nourishing dew to the pastures. Here, Ruskin returns us to the Erechtheum and retells the myth of Cecrops' daughters who were nymphs of the dew—earth, cloud, and heaven, and who helped bring up Athena's adopted son Erichthonius. He recasts the Erechtheum and its porches not only as the place dedicated to Athena but also as a temple of dew and the air that bears it. Air is also the element that powers sailing vessels, and Ruskin reminds us that the *peplos* was carried on the mast of a ship as it made its way to the Erechtheum. And the temple's lamp—the one I saw from the Tower of the Winds—glows with the air that nourishes fire. Like a ship's lantern.

I had never considered Ruskin an ecologist, but in the ozone of a nearing squall, I remember that he called his approach "field work." He interprets myths as they relate to natural phenomena and focuses on clouds and storms to discover the atmosphere behind the stories. We do that every time we venture out on the porch. Ruskin writes the book in the Swiss town of Vevey. Amid the fresh air of spring, he looks out over Lake Geneva toward the snowy peaks of the Alps and beyond to Italy and Greece, where he will soon go. His study window connects him to nature far and near.

The last example Ruskin gives of Athena as the agent of air relates to sound. She carries its vibrations. And he finds them in the songs and throats of birds, in the murmur of insects, and in the quivering tail of the snake. These are "air incarnate," and they are also the "voices of war and peace." The squall's first drops of rain ping on the porch roof, and gusts from the south are musky, like brackish earth. When southerly winds blew across the Erechtheum's porches, they carried sounds of waves from the saltwater well of Poseidon's trident. They rose from the porch into the Acropolis and out across the city of Athens.

Our myths are more mundane, but we tell a few to our guests on the porch, in the midst of the storm. We tell them because porches hold stories, and because stories embody reciprocity. I ask if they saw the Bait Lady this morning. Bonnie Van Buren sells live bait and ice cream from her pontoon anchored near marker 26, where the river's mouth meets open water. Her boat is a waypoint as important as the markers themselves. A few years ago, a boat ran too close and waked her, flooding her deck and its coolers and tipping pinfish and shrimp back into the gulf. And just last month, rough seas sank her boat, and Bonnie had to tread water for almost two hours until a fishing guide happened upon her. Did I mention that she's eighty years old? Thirty years ago, she moved here from New York City to continue her career as an artist, and she built a welding studio for metal sculpture work on a remote island. She had remembered fishing the river with her father, and her sister is a local shrimper. But the Storm of the Century destroyed everything, so she started selling bait to survive. Fishermen bring her the *New York Times* each morning. When the guide found her treading water, all he could see of her boat was the white metal shrimp she had sculpted for its roof.

Other stories: The Gerber Baby lives somewhere along this river. She is also in her eighties now. This coast used to be a haven for drug-runners, and she has written a mystery novel about those days called "Homosassa Shadows." I wonder how many of those runs and exchanges this porch saw? A few summers ago, my son filled chum bags with chicken offal, attached them to rope and buoys we had salvaged, and dropped them in the back creek's inlet to attract fish and crabs. We don't talk much with our occasional next-door neighbor but one day he stopped us at the inlet's mouth to tell us about the mysterious mesh bag and rope that had fouled his boat's propeller. He had been coming back late from a bar and he saw a Grady White—a high-end boat for locals—doing doughnuts around the inlet. He told us that he tried to T-bone their boat to make them stop, but they gunned off downriver. We've called him "T-bone" ever since.

Telling stories on a porch has a way of adding gravity to the everyday. They might become allegorical but can still be laughable. And there is a kind of freedom in the telling that porches afford. Even if your audience isn't paying attention, the air still catches your stories and the world listens. I tell our guests about T-bone's helipad. It's a ramshackle wood platform, not much bigger than a king-size bed, where his father, who had been a pilot in the Vietnam War, landed his lightweight helicopter until he crashed into the gulf after faulty repairs. He survived and won a large settlement. I also tell them about the alligator that used to live in the back creek. It was blind in one eye, and the previous owners fed it marshmallows. Over the years, it grew from three to six feet, and the "things you need to know" document asks us to "let it be." It has never come ashore, they wrote, "even when there are small dogs and small children around." I have wondered if the gator that sometimes drifts up and down the river has one eye and a sweet tooth. From the porch, it appears to be about nine or ten feet long—the right size for the time that has passed.

I also ask the porch to tell its stories. Some of these stories start with what I can read into the porch, in the sense that the word "legend" has its roots in the act of reading. How it was made, who occupied it, and what happened here. The flecks of paint on the floor narrate movement as they echo each chapter of the cabin's story. I want to know who walked across the red floor. I want to hear what they saw. What can they tell me about the squatters who set a piling in the creek across the river? About the accidents and close calls at Hell Gate. About the low budget films made on the river. About drug-runners and artifact-hunters. About huge tarpon running the Homosassa's length. About the Timucuans and Seminole Chief Tiger Tail. The ghosts of Winslow Homer and Grover Cleveland. And legends of goliath grouper deep in river holes. I ask the porch what it has witnessed.

✳✳

Beach towels hang in the porch's air, muggy but drying, draped over chairs, sagging from hooks, pinned to the clothesline in the corner. They drip, as our guests talk. Usually the towels dress the rails outside on the deck, signaling summertime and scallop trips, but the storm has chased them inside where they crowd among us. I remember John Cohen talking about the quilts that curtain the porches of eastern Kentucky after the first frost. There, fresh mountain breezes, carried by fall's cold fronts, dry out the mustiness of the quilts that had been packed away in the spring. Hanging out the quilts is as much art show as practical act. Porches are for airing things out. And in doing so, we lend ourselves to the world.

Two dogs pause, heads turned as if to listen. Through veils of dust and fog, we hear the notes start. Slowly at first, then faster. Our view—the unsteady camera's view—turns across yards, in front of tenements, below leafless trees, toward the porch. Here is the music. And here are four figures. Two are seated, the one who stands has started dancing, and another reclines on the steps. The porch is all lines to their sculpted presence, metopes for a story told by the banjo we hear and the family we see.

John Cohen, musician and documentarian, is filming Roscoe Halcomb as he plays, with his stepmother Mary Jane Halcomb and nephew Odabe. This is a lumber camp in Daisy, Kentucky, on a Sunday morning after church. The fog slowly burns off as laborers rest. Cohen filmed this performance from his car, behind its windshield dusted like the yard, at the end of his time with the family in midsummer 1959. The musician remains at home on his porch and the filmmaker, an outsider, is about to drive away. The distance between the two offers a necessary distance from guest to host, documentarian to subject, outsider to resident. But the porch also supports a connection that is deeper than vision, even deeper than the sound that twangs the high Appalachian air.

The porch allows Halcomb to play and Cohen to film. The documentary could not have been made without the porch. Its open deck offered Cohen access. He never would have found the musicians without it. It is where people hang out. It's how Cohen met Odabe and Mary Jane. It is where they hailed Roscoe walking home.

Halcomb had played once before, five weeks earlier, when they first met. After that first performance on the porch, he refused to play again. *That High Lonesome Sound*, Cohen's documentary, is as much an exercise in patience and trust—all of which plays out on porches—as it is an explication of the Appalachian sound. Earlier in this final sequence, the camera pans from dogs playing around the water pump to the long row of porches down the dirt road. The repetition of porches affirms that each holds extraordinary stories, despite their formal monotony. After this long take and a brief return to the dogs and their play, Cohen appends a final look toward the mountains. They rise up from the ground, bound as it is in dust and fog, to meet the sky. It is as if he is trying to see what the Halcombs see. It is the view from the porch.

Cohen himself wrote of the many possible reasons for Halcomb's final performance. By playing when he did, he and his family were reminding the departing stranger what they do. Who they are. The porch is public, but only on their terms. They choose when to play.

✻✻

Air fills again with conversation. Our guests are comfortable on the porch. The thunder is far off now, but they don't seem to want to leave. More coffee is brewed, and cookies are eaten between stories. Their words ride the humidity in the storm's wake. Sound travels faster in humid air, and I wonder if traditions of storytelling on porches might rely in some part on that thickened medium. And I remember that Jack London wrote that air freshens with conversation.

Stories are told on porches, but they are also told *from* porches. Zora Neale Hurston knew a porch's capacity for storytelling when she conducted her Works Progress Administration interviews on the porches of African Americans in her hometown of Eatonville and across Florida and the South. Another way of saying this is that stories want to be told on the porch. On a camping trip, talking seems to inflate a tent's canvas or fills the space animated by a fire's glow. Telling stories on the porch is akin to stories around a campfire; there is the sense that time has paused and an older narrative time takes hold, one that sits apart from the constraints that order daily life inside a house. Porches and camps inhabit an air saturated with words and tales and music.

To Kill a Mockingbird is full of porches. Night sounds suspend Scout and Jem in restive sleep on the back porch in summertime. Maudie Atkinson rules the street from her flower-fringed front porch. Mr. Avery sneezes and pees off the side of his. Shadows on the Radleys' moonlit back porch scare off Jem. Mayella calls out to Tom Robinson from her porch, and sets in motion the book's pivotal conflict. Sam Levy confronts Klan members from his front porch. The new courthouse is built around the original building's south porch, another piece of the past the town is slow to let go of. Scout punches her cousin on the Finch Landing porch. Judge Taylor's front porch light is on when Bob Ewell trespasses his back porch. Mrs. Dubose shouts at Jem and Scout from her porch. Characters watch, appraise, gossip, yell, dream, and imagine from their porches. The porches house points of view. The town, like the book, is full of porches. And the book, like the town, would not work without them.

The final scenes of Harper Lee's novel move between two porches. Lee doesn't describe either in great detail, but their presence, as with the story's other porches, holds the narrative, linking it to the place and binding the characters to one another. Each porch establishes a different point of view. In the next-to-last scene, nine-year-old Scout Finch watches her father Atticus and Sheriff Heck Tate pace her family's front porch from edge to corner as they discuss the attack that left her brother Jem with a broken arm. Her reclusive neighbor Arthur Radley, known as "Boo," sits with her in the shadows at the other end. Scout's porch faces Boo's porch, and their pairing sets up the story's final insight.

When Scout views the town from Boo's porch, she grows old. In this final scene, she reels back through time and narrative, each season and each event, from the perspective of the other. Two years ago she play-acted a life for Boo and his family on her own front porch, and now his porch affords Scout another way of seeing. She wears it like a pair of shoes. From Boo's porch, she can see the porch swing where her father, consoling her after the first day of school at the beginning of the story, offered a "simple trick": "You never really understand a person until you consider things from his point of view." It could seem trite, but Lee's narrative makes it true. On Boo's porch, Scout acts on this and can "climb into his skin and walk around in it." Porches hinge on seeing—seeing ourselves and being seen by others.

⁎⁎

If a porch is a skin, it is also a stage. Climb onto a porch and you put on a costume; for a moment, you wear the house of another. Walk out onto your porch, and you present yourself to the world. Pose on a porch, and it's your portrait—it just might have hosted the original selfie. It is a place for you to tell your story. Scout and Jem know how their neighbor Maudie Atkinson is feeling by the way she stands on her porch. When a wagon of angry townspeople approaches Maudie's porch, Scout, from her own porch, knows her mood: "She was now standing arms akimbo, her shoulders drooping a little, her head cocked to one side, her glasses winking in the sunlight. We knew she wore a grin of the uttermost wickedness." And Scout can identify her other neighbors by the sound of their feet across a porch floor. That link between people and their porches is evident in thousands of porch portraits.

Porches are readymade for family portraits, and though, like the porch itself, they might be dismissed as relics of the past, they remain common in practice. A porch is often the house's public front, so there is already something of the family's identity in its countenance. Roof, floor, and columns frame domestic life as they also reflect how a family lives. And, for photographers, porches offer diffused light and an architecture of steps, rails, and platforms to arrange rows of people. In one portrait from 1865, a woman and her child pose on the porch roof while another family member, top hat in hand, has pulled his chair off the porch into the street. In between, another man sits on the porch next to a young girl who leans against the column, and a housemaid stands near the front door. Vines grow up the columns, and potted plants and hanging baskets frame this portrait as a glimpse into a lush jungle of leaves and flowers. A neighbor sits on her porch and gazes quizzically at the camera. This might be the first case of photobombing, aided and abetted by another porch.

Porch portraits play between the formal and the informal. For many family portraits, the porch is often a fixed, rigid backdrop to compose a picture straight-on. It is as if the family has emerged en masse to greet an arriving guest, in the person of the unseen portraitist. For other portraits, the porch affords a venue where subjects can be themselves and where the view is often oblique, capturing the environment as well. In these pictures, we are guests who have caught our hosts unaware, during a private moment on the porch. Albert Einstein wears fuzzy slippers on his Princeton porch, U. S. Grant reads the newspaper in his porch's wicker chair four days before his death, Joaquim Miller perches above the jungle that surrounds his San Francisco porch, W. C. Fields—in cowhide chaps and with a sheriff's badge—leans against a porch post during filming on a Hollywood set, Sandra Cisneros sits on a slab of stone, in sandaled feet, with her dog, and Cudjo Lewis sits relaxed but erect, smoking a pipe on his Alabama porch, where he recounted stories of the Middle Passage to Zora Neale Hurston. These photographs tell stories that traverse biography and geography, from Wisconsin to Florida, from New York to California, as they document a nation's wide range of experiences as well as its most painful histories.

Our guests stayed, and the older man's stories shifted to his family's history. A portrait in words. He moved here from Illinois, he worked as a mechanic, and his son was in college. Warmed up and talkative, waterlogged clothes drying with the clearing air, as if that air, wrung of its sogginess, has in turn cleared their heads. How quickly the strange might become familiar. Our guests began to feel at home. More used to a cabin built for solitude rather than for company, it took longer for us to acclimate to their presence, and I was worried they might see the clock above the door and further extend our initial invitation. Out of batteries long ago, its hands idle at one minute before five. I wish that we had taken a picture with our guests on the porch. A narrative touchstone that might also freeze time for a moment.

Being from Nashville, I am partial, but one of the most compelling porch portraits was taken on a nondescript porch in the Eastwood neighborhood in the early 1970s. This image has the feel of an album cover: the Allman Brothers on that Macon porch for their first album, or Crosby, Stills and Nash on a porch in West Hollywood, or Joy of Cooking in Berkeley, or even Eminem in Detroit. Four songwriters and artists ride the East Nashville porch. It's midday and Townes Van Zandt, Susanna Clark, Guy Clark, and Daniel Antopolsky have just woken up. Townes lifts the bow to a fiddle, and Guy sits on the corner of a low wooden chair, guitar on his knee. He might have just strummed the first chord of *LA Freeway*. He wrote the song here soon after they moved from Los Angeles. Al Clayton snaps the photograph as a G note hangs in the air. "Pack up all your dishes ... make note all good wishes. . . ."

Their figures are notes rising and falling along the porch's ledger lines of floor and roof, and the columns are bar lines. Though it has an integral role in portraying character and mood, the architecture of this porch could not be simpler: twelve feet wide, six feet deep, three square posts, flat roof, concrete slab cast over earth, held by two courses of raw concrete block. Townes stands to the left in white cowboy boots; his sunglasses slip down his nose. We can't see his eyes, but he's probably looking at Susanna on the front edge of the porch, her bare feet tickling the low ivy fringe, her coffee cup a white mark, a breath mark. She and Guy have just married (Townes was the best man), and the porch column is the middle line that separates and connects them. Brow furrowed, Guy looks at Susanna, but he also looks out of the porch into the distance. The toes of his right foot rise next to a fifth of Southern Comfort, keeping the beat, marking the porch's time signature. To the far right, Daniel stretches out his arm toward the rest as he plays with a Siamese cat. His floral pants blossom like a potted plant on the otherwise spartan porch. He is the ghost note.

The air is charged not just with music but with human relations, and the porch supports these dynamics, not as a neutral scaffold, but as an active participant. This porch portrait depicts the delicate balance of people and place, caught up in a process of tuning, though not always in tune. The porch is a pressure valve for its residents. Clayton composed this portrait of musicians at the cusp of their careers, but the porch is also where their daily lives play out.

Al Clayton took these pictures in 1972. Three years earlier, he had published *Still Hungry in America* to document the lives of impoverished families in Appalachia and the Deep South. From Atlanta to rural Mississippi to eastern Kentucky, Clayton found the fate of these families on the lean-to porches of tenements, in the laundry hung across porches tilting above garbage-strewn floodplains. He found it behind the netting strung between porch columns to keep toddlers from falling off the precarious deck, shored up and raised five feet above a dry creek bed, and accessed by ladder steps. He found it in babies held up for a picture with equal degrees of care and fear and exhaustion, in grainy mountain air silted with mining dust, and in the serious and mischievous gazes of toddlers playing on raw pine floors weathered with dirt and rain and soot. In another portrait, a young girl in a rocking chair holds her baby sister in her lap, but she doesn't look at the camera. Her gaze extends out of the frame across the porch and beyond. A young boy sits on a rug thrown across planks scattered with shoes, boards, and appliance parts among fluted columns that still support the sweep of an ornate mezzanine in the airiness of a plantation house's ruined veranda. A woman shells peas on her porch, and the husks spill across the floor to the ground. Clayton moves from porch to porch to portray hunger in America.

The final picture in the book wraps four children in shadow. They sit and stand on a small urban porch caught between light and darkness. A seated girl squints in the full sun, and the top half of the face of the boy, standing behind her, is in shadow. Another child has moved into the recess of the porch. Farther in, only the arm and shoulder of the fourth presses out from the dark. A tempest of hunger melts these children into the air, on this porch, in this city.

While Clayton photographed the porch in East Nashville, a photographer in eastern Kentucky was making a portrait with a family whose life he had documented eight years earlier. In this follow-up porch portrait, William Gedney joined the Cornett family on their porch. He is there sitting on the steps next to the Cornett daughters who are well into their teens. Others sit and swing their legs through the crawlspace air at the front of the porch. The family has grown, and its twenty-two members swell across three bays of the porch. In the wake of such portrayals, porches remain as active agents in the life of a community—what John Berger calls "living" and "communal" portraits. Portraiture tells stories like porches, and the caryatids of the Erechtheum embody spirit and identity in their own timeless porch portrait.

Porches scaffold air, and posing on a porch constructs not just what we will see, but how it will be seen. The subjects attune themselves to the architecture of the porch. They gargoyle its roof and caryatid its columns—think of Helen Levitt's famous photograph of kids climbing a New York City portico's columns and play-fighting on its roof. On a porch, in the relative freedom of its open air, we become the architecture. More precisely, the scaffold of a porch lends itself to the performative nature of architecture. We lean on posts, grasp balusters, recline on chairs, swing our feet over its edges, perch on railings, glide on its swings, cascade down its steps. On a porch, we construct an image as we also constantly rebuild the porch with our presence.

The evocative imagery of porch portraits remains, and porch air is the barometer of a social climate. Near the end of her visual album *Lemonade*, Beyoncé joins six African American women on the front porch of a slave cabin on the grounds of Destrehan Plantation. The film's penultimate still image, this long take endures for forty-five seconds. It portrays defiance, power, and redemption. That porch evokes previous generations of slavery and hardship as Beyoncé recalls how her grandmother "spun gold out of this hard life." The image of the porch is introduced at the same moment as the album's heart is spoken: "I was served lemons, but I made lemonade," and a voice-over echoes its themes—"true love brings salvation" and "nothing real can be threatened"—as it also underscores the specific meaning of this gathering on the porch—"I found healing where it did not lie." Janie Crawford, in Zora Neale Hurston's novel *Their Eyes Were Watching God*, also finds redemption on a porch. Previously, others—primarily men—viewed and sought to define her from their porches, as she was also prohibited from socializing on the store's public porch. Now, she occupies her own porch, where she can carry out courtship on her own terms and shape her own identity as an African American woman: "So she sat on the porch and watched the moon rise. Soon its amber fluid was drenching the earth, and quenching the thirst of the day."

✱✱✱

To make room for all our guests, I have pulled a stool out against the front rail so that I face the back of the porch. The rain has lifted, but steam mists through the drying screen. It is an unusual position, like sitting backward on a train, looking toward where you've been, sitting and studying the house through its doors and windows. Our guests' conversation turns inward and private as they plan their return. I feel like I am eavesdropping on my own porch.

Sound carries over water, and on the porch, we are privy to conversations not meant for us. Being outdoors, in the wildness of this place, loosens inhibitions. We have heard stories of work, parties, romance, heroism, and fishing. Crabbers shout over their motors about bosses and weekend plans—and I still wonder who it is the crabber I overheard wants to throw in the water. Locals yell at boats from Tampa to slow down and watch out for manatees. Before dawn, shrimpers call home on their way upriver. Last week, a tourist returning from the scallop grounds tillered her skiff close to the lagoon's inlet, pointed right at our porch, and told her crew definitively, if not defiantly—that's my place, look how it's tucked back in the trees, don't even know it's there; it's mine. Frozen in the still air of the windless porch, I wondered if she could see our silhouettes behind the screens. She reminded me that the porch, even within its natural seclusion, still has a presence in the public realm. Our porch is a mirage, invisible to most, fantastical to some, a private vision to others.

Porches collapse distance. It is from the back porch at Finch's Landing that Aunt Alexandra overhears Scout's tilt with Francis. And, as Scout points out, her aunt is the consummate "back-porch listener." Our front porch is hidden like a back porch. Every once in a while, a small fishing boat will run close to shore and lower a silent trolling motor, its crew casting over the rocks and talking quietly of sheepshead and speckled trout, reverently of tarpon and snook. If the light's right, the boaters will see us behind the screen on the porch and say hello. Privacy's curtain softens, and with it, for a moment, a veil of anonymity lifts. Whether they see us or not, neighbors sometimes call out to us from their boats. Their greetings liquefy as they float through air and across mangroves, like the dampening wake that runs out ahead of their boat and twists into our lagoon.

Eavesdropping offers a way to rejoin the world, to shorten the gap between our interior life and the world around us. That is how Scout, cloaked in the shadows of her porch, eavesdrops with Boo in that final scene of *To Kill a Mockingbird*. Eavesdropping on a porch affords a means to return home, an incremental movement from estrangement to homecoming. When Odysseus returns home, the disguised hero sleeps on his own porch. He is a stranger at home. Along the ash and stone thresholds, between the megaron's main hall and the portico, which Homer calls the *prodomos*, Odysseus listens to the suitors who throng inside, pursuing his wife, Penelope. Here, where animals destined for the feast are tethered, the goatherd teases and insults this stranger. On his palace's porch, Odysseus also overhears Penelope crying in her bedroom as he lies awake and plots his return.

⁂

Our guest's last story begins with their day on the water. When they rented the pontoon, the marina did not mention the channel markers and told them to follow the other boats out to the gulf. On the way back, there were no boats to follow, and in the confusion of the storm, he forgot the mariner's mnemonic of "red right return." Keep the red markers on your right, starboard side, when you travel back to port. He said he wasn't going to tell the marina about the accident. Our guests discuss the finer points of accountability and responsibility in the wake of the storm, and here on the edge of the porch, the natter of raindrops falling from cedars remixes the tempo of their debate.

Many of the stories coming from porches these days are about pirates. Because they are good places for watching, porches are also good places for stealing. Their vulnerability is both strength and weakness. Most news items on porches are about porch pirates. For many, the porch has become an outsized mailbox for delivered packages. The porch shelters those parcels, and it hosts thieves who might easily steal them. Porch piracy has increased dramatically, but the practice itself is not so new, because porches have always been vulnerable. In the 1930s, Nelson Algren stole milk from porches in Chicago when he was a struggling novelist. His rounds shadowed the milkman, mounting the rowhouse steps in the pre-dawn haze.

Whatever is on the porch can be stolen—plants, bikes, furniture. The name of the phenomenon itself casts the porch as a ship on the high seas, filled with valuables. Storming the deck has been replaced by charging the tilting floors of porches, which are not so much abandoned as no longer inhabited daily; and the open seas of neighborhoods no longer have their lookouts who once kept watch for dangers or bandits. Doorbell cameras play the role of the porch-sitters. The panorama of a crow's nest is now the fish-eye lens across a porch's deck and the sea of lawns beyond. I watch footage from these cameras, and I vicariously occupy the porch from a distance, like the owners sitting and watching from their offices, cars, and phones. In recent advertisements, homeowners have conversations with would-be thieves who talk to the doorbells.

We watch from the porch, we are watched on the porch, and the porch watches dramas unfold. Porches are still bellwethers for society and its economies. Where they once served as platforms for the local exchange of news, they now register a globalized economy, and the attendant fragilities of consumerism. This cannot be nostalgic. What is fascinating is that the porch remains. It still waits for things to happen—whether stealing or storytelling. The porch is an anachronism, and like any device introduced by an author, it is a vital part of the plot.

Out here, with no deliveries, we have no porch pirates, but we still share our porch when we are away. We know the neighbors' kids swing on the hammock by the lagoon, and they have surely snuck onto the porch on a dare, but our regular pirate is a field mouse who lives under the wooden walkway that tracks through the cedars. Last week, he tried to steal thread from a basket on the porch. Bundles of bright cord lay across the floor like so much forensic evidence. Orange, mauve, electric blue, black, amethyst, garnet, and dark blue stretched along the mouse's path. This scene was more craft than crime. Under the screen door, a knot of yellow snagged on a metal edge of the threshold. Caught between inside and outside, it reached toward the hidden nest. I moved some of the strands onto the deck, and the next day they were gone. These strands are now probably woven with flotsam and jetsam, caches of multicolored plunder shared among mouse siblings: shredded tarps under an overturned canoe, reeds of dried seagrass matted between wall studs, the bill of a sun visor blown from the deck of a tour boat, then repurposed between logs of cedar. And now thread from a porch.

*
**

Our guests' pontoon floats calmly where we docked it. We trim up its motor and discover that only a fragment of a rotor remains on the prop. The spare in the boat's locker doesn't fit, so we bring our own pontoon around and begin towing them upriver to the marina. Pontoons are a lot like floating rooms—technically they are pieces of a floating bridge—and their deck seems like an extension of the porch. On the pontoon, as on the porch, manners and hospitality are tethered by degrees, and the conversation between our two boats, connected with a tow rope, ebbs and flows as their boat comes closer and pushes back.

Before I drop them off at the marina and cruise back toward a lowering sun, I tell them the story of the tilted house, which is one of the larger road-access houses fronting onto the river. We pass it going to and from the mainland, and on one trip, a tradesman asked me if I could see its sloping foundation. Impossible to miss, it looks like one whole end of the house is sinking. He said the builder would not acknowledge an error and kept building on the slant, as if it was level and the rest of the world was off-kilter. On lunch breaks, the subcontractors would roll golf balls from one end of the slab to the other. Locals ran the contractor out of town, but not before it was finished.

As I write this, I can hear the slurring voice of the older man, I feel the shiver of the woman on the rocking chair, and I watch the shirtless son's disbelief—or is it amusement?—at the telling. Memory of their visit brings an uncanniness to the porch. We tell the story of the castaways on our porch as though it were an allegory, more fable than fact. Our guests have become ghosts.

Porches play host to guests and ghosts alike. Both find a home in the air that immediately surrounds a house. On a porch, hospitality is a process of acclimation, more of a working method than a hard-and-fast system. A porch welcomes guests to a house without fully admitting them, yet its openness limits a host's control. It allows visitors to be close but not too close; it is even a place where presence and absence intertwine. Like a ghost. In Greek traditions of *xenia*, suitors joined guests, strangers, and unwed sons of kings on porches. Near the end of the *Odyssey*, when the seer Theoclymenus has a vision, he adds ghosts to that list of guests: "Ah, wretched men, what evil is this that you suffer? Shrouded in night are your heads and your faces and your knees beneath you; kindled is the sound of wailing, bathed in tears are your cheeks, and sprinkled with blood are the walls and the fair panels. And full of ghosts is the porch, full also the court, ghosts hastening down to Erebus beneath the darkness, and the sun has perished out of heaven and an evil mist covers all." Theoclymenus foresees a porch crowded with guests who will soon be ghosts after Odysseus reveals himself and punishes the suitors. Porches are places of mystery and familiarity. They host estrangements as well as homecomings, and Odysseus occupies the gray area between the right of the visit and the right of residence, because he doesn't want to blow his cover.

When trick-or-treating at Halloween, we play the roles of guest and ghost on the porches of strangers. Some say the night before St. Mark's feast day in the spring is even spookier than All Saints' Eve. If you keep vigil on a church porch before that feast, you will see the spirits of all those who will die in the coming year. John Keats, in his poem "The Eve of St. Mark," wrote of arched porches filled with "whispers hush," and the American writer Washington Irving, living in England, borrowed from local legends for one of his classic short stories. "Saint Mark's Eve" begins at the Bracebridge family's dinner table where a superstitious parson recounts the vigils of townspeople on the church porch. A person must sit on the porch for one hour either side of midnight on St. Mark's Eve for three consecutive years. During the last vigil, shades of those who will die the following year will appear. The parson closes with the story of a man who carried out the vigil and died the next day. The town said that he had seen his own spirit. Irving's story and the folklore it adapts claim the porch as that space of transition where the material and the spiritual worlds intersect. Here, attentiveness and watchfulness meet.

The stories of Keats and Irving tap into traditions of the

early Christian church and how its architecture hosted penance. The basic layout included three main parts still in place today: apse, nave, narthex. In the apse, the choir and sanctum focused the religious service at the head of the church, typically facing east. Its origins in the Latin word for ship, the nave formed the main body under a roof that was framed like a vessel's hull. The narthex—the foot to the apse's head—served as the entrance to the nave. Here, the organization of the church parallels early residential architecture, particularly palaces and megarons, with their simple layout of an external porch and an internal room, much like the core of Alcinous' palace. When a megaron's porch area has both an *aule* (columned vestibule) and a *prodomos* (vestibule), they form an entry sequence similar to a church's narthex that has itself been further divided into outer and inner parts.

Just as its internal rituals were scripted, a church's porch dictated how it met public life and how its visitors were organized. Generally, members of the public who were not baptized and those who were undergoing penance were treated as guests and could assemble outside the doors of the church, but still inside the outer porch of the narthex. This organization of the church dates to early Christianity, and St. Gregory of Thaumaturgus outlined the four stages, or degrees, of penance in the third century.

Weeping was the first degree. The "Flentes" wept outside what Gregory calls the "Porch of the Oratorie," later the outer narthex. The weepers begged those entering the church to pray for them, and here on the open-air porch, at the far western perimeter of the church, they were exposed to the elements as well as the mercy of the parishioners. This outer porch is akin to a portico with its open front and arched or vaulted ceiling;

it was also a place for indulgences and reductions in punishments for sinners, often presented as inscriptions engraved in marble slabs. Other outer porches held tombs because it was considered an honor to be interred here.

The second degree was hearing, which occurred, Gregory says, "within the Porch, in the place called Narthex," where penitents listened to scriptural readings. Known as the "Audientes," the hearers listened to but did not join in prayer, and they left with the unbaptized. The porch of the hearers was the "locus audientium," the hearing place, and it came to be known as the inner narthex. Inside the church but still outside its doors, the Audientes could participate vicariously in the service within clearly defined limits. Their view was blocked by the church wall and its closed doors.

Time plays a part in this process, and those who repented their sins had to spend three years in the narthex as hearers. Gregory tells us that those at the third and fourth stages of penance were allowed beyond the porches into the nave. The duration of these parts varied depending on the severity of penance, and the next step of "Genuflectentes" or "Substrati" could require ten more years. This third group was primarily known as the kneelers, but Gregory took their posture even further to prostration on the church's floor. This group left a service before communion. The last order of penitents, the fourth group was the "Consistentes," or standers, who could stay for the whole liturgy but did not receive communion. The fifth and final stage was participation in the Sacraments and full membership with the church community. For those who had fallen away from the church, this system of penance was a process of re-acclimation.

I feel the vestiges of these degrees of penance when I walk

through a church's narthex. I have always felt at home in this place where winds and sounds enter alongside parishioners. And smells from the church linger around umbrellas, stacks of hymnals, and people shaking off the outside world. Unguents and exhaust, perfume and dust. A narthex has its own weather. It is a hopper of atmospheric change, its air pressed between secular and sacred. Typically long and narrow, its low ceiling hung under a mezzanine, the narthex, a kind of enclosed porch, would have reminded earlier visitors of its Greek word's dual meaning: the slender length of a fennel and the casing of aromatic oils. A typical narthex has large front doors, and they usually remain closed so that you enter from the side through smaller doors. Before and after a service, the opening and closing moves air sideways, and this cross-ventilation mixes church air with street air. Even though, in its later forms, the narthex tilted toward a vestibule's closure rather than a portico's openness, it still holds all of a porch's transitional nature.

*
**

Our guests have returned deep into the mainland, the storm has crossed the peninsula, and it is the golden hour. The air in their wake has settled, and we are again guests of nature. The sun is behind us over the shoulder of the porch. It casts a soft but brilliant red light in the tree line across the river. The air is amber. In its lucidity, the far shore comes near. This time of day, the fish are active. The lagoon flashes with sloshing, splashing, slipping, slapping. I hear the shape of their fins. Spooked needlefish rip the surface. A redfish turns slowly over the rock. Snapper lunge at insects, flapping on the water. Mullet leap and smack. An osprey calls in her high voice, and a bald eagle seems to answer. Flutters of birds fill air already saturated with color. We become the audientes. The hearers. We listened to our guests, and now we listen to nature.

That hour before sunset is my favorite time on the porch. The view is spectacular. And when warm, calm light fills it, I feel like I am swimming in air, immersed in its glow. But how we really see as the light fades is through hearing. In the golden hour, illumination comes from indirect light, and for a porch-sitter, insight comes from senses other than sight. Hearing without seeing is a reminder that we are visitors in nature. I have sometimes thought of wildlife as our guests, but it is the other way around. We are the penitents in nature's nave. We don't host the funnel weaver in the corner of the porch; our porch casts itself into her home. When we hear manatees breathe in the lagoon and dolphins puff at its mouth, their visits are unannounced but not surprising. It always takes our breath, but there is a calmness and ordinariness to these en-counters. As guests, our porch skin presses gently out toward their daily and nocturnal lives. In these moments, the screen evaporates and our porch moves in close, we listen to air and place an ear to the water.

There are interludes in the golden hour when nature is quiet. When the air is wet, the cicada's click tapers slowly in expectant air. When north winds blow water out of the river and moisture out of the air, the squawk of a great blue heron dissipates quickly like a sun shower's drops on the hot metal of the porch's roof. Then silence. Nature rests, and I think. I listen to the spaces between sound. Some inkling of water is still there on the edges of air—the liminal sounds known to musicians. I hear breath and thoughts pass into the air.

Musicians and architects talk about these in-between

areas as negative space. It is an open ground between solid figures. But a porch's air is so dense with stories, humidities, sounds, spiderwebs, breezes, afterimages, memories, guests, palmetto bugs, wet towels, leaves, shadows, reflections, smoke, musk, pollen, and light, that it wholly reverses this idea. It reminds me of the wonder in students' eyes when I ask them to reverse figure and ground in a plan view they have drawn. What was solid becomes air, and what was open becomes filled with molecules of graphite. The air of a porch is like that. It is also like the humming airiness of the page where I sketch those wandering lines. They drape and hang there, and this medium of air makes the space between us and nature. It is what links us.

We can learn a lot from a porch's hospitality. In ancient Greece, rules of *xenia* did not require a guest's reciprocity, but being on a porch, as guests to nature, is a reciprocal endeavor. Church architecture turned its guests into an active form of penance, and porches make room for active participation in nature. Not strictly as penitents, although we have much to repent, but more as active witnesses, more like the vigils that waited and watched for ghosts. And we wait and watch, haunted, on the cusp of climate crisis.

In this golden hour, there is still time to revive those connections. A porch's ambient air is filled with opportunity and promise. Like the glow of a porch family portrait. Like the visceral emotions of youth forged in Welty's stories. Like the comforting glow of a porch light and the Erechtheum's myths of lightning and stone, olive trees and dew. In the golden hour, light on the porch comes from all directions.

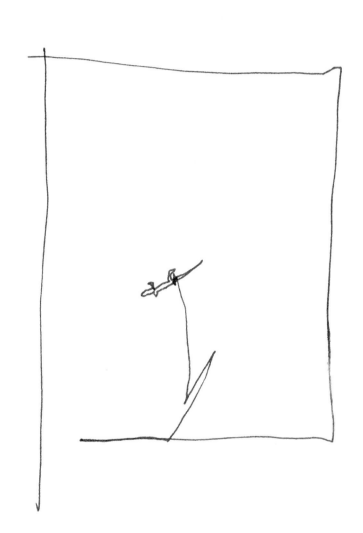

4

SCREEN

This morning late in December is damp but warm. Fog swims the river air, and the dogs climb onto the deck and shake the mist from their coats. Lines of dew etch the porch screens from top to bottom as they seine the swollen air. Their drip seems to begin from nothing, and I see only movement, shapes without edges behind cataracts of falling water. It's a quiet morning and few sounds fin through the mesh. Drops from leaves drop onto other leaves, drop onto soft ground, drop into water. Some are close, others might have drifted from across the river, although there is no breeze, only breaths of vapor. Long pauses follow dense cadences as a kingfisher's calls are more bycatch. My pants are wet from the couch. And the screen is a wet caul around its room.

A porch protects as it exposes. It is open and closed because it screens. If tilt is the foundation of a porch's resilience to weather the elements and engage the warp of the world, if a porch's captured air is its capacity to accommodate social change and broker a natural contract, then screen takes you to a porch's edge and its porous walls. If the porch occupies the air next to the cabin, then the screen is the frontier where air first touches the porch. Porches let you out into the world, while still under cover. You can be susceptible and sheltered at the same time. Candid yet reserved. A porch pulls you in close and fastens the ropes as it also shoves you away from the dock. That's not something architecture typically does. What makes this possible—its practical solutions and its contradictions—is screen.

Screening a porch varies by degree. The ends of floorboards and an overhanging roof imply one limit. Columns and railings provide another, and wrapping a porch in the woven mesh of screen material sets a filtering edge with a higher degree of enclosure, further shielding from the elements and insects. As screening manages the frontiers of fresh air along its edges, a porch screens its inner house from sun and rain. A wraparound porch locks a house in a protective embrace that still allows it to breathe. A south-facing porch, in the Northern Hemisphere, focuses its efforts on the sun's arc, and more modest porches simply but honorably shelter entrances. A screened porch offers just enough closure for shelter but not too much definition for fresh air to lose its fidelity.

I don't know exactly how long the Homosassa cabin's porch has been screened, but the porch has, with and without this screen mesh, softened the impacts of sun and storm. That porch gives itself over to air and water. It is the cabin's tithe to nature, and at some point in the future, it will be a first offering to the sea. It is a ruin in waiting. At the back edge of the porch, the cabin's walls—its boards and battens, their paint, and its windows—have weathered more slowly than the rest of the cabin's façade. And the mesh of the screen is a wise choice in a marsh where insects swim the air like schools of minnows. Mosquitoes in the summer, no-see'ums in the winter, and wasps and spiders all year. It might be a necessity, but it is also a compromise. The screen mesh is a further reminder that I'm a guest, not fully equipped for nature's trials. I wear that screen like a slicker, a beekeeper's veil, an introvert's cloak. It also makes me aware of vision itself.

**

Screen originates from *screna*, a partition, particularly one that moderates the heat of a fire. This type of mobile and temporary screen could be moved around and adjusted. Which makes sense because of the fluidity of air and heat. But how do you translate *screna* into more permanent architecture? Wood and steel can readily make open frames, and they lend themselves, particularly wood, to the domestic scale and the everyday methods of residential construction and its open-air porches. But when your vision goes beyond just solving a problem, a porch takes on what architect Louis Kahn called the "very simple everlasting presences that should constantly talk to you in architecture." Kahn mostly worked with concrete and brick and, despite the heaviness of those materials, his architecture was sensitive to air and change, responsive to what is ephemeral and temporary. He called these responses "porches," even though some are themselves as large as buildings.

Kahn was a master storyteller. Students would sit in rapt attention as he spun simple yet poetic tales of architecture and life. Materials came alive in his hands. Famously, he held up a brick and asked what it wanted to be: "You say to brick— 'what do you want, brick?'" The conversation proceeds from there. It follows a simple yet elegant logic of honoring a brick's aspirations. Students laugh when brick responds that it likes an arch. While Kahn venerated brick, he also knew its limits and partnered it with concrete in projects like the Indian Institute of Management. There, concrete told the architect it could let the porches open wider and consequently draw in more air. The way Kahn put it—to make a "bigger mouth"— tells us that the absence was as important as the presence of material. Kahn built with air as much as with bricks and concrete. With porches in particular, he made climate visible with his materials. He made what was delicate and largely unseen into an architecture that relied on the lightness of screens and that also spoke of solidity and timelessness. For a screen, timelessness means an awareness of changes over time.

As screens, porches tell the story of their efforts to hold air and light and their work to protect from storms and sun. Of the many porches Kahn designed around the world, one project asked him to consider a unique mix of requirements for security and openness. For an embassy in Angola, the intensity of light called for a solution that transcended simple shading attachments to windows. Kahn wanted to "find an architectural expression which somehow tells the story of the problems of glare"—a solution that celebrated the problem while solving it. He found it in ruins: "I thought of the beauty of ruins . . . the absence of frames . . . of things behind which nothing lives . . . and so I thought of wrapping ruins around buildings; you might say encasing a building in a ruin so that you look through the wall which had its apertures by accident." Kahn's solution fully wrapped the embassy with porches. These partially shaded, sun-filled rooms essentially screened the interior rooms from the light's brightness. They acknowledged its intensity as they also tempered it so that it could be comfortably brought inside. Looking out, you see the glow of sunlight as it bounces along the walls of the outdoor room, along the screen walls of the porch that is itself a screen.

Wrapping ruins describes the richness of Kahn's composition in concrete and brick and air, mixing architecture's fragility with ostensibly permanent materials in the face of nature's intensities. It also highlights the temporary nature of porches, recalling that such screens have their origins in the movements and adjustments of *screna*. A porch's exposure to the elements and its typically light, wooden construction—unlike Kahn's material palette—make it a temporary screen. It is not unusual for porches to list, sag, and even fall from the sides of their buildings. Walk along historic American streets with houses of brick and stone, and you will see traces of porches. These erstwhile attachments to their houses have long since rotted and fallen away or been removed.

When I recently walked the streets of historic Fredericksburg, I saw outlines and faint shadows of long-gone porches across the fronts of houses. I was reminded of Rainer Maria Rilke's meditations as he drifted through Paris. On one particular walk, he described the wall of an apartment left exposed after its neighboring structure had fallen away: "What was most unforgettable, though, were the walls themselves. The dogged life that had been lived in these rooms refused to be obliterated. It was still there; it clung to the nails that were left, it lingered on the remaining strip of floor-boarding, it was huddled up under the little that was left of a corner section. . . . it had traced and retraced their outlines amid the spiders and dust even in these hidden places that were now exposed." Even after it is gone, the memories of a porch cling to its house.

Porches pose unique problems for historic preservationists, who must sometimes determine the provenance of a porch that is no longer there. This dilemma is part of a larger question of pinning down the flux of architectural history. It is made particularly difficult when the architecture is not wholly permanent in its materials, and when it is characterized by mobility, like a ship that must be maintained in the face of chronic weathering. The enigma of lost porches vexes preservationists and historians, as it confounds unwitting residents. I have heard stories of owners who have moved into houses that once had two-story porches and who have since marveled at the second-floor door that now offers a precipitous exit into thin air.

Across the Rappahannock River from Fredericksburg, Chatham Manor rides the crest of a ridge that marks the geologic change from alluvial plain to continental bedrock. Standing where the colonial house's front porch used to be, my view tracks westward across the town's church spires to a tree-lined horizon and then downward into the river's course where the falls mark the "fall line" that set the nation's first frontier. This view from the ghost porch anticipates a nation's expansion, as the porch's absence tells other stories of the ebb and flow of frontiers around the house. In 1770, tidewater planter William Fitzhugh built the brick house without a porch. Four decades later, the second owner, Major Churchill Jones, wrapped it in porches. On the front, Jones added a two-story porch in the popular Greek Revival style along with two smaller, flanking porches that mirror the larger one's mix of austerity and refinement. In the 1920s, the house was sold and the porches were removed, but their outlines and traces remained. When architect Oliver Clarke redesigned the entrance, he used the ghosted boundaries of the front porch to determine the precise outer limits of the new steps.

Today, I feel as though I am a witness to a crime scene. The architectural criminality of removing the porch and replacing it with an unwieldy array of elements—such as a broken pediment with a pineapple—can be debated. You cannot, however, look away from the forensic evidence of the transformations to this house's leading edge. Clarke's semicircular steps spill out from the front door and fill what was once the porch's generous volume, but the real evidence is the silhouette of the porch's columns and floors on the red brick. This white figure across the bare façade is an early coat of paint—possibly the first—that was preserved when the pilaster columns were pressed against the main house during porch construction at the start of the nineteenth century. Over centuries of exposure, the rest of the exterior paint peeled and wore away. Now the outline of the porch looks like it was screen-printed there. Closer up, I can read the profile of the millwork and the sharp edges of column bases and the angled and squared parts of the column capitals, their abacus, echinus, and even what looks like the necking between capital and column.

When the builders removed the porch, they stashed its columns in a loft. Was this a heroic act of archiving? Or was it a surreptitious deed, hiding the evidence? Either way, the columns are significant artifacts—as is the silhouetted paint— that have helped preservationists understand the history of the house. Those who added the porch had also contributed to this archival record. These craftsmen frugally saved the pieces that were removed when the porch was installed, such as segments of cornice trim with wrought iron nails still intact, all of which was stored in the attic. The single coat of paint on these pieces, like the silhouetted paint on the façade, provides an important record of the house's original materials and finishes. Most telling in these stories, though, is the coming and going of the porch, as if it were an outsized piece of furniture, an occupiable *screna* of sorts, that can be added and removed, even packed away, with the caprices of style, the whims of owners, or the impacts of weather.

Perhaps Kahn anticipated the ephemeral nature of porches as screens. It was not that he expected his design to be altered or the porches to be removed, but he did understand the environmental changes that porches hold. Porches make room for air, and their edges hold light. And so Kahn's wrapped ruin is also a *brise soleil* that can be occupied. It is one take on the defensive layer of architecture that "breaks" the rays of the sun. Before designing the embassy in Angola, Kahn had seen architect Edward Durell Stone's embassy in New Delhi, a project he critiqued for the patterning and flatness of its *brise soleil*: "He could have gotten something extremely beautiful by letting the water make the porch"—just as the sun would make Kahn's embassy porches in Africa. It is an extraordinary idea that elements quite literally make the porch, and the porch in turn re-makes these natural elements into space. By living within Kahn's version of the *brise soleil*, we don't simply occupy a neutral space, we inhabit light-filled air and the sunlight itself. Taking that idea back to *screna*, the screen doesn't simply separate us from the fire, filtering its heat, and we don't just see the fire through the screen. We feel the fire. Kahn's ruin—his occupiable *brise soleil* that is like an occupiable *screna*—tempers the heat and brightness of the sun, not by separating us from it, but by creating a room that connects us—a room where we can fully experience sun's light. Kahn's logic is the logic of the porch itself. His solution to the problem of the screen yields porches that are as poetic as they are practical. They are built of light and air and imagination just as much as they are conceived of concrete and brick and function. It is a logic at the heart of architecture itself. Kahn says: "The order of light tells you that the porch belongs to the sun and the place inside the porch belongs to man." This story of architecture, and how it seeks to connect human and nature, is the story of the porch. And with the porch as an occupiable screen, the logic takes an environmental turn, one that also yields the metaphysical. Building isn't a foregone conclusion; it is a contract not only between those who occupy, design, and build it. It is also a negotiation with nature, which is why Kahn called the porch "an offering to the sun." You offer something up when you are taking something else and when you owe something back.

The late December morning warms and the dew on the screen slowly dries. The screen's mesh makes its own capricious façade. In some places it remains a wall of moisture, and in others it is a freshly polished window, looking out on the wisps of fog that still float above the river. What I have seen as the screen's play is really what it can reveal about the atmosphere. Here are the sun's rays, there is a tree's protection, here is a pocket of water-warmed air, and over there are patches cooled by damp soil. Whether capricious or climatic, that screen indexes the passage of time, just like this porch anticipates the erosion of the cabin's edges. In front of me, everything is changing—by the minute. Behind me, the cabin wall is only lightly touched. I am wrapped in a ruin.

**

An orange life preserver hangs on the back wall of the porch, and its inner curve wrinkles with time. Crumbly foam falls away where the paint has chipped. The white of stenciled letters affords a geometric clarity to someone, like me, who is unfamiliar with its alphabet, but cuts and scrapes have obscured this logic, further encoding an already enigmatic message. Even if I could translate its text, will I ever know its full meaning? So far, I know only that the lower part of the ring identifies Vladivostok.

The porch holds many things. Some we have inherited, others we have collected. Most others, like the preserver, we have no idea how they got here. We do know that each arrived either by boat or by sea. All of the objects that the porch holds have an air of repose, even amid an equal sense that they are all in transit. As if their movement has slowed down and momentarily stopped. They are in limbo. Some of the objects seem to have been on their way out, sloughing away from the house into the outdoors. Others are on their way in. They have been dropped here, like heavier sediments from a river's current, like the marsh mud that storms push into our lagoon, or they have been deposited more intentionally, either not yet ready, or too much a part of nature, to be brought fully inside. As if they have been screened by some form of appraisal, whether sentimental, rational, or accidental.

When a house that is accessed only by boat changes hands, most of its contents remain. There are no moving trucks or quick trips to a storage container. Pontoons and burn piles offer two options: the labors of trading something out with a long trip up and back down the river, or the finality of incineration. Each risks the later realization that the castoff was in fact useful after all. What's here is here. When we moved in, we didn't hesitate shifting or storing what was inside the house, but the contents of the porch stayed put. Maybe because our general sense that we are visitors in the estuary's delicate balance ultimately took up residence on the porch. Maybe the porch marks the edge of a home that is already away from home. Maybe it is the way each object displaces air in a place built of air. The porch is a place of chronic holiday, where tenure isn't defined so much by the ownership of things but in the idea that you return there time after time. I think I feel most at home on the porch because I have to change so little about it.

When I inventory what the porch holds, I have a sense that each thing—precious or dispensable, enigmatic or everyday—has its place. It is a kind of open-air museum where things are slowly, inevitably accumulating. And just by being here, things take on a hallowed quality. They garner a reverence that we can add to, but that I hesitate to subtract from. Each object has the weight of desire, and the porch is filled with votives, flooded with wishes. Each object added is a further offering. A sign of devotion. If the porch is an offering to the sun, as Kahn said, then these objects are gifts to the porch itself. I'm not surprised when I learn that screen also has its origins in scrine—a chest of valuable objects or particularly sacred relics. And so, scrine links screen to shrine. It protects things that are displaced but carefully placed. It holds memories. This porch brings together the memory and desire of a reliquary. Its screened room, along the side of the river's nave, brings distant things close, makes immediate what is obscure, and leads us to divine larger meanings from very small things. This is what the porch holds:

Shells line the thin shelf made by the top rail: oysters, scallops, blood arks, knobbed whelks, tiny seriths, purple limpets, eggcockles, and moon snails are joined by coral, fragments of limestone, potshards, and bits of chert—some from middens, others collected in the river. Between a scallop shell—one of the rare orange ones—and a banded tulip shell, there is a seagull painted on a wood cutout, white and gray. It looks more like a pigeon. It leans against the screen until wind blows it off, which is how we first found it. Each time, we have returned it to its perch. On the floor are oyster clusters and heavy pieces of limestone. The bouquets of oyster shells grow along river and creek shoals where fresh and salty water meet. One chunk of limestone has a perfectly round hole three inches in diameter.

On the porch's tables, bowls of collected pottery, chert, and coral await a sorting that may never come. The shards of pottery have one side burnt from when they were fired, and the bits of chert are chips from making stone tools. We collected some of these pieces downriver on a small island that we think must have been a workshop because of the unfinished, and seemingly rejected, arrowheads we have found there. We imagine an Indigenous craftsperson rejecting them for their geologic imperfections or for their human flaws of craftsmanship. I sometimes think we have reconstructed the river's geology along with the material culture of its first people, here on the porch. And the porch rails with artifacts below the screen are the vitrine of an amateur archeologist's museum.

The porch may be a cabinet of curiosities; it is also a vessel of everyday life. At the far corner, a stack of wood awaits the fireplace. Some is cedar cut by a previous owner, perfectly dressed to length, as if a symbol of firewood. It lingers at the threshold between forest and hearth. Here, next to the screen door, shoes and sandals are piled in a basket. On the shelf below, thread from a craft project has twisted together in a basket—this is the bin where the mouse found the bundle of yellow thread. A stray board from the deck leans on a post. It is one of those pieces dislodged and orphaned from our wooden walkway by the king tide last month, and I can't remember where it goes. Towels hang on a line strung across the corner near the door.

Other things hang on the porch. Two mobiles marionette in the breeze. One we made with the kids when it rained so hard we had to move our workshop from the porch into the cabin. Broken shells dangle from its driftwood arms. Another mobile predates us. Its six brightly colored fish swim next to the cabin's wall, circling just below the ceiling. On the other end, a red birdcage holds air in its lattice of thin dowels like prison bars. Sitting on the porch, we wonder what birds roosted under its delicate gables. At the far southeastern corner, a chandelier made of shells tempts wind and rain. Only in strong gusts do we hear the tinkle of its cowries and shell fragments. The shells cluster grotesquely like so many fish bones, and every other ring of shells is dyed with aqua. It was a kitsch birthday present from one of the few roadside gift shops that remain on Highway 98, on the way from Gainesville. When I turn them on, the porch's two ceiling fans spin the fish and wobble the birdcage. An osprey feather see-saws on the coffee table. It balances between the fan's breath and the intermittent breeze.

A porch and its artifacts hold many mysteries, and we still haven't figured out the original use for the wooden brackets at the top of each post. Their profile has angled ends and a notch that might have held a bar for blinds, but the deeper slot is upside down. On one of these brackets, we have hung buoys salvaged from ghost traps and flotsam and jetsam from storms. These are eight of the hundreds we have. Six of them are relatively unscathed, one is pocked to reveal white foam, and the other is a half sphere. All are yellow with midnight blue stripes, wide around their equators. We call them the Swede buoys for their color but also for the crabbers, wearing oilskin overalls, beards flagging in the wind, who for many years attached them to their traps and plied the river in a similarly painted boat. We smelled the boat before we saw it. The screen mesh was no defense for the putrid chum that was their bait. It lingered on the porch long after they had passed.

Three hats, a clock, and a fishing bobber hang on the porch walls and posts. We rescued the straw hat from the wake of a rented pontoon. The bright yellow popping cork swings side to side next to the Yeti baseball cap we found floating in flooded spartina on a kayak trip last year. The bobber's weights click like crackling shrimp, and the hat's mesh is frayed and its brim is curled from too much sun and too many tidal cycles. Another salvaged hat arrived in better shape. It must have floated downriver from the state park to the mangrove tree where it dangled. Its forest green blended in, but now it stands out when we wear it kayaking. We wait for other boaters' reactions when they recognize the "environmental protection" emblem. Above the hat and the cabin door, the clock on the wall freezes time just before five o'clock. Like the song, it's not just five o'clock somewhere; it's always five o'clock here. Maybe the birds painted at each hour could sing this tune. In frozen time, the little hand points to a tufted titmouse and the house finch rides the big hand. Only once in late fall have I heard the finch's seet and wheet calls, but titmice whistle through the porch's mesh all year.

Driftwood is everywhere on the porch. It has been put to work in the arms of the mobile to support strings of dangling shells. It leans against the posts like a petulant teen, bored by the porch's slowness. And it hangs from nails, a simple picture of weathering: wood's skeleton and time's passage. Another larger piece of driftwood that rises from the corner is a dolphin's joyful leap and stretch to breach air. If winds have polished the driftwood, water has smoothed—albeit more slowly—the bottles we have collected. They line the floorplate below the railing. Green, brown and clear, some with labels, others filled with silt, some with caps, corks, or tops. A few have wax from the candles we made two years ago.

Next to the bottles are signs we have inherited. The newest reads "Lost Lagoon" in raised lettering. Its oval shape and lavish manufacture have the feel of a golf club's placard, out of place in this wildness. The text, though it describes the setting, brings with it a tiki bar's kitsch, but the previous owner assured us he found the words carved into a ragged—and long lost, it seems—piece of driftwood on the porch.

Nearby, *Privatweg der Bay* once marked a private path in the state forests—the *Bayerische*—along the border between Austria and Germany. Here, it underscores the cherished privacy of a hidden spot. Like most of these artifacts, it is a puzzle piece, a fragment that fits with larger ecosystems of meaning and function. Overall, it has the simple efficiency of a metal street sign, black lettering on white background. The lower part of it reads *Saalforste*, which recalls the icy resolve of Tyrolean forests and the landlocked rise of the Alps and gives the sign a more precise location near the region's Bavarian salt mines. And now its edges rust with salt air five thousand miles away.

Next to this sign, as if curated to celebrate its rough-hewn, down-hominess by contrast, *Crabs* has been carved into a piece of local cedar and painted in blue. The red silhouette of a stone crab accompanies the text, and the ends of the bare block of wood have been serrated. A smaller wooden sign with the names *Nette—Bob* identifies—and, in a way, memorializes— the owners who once fed marshmallows to the alligator in the back creek. For the longest time, I thought the sign rendered Bob's nickname—maybe he expertly caught and netted twisting Spanish mackerel out in the gulf? The porch affords time to make up such stories, frivolous and serious alike.

Understanding these objects and the signs—whether or not in English—is a process of translation. Over time, I returned to the life preserver that hangs on the porch's back wall. It's on the left when you walk out onto the porch. It has remained in the corner exactly where we inherited it. The ring looks like it has been there since 1950, and I think the irony— and the eventual shock—of its presence has made it untouchable, hanging a delicate balance between what we know about this place, and what we don't—some of which is also what we don't want to know. Here on the cusp of sea level rise, it is ready for disaster, close at hand, to be thrown to someone who might fall overboard from the porch. Its position makes the house a ship and the porch its deck. It tells stories. It is an emblem of rescue in an ever more vulnerable place.

The life ring is old. Eggshell cracks vein its orange skin. Chips, gouges, scratches suggest impact. It is mottled with spots where barnacles have been removed. Its white text sent me on a journey of translation. I eventually confirmed its provenance in Vladivostok. Where has it traveled on its way to this porch? I imagine heavy steamships splitting the cold waters of the northern Pacific. Trying to sound the meanings of this artifact, I look back at the only other Russian life preserver I have ever seen. Avant-garde artist El Lissitzky collaged a life ring in his tribute to a Soviet expedition that tested whether a ship that wasn't an icebreaker could travel from the country's northwest to its far east through Arctic waters. Despite a thickened hull, the steamship *Cheliuskin*, named after the eighteenth-century explorer, bound up in ice in late fall 1933, and later sank. Its crew and their rescuers became heroes, and in Lissitzky's collage, biplanes hover above a crowd waving celebratory hats, and fly through the preserver that floats in an ice-gray sky. Its center holds a photograph of the makeshift airfield of ice, and around its ring are the words Vladivostok and Cheliuskin. In the ensuing decades, seas have warmed, memories of this heroism have receded along with the ice, and even ships that aren't icebreakers can now make the trip with little resistance along what is called the Northeast Passage. Could this ring on the porch have outfitted the *Cheliuskin*?

I learned that the text on the lower part of the ring indicates the ship's homeport and the upper text identifies its name. I figured out from the script in Lissitzky's collage that it wasn't from the *Cheliuskin* as I had hoped. When a friend translated the upper part for me, another story from the 1930s emerged, and the preserver took on a much darker meaning. The letters are smudged and barely legible, but this ship's name seems to have been *Postyshev* after Pavel Postyshev, the Ukrainian communist leader. An ally of Stalin, he orchestrated the famine in his home state, and now this specter haunts a porch seven thousand miles away. Somehow making its way from Peter the Great Gulf to the Gulf of Mexico. From totalitarian horrors to a small cabin on a river. Its ring holds the absence of a body, but air held in that ring preserves the memory of many more bodies—not the recovery of stranded mariners on the icy airfield in Lissitzky's collage, but the recollection of pain and loss in withered Ukrainian fields. It turns out that many ships—some still in use—bear the war criminal's name, making it difficult to trace this ring's origins any further. I think about how we can't always anticipate, much less choose, all the meanings that gather on the porch. The transitional and vulnerable places we inherit don't always tell the stories we want to hear.

Couches, chairs, and tables crowd the rest of the porch. An alligator scute rides the marble surface of the side table. Ancient like a fossil, as old as stone, it is one of hundreds of bones we found on the other side of the river, within sight of the porch. From its skull, it figures to have been an eleven-foot gator that might have perished decades ago, or, given the force of a marsh's decay, it could have died last year. Its skeleton was fully draped across intertidal limestone. This discovery, in our first year out here, echoed our mix of wonder and caution. The limestone bowls and crevices held vertebrae, tailbones, teeth, and handfuls of scutes. At low tide, we had to feel for the last few pieces, plunging our arms into holes, feeling, grasping, clutching. Like a raccoon reaching for clams deep in lagoon mud.

The scute on the porch is two inches across. It was one of the many plates under the skin—those bumps along an alligator's back, like the spikes of dinosaurs. Its surface is pocked with holes, a smaller version of the limestone where we found it. Out of context, here, it might be a piece of ancient coral. The holes are the sutures where the skin was connected. It has a ridge in the middle, as if the mesh of bone has been pinched like clay. Herpetologists call this the keel, and the scute is a tiny boat, flipped over, riding the alligator. It might be obvious that scutes offer protection, but they also help regulate temperature. Tiny offerings to the sun, this lattice of bone has floated on the backs of gators for millions of years.

As I read on the porch, I hear a crack from the top of a cedar that has begun its decline amid saltwater intrusion. An osprey lifts across the mouth of the lagoon with a silvered branch in its talons. Its flight turns upriver toward the nest built amid the green metal of channel marker 63. I wonder about our inclination to collect things on the porch. It does offer an intermediate place, neither inside nor outside, where sand sprinkling from shells or dirt and cedar needles falling from driftwood can blow away as easily as they are swept up. The porch is a screened vessel that pulls things in and protects them while not fully removing them from nature. But seeing the osprey with the branch pulled from a dying tree to make her nest on a rusting channel marker, I wonder if collecting things here also makes a nest. In one sense, it is a delicate membrane between what we own and what we have borrowed, between what we can control and what remains out of our hands. And in another, our porch nest holds small bits of knowledge sieved from what is around us and suspended here on the edge of the world.

※
 ※

> The much approved *Daton*, and the common straw cutters, together with very superior *wheat fans, root cutters* or *turnip slicers, cultivators, hinge* and common *harrows, drill machines,* garden tools—the *Spring Steel, Hay* and *Manure forks*—*screen, safe*, and *window wove wire*.—The well-known Kinsey axes, and a very useful tool and implement that farmers ordinarily want, may be had at all times at his factory. Of garden seeds, he has on hand at present a very general assortment, . . .

There it is, wedged between food safes and Kinsey axes. What many consider to be the first mention of woven wire cloth's use for window screen comes in an advertisement from Robert Sinclair and his successful factory and nursery in Baltimore on November 28, 1823. This was a time when frontiers were being proved and defined. Stephen Long had recently published the report of his expedition into the West along the Platte River, Spain recognized Mexico's independence, and four days after Sinclair's advertisement, James Monroe's annual congressional address outlined the doctrine that would frame American attempts to control the Western Hemisphere. So, as the president went to and from the White House across the newly added south portico and as he defined expansive, geopolitical thresholds, the manufacturing advancements in screening technology further bolstered domestic boundaries. Sinclair's advertisement also sends out threads and clues about the origins of modern screening material. Screen wire and safe wire were also available; and window screens generally developed from the agricultural use of mesh, and, more particularly, from the invention of screened safes to keep food ventilated, relatively cool, and protected from insects and animals.

Firsts are typically hard to pin down. Two years earlier, Thomas Massey, on his farm in Delaware, had already enlisted "wove wire" to screen his dairy's windows from flies. In a letter to the *American Farmer*, Massey describes the ideal dairy for thirty cows. It is not clear whether screens and porches had yet been combined, but Massey had both; the plans and sketch accompanying his letter include an open porch on the front of the milk-house, where all the work of milking would take place. That work excludes skimming, which the farmhouse could still accommodate, but it does include straining, which, Massey says, should be done out of doors in the porch, because otherwise the warm milk of thirty cows would raise interior temperatures to unhealthy levels, particularly during the summer. For screening the windows, he proposes two alternatives—the wove wire later advertised by Sinclair, or millinet, a high grade of cheesecloth. These were practical solutions because those materials would have been close at hand. Dairy farmers already strained milk and skimmed cream, so why not also sieve pests from the air?

Porch screens began as sieves. Before sifting air, they separated debris from milk, meal from bran, and fiber from pulp. They lined the windows of train cars to protect passengers from airborne steam engine cinders. The application of wire cloth began in earnest in the middle of the nineteenth century when manufacturers like Gilbert and Bennett sought durable alternatives for horsehair sieves in their tannery business and cotton mesh in the glue drying process. Early production struggled to find machines to weave the metal wire and initially relied on looms used for lighter materials. As the industry grew, it targeted burgeoning markets for window screens around the time of the Civil War. Machines for drawing and plaiting wire became common, but the simple principles of weaving remained.

Weaving persisted as materials continued to change. The screens of the Homosassa porch are fiberglass—often the preferred insect screening material. The mesh is woven from glass yarn coated with vinyl. It solved problems of cost as well as durability and glare. Typically available in silver gray or charcoal finishes (we have the latter), fiberglass mesh is the least expensive and most readily available option. Earlier metal wire screens rusted, particularly in coastal settings. In the early twentieth century, galvanizing helped combat weathering but added to the cost. For about twice the expense of fiberglass, you can wrap a porch in aluminum mesh. Its silver finish glares in the bright sun, but virtually disappears from the inside. Stainless steel, bronze, brass and copper are also options—the first increases strength and corrosion resistance, an ideal choice for marine environments, and the latter two are forty times the cost of fiberglass, way too precious for a modest river cabin.

When I replace a panel of screening, I am stretching a canvas. Like a painter readying a work surface, I move outward from the center, adding tension and pulling out wrinkles. Some screens are tacked to porches just as a painter staples fabric to a wooden frame. That would have been the technique in this porch's early days, but now it has an aluminum frame with grooves for the rubber splines that pinch the edges of a screen into place. The coiled spline looks like a really long licorice Twizzler; its ridges and grooves are the lines of screen spun on its axis, a tactile reminder of the mesh's texture and pattern, as I press them into the frame's grooves.

The link between porch screen and canvas isn't just about technique. Porch screens have been actual canvases for painters. In the nineteenth century, artists and homeowners painted porch screens with natural scenes, and in the early twentieth century, Baltimore resident and commercial artist William Oktavec painted window screens that hid interiors but still allowed views outside. If the contemporary porch feels like a renewed experiment to interface with nature, recapturing all that we're missing in an increasingly virtual world mediated by electronic screens, then these screen paintings—many of them made more than a century ago—already indicated a growing sense that nature, and the fresh air and wildlife that go with it, were being lost to industry and growing cities.

Painting a view of nature across a porch that already provides its own views carries a certain irony. The screen becomes a double-sided mechanism that plays with viewers' expectations. The screen painting is invisible to porch-sitters, but to those on the outside, the screen turns opaque with color and imagery. Looking toward the house, rather than out to nature, the porch screen became a picturesque sign, and the scenes effectively domesticated nature by mapping it onto the open-air architecture of porches. Sitting on screened porches today, an outward view likely pairs this actual view with a phone screen's virtual view—a digitally mediated, information-laden vision of what we're seeing. Today's porch screen has the potential to make our vision wild again, reminding us of the wonders of real-time nature and of how little control we really have, as it is also painted with the flicker of all the other images that stream across our digital screens.

The density of a screen's weave is a balance of vision and protection. The wider the spacing, the clearer the view. Pull it tighter, and fewer insects crawl or fly in. The wire count in each direction—warp and weft—measures a screen's density. In the early twentieth century, public health agencies promoted the screening of windows and porches to prevent the transfer of insect-borne disease, as they also prescribed fresh air for general health and as the sleeping porch became trendy. Little quantitative research was carried out, and recommendations for densities varied. Some researchers found that fifteen by fifteen wires per inch was the smallest mesh the *Aedes* mosquito could negotiate. The US Army corroborated the opinion that even sixteen by sixteen was too wide and proceeded to specify eighteen by eighteen. Yet a grid of sixteen by sixteen became the industry standard by the middle of the twentieth century.

In 1946, after ninety years of relative consistency, production of screen material changed. In the new material, eighteen warp wires ran the length and fourteen weft wires ran the width. This change was a function of post-war efficiency. In a loom's setup, the warp is fixed, and the weft moves under and over it. Fewer weft wires mean that the loom's shuttle has less distance to cover, saving two trips per inch. And as the holes changed from square to rectangular, their number dropped only by four.

The Insect Wire Screening Bureau was formed in 1941. Its name has the ring of a Monty Python skit about overwrought bureaucracy, but the IWSB was an industry-led group charged with responding to changes in screen manufacturing. Five years later, the Bureau sponsored research at the University of Florida to study the effects of the new mesh configuration. This research measured not how many mosquitoes and gnats got into a screened area, but how many escaped from a small screened box. They found that sixteen by sixteen mesh is only slightly better than eighteen by fourteen. For small insects like sandflies, abundant in wetlands and saltmarshes near the research site, neither mesh size was sufficient. They recommended an even tighter mesh, which led to the twenty by twenty screens produced today. The researchers cautioned that any further increase in wire density would noticeably reduce visibility and air circulation.

Two other recommendations came from that research. It turns out that manufacturing tolerances—how precisely screens are made—have a powerful effect on screen performance. Industry tolerance is a quarter of a wire's width in the warp direction and half a wire in the weft, which is called the "filler" direction. That doesn't seem like a lot at ninety widths per inch, but it matters when your porch takes an expedition into clouds of mosquitoes and gnats in a land of water and sand and mud. And those researchers here in Florida knew about this firsthand when they urged care in the spacing of filler wires. They found that eighteen by twelve mesh oriented horizontally allowed a significantly greater number of mosquitoes through. Such attention to micro-dimensions and details brings the porch into focus from the perspective of the creatures it meets. Here, even though framed by the numbers of scientific analysis, we can imagine how a bug's body actually meets the screen. As you would expect, insects typically fly and rest upright, but their wings extend out from their sides. So, mosquitoes prefer horizontal doorways, and when I think about the warp tolerances perhaps not being met, and the even greater variability in insect size and species outside the laboratory, I resolve—even though I have never heard of anyone checking the grain of their screen mesh—to double-check that I'm installing screen with the vertical orientation. Because screening a porch is a game of millimeters.

**

I just watched a no-see'um climb through the screen. It wasn't easy. The watching or the climbing. Despite their name, you can see them. They are white flecks drifting, then sailing and clouding, around your body. They are small, but how small is hard to tell. To get a bearing on their actual size is elusive, as they float and spin, riding your breath and pulses of air. They are a blur of indecision, like tiny airborne jellyfish, until the screen brings them into focus. The grid of the mesh scales them into something you can get your head around. It structures their movement, it slows them down, pulls their loops and curlicues into rectangles and squares. They must hate this rationalization and structure. I watched this one wriggle through a sunlit square of screen.

The Homosassa porch's screen is the twenty by twenty mesh recommended by the researchers all those years ago, but I wonder: In seven decades, have the no-see'ums adapted? Do we need to reconvene an Insect Wire Screening Bureau for the new century? Is this an issue of tolerance? A flaw in the screen? But each twenty-fifth of an inch of air seems the same as the rest, and I watch her cross the sunlit threshold where vinyl reflects the sun white. The glare of the material and the blurry white of her body make it hard to be certain of the ins and outs of her crossing, but it worked and she is through.

Does she care whether she is on this side or that? I do, but I have little say in the matter. She must have hated the exposure of the sunlight. Mostly, no-see'ums prefer shadier air and the leafy protections of undergrowth. I have said "she" because later, having lost track of this no-see'um world, I will feel the slightest flutter in the hair of my hand and the sawing of tiny jaws on my skin and the sting of an anticoagulant bite. She seeks the blood that will sustain the eggs she lays. Seeing that struggle at the screen humanized a creature I knew only through discomfort, a kind of abstracted pain and itch on breezeless winter days in the mudflats, and even sometimes on the porch when the sky is gray and the air is still. Until now, I saw only a stochastic cloud of abandon. I had assumed they blew in with the screen door's opening and shutting, but now I understand an insect's deeper resolve against the screen's porous barrier. I watch as perhaps that same gnat, alone, on this side of the screen, watches a herd of other gnats on the far side. What effort of navigation and gymnastic precision will it take to reunite? Sure as I write this, she answers again, unseen, with a bite.

A porch can come down to this detail, to this level of intimacy. That no-see'um might have flown across the river, the same relative distance I will travel when I go back to Gainesville and tell whoever is studying bugs and screens what I have learned.

*
**

That's the compromise. A screened porch puts you out there with the insects. And the wind and the rain, hot and cold, birds and gators. Then, it slowly lets them in. Leaking bugs. It is a compromise between nature and control, wildness and domestication. If a denser screen doesn't really keep no-see'ums out, how about two screens?

Jack London wrote tales on the edges of civilization. In "When the World Was Young," he deployed the porch as a space of "compromise" between the savage and the civilized. When James Ward goes to sleep each night on a porch wrapped in two layers of screen, their purpose is not to keep insects out, but to keep Ward in. The successful businessman is afflicted by a haunting "atavism" that sends him far afield, werewolf-like, each moonlit night. As a result, Ward is wakeful at night, inarticulate in the morning, and "brilliant" in the afternoon. To compensate for his mercurial nature, Ward builds the sleeping porch on the side of his bungalow. Safely double-screened, he can breathe the wildness of fresh air but save nature from his savagery—he has an instinct to hunt animals in his wild state—while also protecting him from himself.

London brings the porch and its screens into the canon of American mythology. On the porch, James Ward enacts the mythical struggle between the night-born and the day-born gods whom Thoreau had summoned as avatars of a nation's effort to define its place in a monumental—sometimes sublime—landscape. Thoreau himself had explored these frontiers at Walden. His cabin did not have a porch, but it essentially was a porch. Its openness to climatic elements and its dimensions of ten by fifteen feet are porch-like, but it is the way Thoreau conceives of the cabin that really confirms its essential porchness. After breaking ground, when he describes his cabin as a porch in front of a burrow, he comments on the temporal nature of his dwelling in particular and the American house more generally.

In another passage, Thoreau's conflation of tent and house further builds on the idea that such dwellings can be defined by their edges rather than by what they contain. In other words, living along frontiers like porches is a condition of occupying edges, rather than being bound up between them: "The only house I had been the owner of before ... was a tent. With this more substantial shelter about me, I had made some progress toward settling in the world. This frame, so slightly clad, was a sort of crystallization around me, and reacted on the builder. It was suggestive of a picture in outlines. I did not need to go out of doors to take the air, for the atmosphere within had lost none of its freshness. It was not so much within doors as behind a door where I sat, even in the rainiest weather." The walls of Thoreau's cabin are like the porous screens of a porch. They place us at the edge of a frontier that is actual as well as mythical. To walk to the edge of a porch, whether to the end of its floorboards, to the boundary of its rail, or to the surface of its screen is to approach a fall line between the known and the unknown.

When Frederick Jackson Turner pitched a tent on the back porch of his rented house in Cambridge, Massachusetts, he was not just escaping the stuffiness of the northeast's aristocracy. He was also connecting back to the frontier he had studied throughout his career. Harvard had invited Turner as a visiting faculty member in 1910, and the famed historian lived along what is called "Tory Row" in one of Cambridge's oldest neighborhoods. The presence of this house along the front lines of American history was surely not lost on him.

Built in 1764, the three-story Georgian clapboard originally accommodated a loyalist who fled before the Revolutionary War, and the house served as a hospital after the battle of Bunker Hill, before it was transferred to a patriot. In the midst of this deep history, Turner spent his nights on the back porch, facing north rather than west, and less than thirty feet from his neighbor's plot. Far from the open range of the West.

The country's frontier had surely closed, but Turner found something on that porch that helped him test other boundaries, personal and domestic. He wrote that he was "lulled by the lapping of the automobiles" on Brattle Street and was "awakened in the early morning by the tinkle of the milkman's bottles." He said that it was like "a vacation from about 11pm to 7am." On the porch, he might be camping along a Wisconsin trail of his youth, or, more abstractly but no less tangibly, he might be edging the residue of a long-vanished western frontier. Today, the neighbors to the north have added a large swimming pool, further encroaching on Turner's old backyard, and his back porch has become an enclosed sunroom. Even this porch frontier may now have also closed.

If James Ward finds a compromise in his double-screened porch, if Thoreau experiments within the "slightly clad" frame of his porch-cabin, and if Turner occupies the residual space of a contracted frontier on his back porch, then George Babbitt limns the frontiers of the suburban house from his sleeping porch. Sinclair Lewis' novel of this "new American stereotype" opens on the porch, lodged between the banalities of Babbitt's daily routine—he is a "total conformist"—and the fairy tales of his imagined life. Like Babbitt himself, the sleeping porch is "unromantic," attached to the second floor of a Dutch Colonial, much like every other stock plan house of the 1920s. From the porch, Babbitt inventories the trappings of Midwestern suburban life: a large elm tree, the green grass of manicured yards, a driveway, and a garage. His survey also looks farther afield toward the town's central district, where he engages in real estate speculation, a business that yields exactly this environment of conformity. The porch is a frontier that connects him to the external world, while serving as a site for introspection, and perhaps a springboard for escape.

When Babbitt dreams, the porch offers a thin veil between the banal and the fantastic. On one side of the screen, he remains vulnerable to the mechanisms of suburban life. One morning, having heard his neighbors start their car and leave for work, Babbitt, "pious motorist" that he is, awakens with his arms raised, clutching an imagined steering wheel. Only when the car moves on is he "released from panting tension." The porch is also poised along the margins of a domestic landscape where he seeks escape from being "extremely married," but it is not far away enough for Babbitt when he hears his wife's "detestable cheerful 'time to get up, Georgie Boy'" from the neighboring bedroom. The sleeping porch is the setting for Babbitt's search for a "fine, bold man-world." It stands in for the camping trip that has been foiled by middle-class responsibilities. On the expedition to the edge of his house, Babbitt brings a specially purchased blanket that symbolizes "freedom and heroism" as he also carries along "gorgeous loafing, gorgeous cursing" and "virile flannel shirts." But when it gets cold, the camper gives up the "duty of being manly" and retreats to his bed inside.

On the porch, Babbitt also attempts a return to childhood, "again dreaming of the fairy-child, a dream more romantic than scarlet pagodas by the sea. . . . For years the fairy child had come to him. Where others saw George Babbitt, she discerned his gallant youth. She waited for him, in the darkness beyond mysterious groves." Babbitt's dreams transform suburban reality into fantasy where the elm and its domestic yard become a fairy tale's grove. If the porch is a soporific device for longing, it is also an emblem for a country's search for lost frontiers, a coming to terms with its identity. Just as Babbitt turns inward on the porch that presses out onto the new frontiers of middle-class suburban life, Americans were coming to terms with their position in a rapidly shrinking globe and country.

In the 1920s, the sleeping porch reached the extreme limits of its influence. In some parts of the country like the Deep South, sleeping out on a porch was a practical response to hot summers. In other parts, it was a health fad that had moved from California's temperate climate and its prescriptions for fresh air into the Midwest and the discomfort of its colder temperatures. To sleep on a porch in Ohio in the heart of winter was absurd, an irony not lost on Lewis. In *Babbitt*, such porches have become a "standard thing" for a newly burgeoning middle class. And like other objects of satire that hold prickly truths, the "normal" sleeping porch becomes a tool for revealing the strange. It is a means for Babbitt to see things differently or at least to access, even if he doesn't recognize it, an undercurrent of "discontent with the good common ways," like when he watches a foggy summer evening from behind the wire screen. In a delirious vision, the screen transforms the streetlamps into "crosses of pale fire." Their light is like the glow of the moon stolen, as Shakespeare wrote, from the sun, and it will later be the "pale fire" of John Shade's burning manuscript that Nabokov asks us to watch from the porch of

Charles Kinbote. Through Babbitt's screen, the entire world becomes "abnormal." And Babbitt comes to inhabit this kind of screen on his sleeping porch, which is not just a break from reality. Its liminal position also offers a reconsideration of what is real. At least until it's time to wake up: "He escaped from reality till the alarm-clock rang, at seven-twenty."

✳✳

The compromise of a screen is worth it. If you have to screen your porch, and many of us do, what is lost with more closure is gained back with what the screen offers. It is a surface alive with all the connections a porch affords. Here are some of the things the Homosassa screen has collected: small shards of cedar bark, flecks of Spanish moss, the quiver of pollen filaments, seeds, bugs, the eggs of some of those bugs, flecks of paint, tendrils from funnel weaver burrows, air plant seedlings, dirt, lichen, leaves, pieces of trees, and knots of old cobwebs—some of them ball up on my fingertips, but most melt away at my touch. One spray of web looks like a dragon, rearing back, ready to breathe fire. Wind brings these things in as it also washes them away.

The wind leaves some things intact on the screen. For three months I have watched a cedar twig change. It is now the color of the water in the back creek. A rusty tannin. It began as the velvet green of a mature cedar tree. I imagine that it broke when a belted kingfisher pushed away from his perch to arrow across the lagoon. The twig's fall mixed wind and gravity. It must have been blown, wobbling with the quick tempo of the kingfisher's voice, riding the spin of the earth. Its needles fit exactly in the squares of mesh, and it becomes another weft, more brittle but perfectly matching the width of air. It pivots where it laces with fiberglass. It is a kinetic sculpture: stiff vibration where it touches the screen's tension, rapid swings where it twists out into the sky, strobes of movement in its needles, and the periodic nudges and geiger twitches of its main trunk that cantilevers and points toward the river.

Broken needles rattle in the webs that further bind it to the screen. A spider has carefully hidden her single egg sac in the crook of one of its branches. A nest in a tiny tree. I study it each day through the screen's grid like an archeologist. I trowel the air around it, asking what it can tell me about time. The twig died when it fell from the tree, but now it continues dying. Its patina is the slow ebb of the rest of the cedars and oaks and the coastal forest—the ecosystem marked by all the things seined into the porch screen. But its steady decline is matched by the way it resolutely clings to the screen. As one system is dying another is being born. A tearing down parallels a building up. Unmaking and making. Because we can still see what is leaving (in the cedar twig, it is the stubborn green of chlorophyll), what comes in its place is a ruin in reverse.

I have tried to photograph the twig, but it resists documentation. How do you capture the slow creep of entropy? I have tried to photograph it set against an intact cedar in its picturesque arch over the lagoon and its mix of green and brown needles on living branches and dying limbs. But I don't have the skills to set the depth of field, and the screen collapses distance as it also collapses time where past, present, and future feel as tightly knitted as the mesh itself. In the growing tannin of its needles, I read the muck's slow decay, which is also the marsh's life. Right now, the back creek is the color of tea because of all this dying. The screen also tells the future. One day in late fall, in a broken spiderweb, I discovered the

petal of a mangrove flower next to a wisp of blue tarpaulin. One points toward a new generation of land-building plants and the other is a river-dweller's makeshift repair after storm damage.

The porch screen is also a living screen. Lichen and air plants find homes on its mesh. Subtle microclimates, at the scale of no-see'ums, warm these plants in the middle of winter's cold snaps. The heat is absorbed and re-radiated from the screen's dark gray material. It incubates those egg sacs held in the cedar twig's branches. Heat also courses along the mesh fibers toward the aluminum frames where it dissipates in a microscopic system of passive cooling. The screen is a habitat in and of itself, a scene of other minute acclimations.

I like to think I can tell the time of day in the light cast across the cabin porch's screen. The seasons alter this timing but here's the rubric: morning sun evaporates the screen, late morning is half shadow and half light, midday to afternoon is all shade, and finally the end screen flares with a lowering sun.

Porch screens collect things, and they also catch shadows. They repel and admit insects, as they bounce and transmit light. A screen's mesh is a playground of light and shadow and shape and change. In certain light, screen becomes scrim. A mottled flicker. A theater.

These interactions mostly follow the rules of veiling reflection. When you're in a place that is illuminated, looking into a place that is dark—whether an unlit interior or the outdoors at night—the screen becomes a wall, opaque. At night, screens turn inward, and the porch nestles between charcoal walls when a lamp turns the fine lattice of mesh into graphite. From outside, the porch is illuminated like a stage. Put another way, the exterior surface of the screen reflects external light, and the interior surface of a screen reflects internal light. The more reflective the surface—whether exterior or interior—the more veiling reflection there is. And so, depending on the light, the porch makes room for introverts or extroverts. In the light of day, our screen is a veil of privacy from outside, and it is, inside, a bright film screen of nature. At night, it is a curtain of security, even though night-born sounds breach the mesh, and I know that the raccoons, the bobcats, and the mice watch us.

The degree of veiling and transparency depends on the kind of light. Places where direct sunlight strikes the screen are less transparent than areas illuminated by ambient light. Most transparent are the shadows cast by the sunlight across the screen. This effect takes us back into the no-see'um's world, where the screen has depth, and the thickness of its mesh matters. The top edges of the screen's warp reflect the sun's rays, like the flaring wings of a gnat crossing a sunbeam. That glare interrupts—or veils—your vision from the porch. Screens of darker material will reduce the glare from this direct sunlight, and thus increase outward visibility through those brightly lit areas, but the difference between a sunlit and a shaded screen's transparency will remain.

Porch screens let you look through shadows. They break the rules of veiling reflection so that you can fully experience what is abstractly referred to as the "play of shadows." The screens nearly disappear in the soft glow of midday's ambient light, and shadows are like windows in the mesh. Rays of direct sunlight add another layer, appearing like thin white plaster over the screen's flickering veil. But what sunlight has troweled on is then easily wiped away by the flicker of shadows that cross those rays of light. Sitting on the porch, watching the screen perform, I have learned what Louis Kahn already knew about how porches temper light.

Mid-morning in late spring, and the sun casts shadows from the screen into the porch. The screen's mesh zebras across its frame. Its warp is a wide stripe of shadow and its wefts are gossamer sinews that stretch across the larger grain. The screen comes into focus on the page where I write. A minuscule graph paper, cutting an acute angle of sun and wind. Just a little bigger than its actual size, it textures my thoughts. Sometimes the weft goes away altogether and the warp's parallel lines twist across the page. My whole body is wrapped in this net. On the screen itself, dapples cast between leaves are windows of light. They hold saturated blues and greens in their miniature frames. As the sun moves higher, the screen becomes a light mist. Its holes are bright like so many droplets of water, like the albedo of white snow in a vast landscape. A closer look, and I find the specks of light are those reflections on the top edge of the mesh. They are the glint of the tiny suns I have seen on the crests of riffled waves out on the river. Now the sun is even higher, and the screen is a heavy gauze, a cataract over my eye. I try to look around it. It's a subtle reminder of that edge between here and there, between almost-outside and outside.

Later, movement plays across the screen like shadow puppets. Mid-afternoon, when the sun begins its descent, a drama lights up screen and floor. In this play, Spanish moss beckons at the lumbering nod of a dying palm leaf. Moss' gestures become taunts as it flags and teases the trees' stiffened trunks and thickened oak limbs. A palmetto's fronds are wiggling fingers, bridging the chasm of porch posts, toward the flicker of pepper trees, falling in love with their frenetic dance. And cedar-tipped limbs bend at the waist, laughing at the absurdity. As I watch, an audience of birds can't keep quiet, quipping and singing their own versions of the story as each act mimics the one before. Wind's organ murmurs. It slips in and out of step with the show. Wind and scene and sound and sight braid and then loosen. For a while, they follow the same storyline, matching what I see and hear, but then the air near me rests, and a silent film glides on unheard breezes, long takes, and quick nods that speak to the way of things and time. Every time I walk out onto the porch, this play is different, but the story is the same.

**

Each day on a porch, you are an impressionist painter. Air is your medium. The screen is your canvas. You return to the same spot, in the open air, to learn the process of seeing. Like Paul Cézanne poised by his easel at Mont Sainte Victoire, the porch screen becomes your étude sketch, where you study the way air and light touch rocks, leaves, and grass, as well as the screen itself. Even if you're not actually painting, you still test vision and study change. I stare entranced over the lagoon, across the river. Each time, the scene—its river, light, water, color—asks me to see it for the first time. Sometimes I sketch, but often the viewing remains a mental study. It asks for a way of seeing reminiscent of Stéphane Mallarmé's call to impressionism in the late summer of 1876: "Each work should be a new creation of the mind. The hand, it is true, will conserve some of its acquired secrets of manipulation, but the eye should forget all else it has seen, and learn anew from the lesson before it."

In the following decade, Cézanne executed a series of paintings that relied on screens of trees for their composition but also for their meaning. In one sense, the trees are a natural architecture of vision; they establish depth and provide stability in their frames, but they also give something else, much more important to Cézanne's intent. The screens of trees af-

SCREEN 157

ford doubt. When you look at *Trees and Houses*, you have the sense that the painter is practicing sight. The painting is not just about seeing, it is about learning and then knowing how to see. The screen promises order, but it raises as many questions as it answers. Leaves are smeared on houses, contours shift as they pass behind tree trunks, mountains evaporate into the sky, windows hang from tree limbs, houses become the color of underbrush, limbs are infused with the color of houses. I have always thought of these paintings as if they were composed from a porch, where the trees are columns and what happens across the canvas is a screen of built-up paint. Like porches, these paintings teach us the reflexive nature of perception.

Cézanne said that "nature is on the inside." Behind the screen of trees, we are neither inside nor outside. The painter instead takes us to a place where we're partway in nature, but most significantly, *conscious* of how we perceive nature. The experience is important—Cézanne ventured into *plein air* just as we go out into a porch's air. But the process of reflection—of thinking about what we are seeing and feeling—is also critical. We see things and we see ourselves in the world. This approach includes what we see and what we don't. On a porch, this way of seeing finds a home, as the philosopher Maurice Merleau-Ponty says, in the "texture" of the visible and invisible.

And Merleau-Ponty also said, "there is no vision without screen." A porch's screen extends the threshold our body makes with the world. It brings things that are far away closer and it allows us to see what might otherwise remain invisible. Just as Cézanne found the thresholds of sight in his painting's trees, the philosopher once marveled at a screen of cypresses "where the web of reflections plays." Whether it has a screen or not, the porch is an anchor for this kind of seeing. And right now, when I raise my head from this myopic cradle of writing, there is a play of distance between near and far. Three feet away, a bright green anole climbs the woven screen. He looks through the openings in vinyl mesh, its apertures about the size of his eye. We see each other for a moment. Beyond, a few juvenile palm fronds touch the breeze, and, farther away, water reflects sky, pleated by a crab boat that passed upriver a few minutes ago. Across the river, the lines of cordgrass, limestone, and trees offer other horizons.

*
* *

I have pored over this image like I sometimes look out from the porch, through the screen, with a mix of rapt attention and blank stare. Nothing is going on and yet everything is happening. I am looking intently, yet not quite processing all of what I see, waiting for clarity. I am looking at an image of the porch that Marjorie Kinnan Rawlings added to her house. A few years ago, I made a three-dimensional laser scan of this porch in Cross Creek. Usually, these scans go through a digital processing phase to sort out the raw data and correct errors. This scan was never processed, so the image has many pieces of information laid one on top of another. It remains raw. I borrowed the scanner from a historic preservationist who uses it to prepare buildings for renovation or sometimes to document them ahead of destruction. This image is not what the preservationist seeks—there are too many anomalies, misalignments, and blurred edges. But it is a near-perfect visual analog for this porch and the broader experiences of porches, both in the past and now.

Scanning the porch took all morning. First, I set up in the porch. About my height on its tripod, the scanner hovered like an uncomfortable guest, a poet perhaps, visiting Rawlings from the city, hesitant along the porch's tilt and this outpost's wildness. Its revolutions were those of a head turning slowly for a sideways glance. Later, out in front of the porch, it stood like another tool in the orange grove, a farm implement among ladders and bird feeders, wading across chickens and ducks. Waiting for the scanner to complete its full rotation, I thought about the ironies of scanning an old porch. It is counterintuitive to document an old porch with such new technology. You could rebuild this porch two or three times for the price of the scanner. Rawlings herself added the porch in the 1930s for a fraction of the cost.

This image I have stared at for longer than it takes the anole to finish his ascent of the screen in the hottest part of the day is not an exact documentation of Rawlings' porch, and yet it is wholly accurate. It demonstrates technology's potential as well as its limits. The porch's physical properties are all here, writ over one another. The image collapses not just inside and outside, but front and back, dark and light, reflected and screened, above and below the porch rail. Horizontal wood siding on the exterior lays over vertical beaded board on the interior. Above the rail, screened frames collage with the house's siding and its two pairs of French doors that brightly reflect the morning sun. Tattered edges of the image reveal metal roofing that runs behind roof rafters and the tongue-and-groove ceiling. Along the ground, a broken grid of trellises criss-crosses through a full spectrum of grayscale shadows, which are the sun moving in and out of clouds while the scanner slowly rotates. The trellis is punctuated by three steps in the middle and the ancient tea olive bushes that flank the entrance to the porch. They are both white silhouettes, all scraggly branches and leaves. A few brushstrokes of sandy earth contour the lower edge of the image. A single stroke of blue captures the eastern horizon.

The porch's insect screens sieve what is on each side. You are multiple places at once. In one reading, you are outside looking in. You've turned off the road, and the front gate swings shut as you approach the house. Behind you, late morning sun has just cleared the tree line to warm your back and to illuminate white siding and reveal its imperfections, while thin shadow lines stripe below the sill and deepen the low wall's shallow relief. This light on the screen would typically veil and obscure your view into the porch, but the scanned image freely discloses the interior, all the way through to the back wall's French doors. Catching the reflected light, their panels are bright, whiter than the siding. The screen of the porch door is a dark gray sheet framed in wood—so many dots that moiré across a paper's whiteness with small errant strokes of green. Above the siding across the porch's width, when the screen does veil your approaching view, it gathers more landscape—sand-filled grass, orange tree foliage, crests of tea olive bushes, the gloss of magnolia leaves—in a pointillist halftone like a serigrapher's print, precisely masked at its edges but tinged by the scanner's algorithmic whims, bleeding like printer's ink.

This image is also the porch-sitter's view. It is Rawlings waiting for your arrival, or me trying to imagine her perspective. From inside, the screen is a layer of glass that reflects what is behind me—those French doors and the wood siding on the house wall. From this perspective, the term veiling reflection takes on even more meaning. It is as if the screen reflects not just light but other images. To my far right, this reflection, in a digital anomaly, rains down in lines of gray dots like water falling from the roof during a summer thunderstorm that will send the ducks under the porch to safety. I have just noticed them in the yard—smudges of brown snared in the screen's net. At the very top of the screened panel—another digital anomaly—just to the right of the door, a thin smudge of blue is the sky, but it's impossibly low, having fallen well below the tree line; it is what Rawlings would have seen decades ago when lower-slung orange groves ranged eastward, before the mature oaks and pines of today.

The digital process has done what Cézanne did, playing with depth and making tangible what would otherwise remain ephemeral, even invisible. Air becomes solid material, windows hang from tree limbs, and those limbs become translucent with raking dusk light. To the left, I see myself. I'm out in the yard, hands in pockets, waiting on the scanner's slow rotation, weaving its impossible net of information. I thought I was out of the frame, but I'm caught in its vision like everything else.

***

There's a gecko on the porch screen. Its sure form clings to tremulous mesh. When I turn the light out, moonlight x-rays an already translucent body. I have seen these geckos on glass, but it's not the same. Even in a darkening room, the window embraces the night's opacity, collapsing the space and hiding what is just on the other side. Through the screen, its faint but regular voice squeaks and chirps as if to assure us of its own spectral presence. It is a ghost, an Old World gecko. Its ancestors drifted across the Atlantic from Mediterranean coasts. Field guides attest to its anomaly with maps that show its range in north and central Florida. An inchoate New World habitat. The porch screen must be its Greek fisherman's netting, its sun-warmed stone wall, its perch on a tiled roof's lip, under an Aegean sky.

I don't know if Marjorie Kinnan Rawlings ever saw geckoes on her porch screens but she might have felt an alliance with these specters who made her insect screen a living screen. An expatriate to the South's social and atmospheric climates, Rawlings might have seen a little of herself in these transplants who are also emblems of migration, refugees of climate shifts, hitchhikers of global trade, and mostly solitary sojourners. She might have fed from their presence just as they were feeding from her reading light's screen-bound insects.

I do know that Rawlings watched lizards on her porch. She met their gaze as she carefully observed their lives on the screen: "They clamber slowly, gracefully, up and down screens. They watch you for hours with bright small eyes."

⁎⁎

I sit at the back edge of the porch when storms throw squalls across the river. They cross the river in seconds. Rain shakes the screens, like the river has turned sideways. Bouncing, pulsing as they dampen both water and wind. Mesh cuts the rain into mist, and this porch fog strobes with lightning. It wets our faces.

A porch's screen sieves rain as well as air. When I sat on the Rawlings porch a few years ago, a chilled winter air carried sights, sounds, and smells into its mesh. I noted: *An errant wasp strikes the screen, third panel from the left. A car passes, a cardinal splashes in the bath, its wings rustle when it lands, and the sun turns on the dial. The ducks, now quiet, peck in the orange trees' dripline where no grass grows. There's a bumblebee's resonant hum, cut by a squirrel's claws scratching over a pecan tree's bark, as moths lift silently, and the scent of tea olive drifts through wire mesh.* I was practicing Rawlings' finely honed skills of reverie. I sought that time when the view through the screen is a projection that plays at half speed. Almost as if the squares of screen are pixels that don't obscure what you're seeing or reduce the information you're receiving, but actually increase acuity in the way that higher definition doesn't necessarily mean greater understanding. I feel certain that Rawlings could have written this line nowhere else but on her screened porch in Cross Creek: "I have lain on my veranda and asked no more of the summer day than to watch, one by one, the lotus petals falling."

A screened porch makes room for reverie. It offers a thin veil of safety for daydreaming. Like sleep itself, it harbors a dream's loose mix of the concrete and the fantastic. Screens mediate distraction but they don't get rid of it altogether. Disturbances are a natural part of porches—a quality that Rawlings lamented and celebrated. On her porch, I watch as a crow lifts from the birdbath and flies right at me, as if it might pass through the screen. Its shadow does. The porch offers solitude, but it does a poor job of isolating phenomena. It can sustain the fury of a ship's deck or the quiet calm and introspection of a chapel. A palmetto frond falls, cracking, then scraping the trunk, scratching glossy oak leaves, and then—at the edges of what is audible—touches down on pine needles. I look up, lose my train of thought, and think about the color of the sky.

When Rawlings writes of her Cross Creek porch, she captures the in and out of screens. When we bring items onto a porch, we interrupt the order of things as we also bridge the gaps between inside and outside. And we learn that those gaps aren't really separations but bonds that have been overlooked or forgotten. A porch screen is a frontier of understanding, and it helps us see ourselves in nature: "The humming-birds come in, to stand on their heads in the red hibiscus cups, to sit like minute bright twigs on the tips of orange boughs, to poise, motionless except for the vibrating wings, outside the screen and stare at me. One day I selfishly picked all the hibiscus blossoms and put them in a bowl on the veranda table. A hummingbird tried to dart through the screen to come at them. His needle-bill caught in the wire and I loosened it gently. He flew away and perched on the fence and shook himself and tried to adjust himself to invisible barriers." Screens reside along the seams of the world where the invisible might become visible again. And, like the hummingbird, it is up to us to adjust.

A leaf blows into the screen. The wind is the early spring curl of high pressure that draws warmth from the south and speed from the east. The leaf holds. And I have time to study it. Its russet skin holds deep brown veins. A luster draws redness from its stiffened form, and it holds the sun along the finely drawn lines of a folded rim. Late winter is fall for the live oaks in this part of Florida, and this leaf must have dropped a while ago because the screen is already flecked with oak pollen like tiny clusters of dried grapes. The leaf hangs there, still pressed by an insistent breeze. Supple leather, thickened and smoothed. Polished with morning light, it recalls its year in the sun. It curls with age and twists where an insect bored a hole along its midrib; its oval is an eye that squints from this wound. It looks at me, concentrating. The wind drops but the leaf remains. Time slows as I try to focus on its detail but the sun is out now and the leaf is backlit. Just before it drifts to the ground, I see that it carries a wisp of pollen, a hitcher from the smooth cordgrass that grows behind ragged limestone. A sojourner from the river's edge.

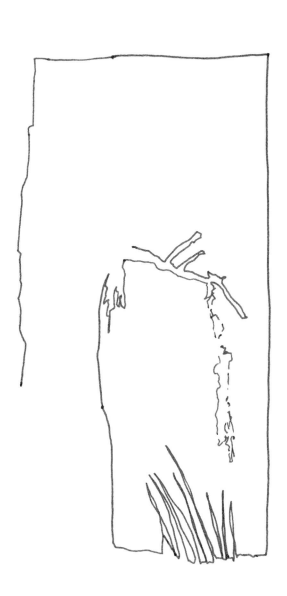

5

BLUE

Mornings on a clear day the porch ceiling becomes the surface of the river. Looking up, you feel like you're underwater.
Sunlight flashes in waves and ripples that shadow across the
ceiling. You can see the wind in the patterns that riffle sheets
of the river's flow. More than that, you come to know the air
that is moving the water, chafing its surface, even if that wind
and those breezes have yet to move through the screen and
touch your skin. As its angle changes, the sun compresses and
stretches light, and the reflections tell of tide and current,
drafts and freshets, where manatees and pelicans, mullet and
osprey act in a story projected on the porch ceiling.

The porch is all sound. Rain taps the metal roof and plays
a soothing beat. Soon, the tympanum resonates louder and I
feel the impacts like so many shots fired from the high clouds.
The drops have been falling for a few minutes, crashing to
earth at twenty miles an hour, having covered many thousands
of miles across land and sea. Which ocean did this water come
from? Which melting ice sheet? On clear days, acorns are another staccato loosened by a gust or one of the squirrels long
marooned out here. I haven't cleaned the porch's gutters in a

while, so after a rain, the sun warms the wet compost of cedar needles, raccoon droppings, and oak leaves, and it smacks as it dries. Like loosened gums along the porch's edges.

Water makes the porch's roof. It binds above and below. River reflections on one side, rain on the other. The roof is a fine membrane; it is a percussive skin that sheds water finding its way back to earth, and its underside is a playful scrim where I imagine a dance of fish, seaweed, and sediment. This porch where I write is all about sea and sky. The tides wash across the page in pale reflections from the ceiling, and the light on the page dims when a storm cloud crosses the sun.

A porch's roof edges the sky. Writing from her porch, Marjorie Kinnan Rawlings watched the eastern sky above the orange grove. And she watched squares of sky cut out at each end of her porch, north and south, where its roof meets the house. Such views were her "irreducible minimum of happiness," and that porch in Cross Creek enabled her "tangible desideratum." Every day, her writing was grounded in the sight of a "tree top against a patch of sky." And on fall days, the color of that porch sky anchored the writer's palette: "When the September storms are over we have some of our most superb weather. The oranges take on color, the red-birds are delirious, and in the morning and evening long shadows lie under the citrus trees. The skies are the brightest of robin's egg blue and the air has a translucent quality, as though the storms had washed it with a fine gold dust."

Robin's egg blue. In the sky, Rawlings saw the color used to paint porch ceilings across the South. Her own porch was painted white, but its roof cut a clean line across her vision.

Between ceiling and sky, that line drew the happiness of "superb weather" onto the page, saturated it with cerulean hues, and underscored the richness of those September days. Blue-green porch ceilings extend beyond the South, but it's here where the traditions run deepest. Two particular colors stand out: robin's egg blue and haint blue. One has storied natural origins and the other links to supernatural stories. Both have attained a mythology that further deepens the elemental nature of porches, tying them to air and water, sky and tree, color and imagination, climate and thought.

Why blue? The answers mix folklore with science, and the motivations blend the practical with the mystical and the actual with the imagined. None of these are proven, except perhaps when repetition becomes tradition, so that over time— and really because of it—the expected results are bound to occur. Porches are more susceptible to insects than other parts of the house. So, one reason for painting a porch ceiling blue is to fool spiders, wasps, and mosquitoes into thinking it is the sky. But I have to admit that I haven't seen swarms of mosquitoes clamoring toward painted wood for a release into the blue; they seek more direct routes through tears in screens and cracks in walls. Wasps already like to build high nests pressed against the sky in corners and under eaves, and spiders follow the other insects.

Another goal of blue porch ceilings isn't to attract but to repel. Porches in general and porch ceilings in particular require frequent coats of paint. And in the past, as porches gathered their folklore, paint was made with milk, pigment, and lye. That last ingredient is a proven insect repellant, and repainting refreshed it. I have wondered if blue's indication of a lower acidity in nature—think of hydrangeas and blueberries—is akin to the low acid content in the lye that repels insects. But wouldn't lye in the ceiling send insects back down toward bare arms and legs?

Why this shade of blue? Blue is considered a calming color. It soothes and cools as it slows respiration and heart rate. And of course context plays a large part in how we perceive color, so that its use in a typical porch's already calming environment surely helps. The touch of green in robin's egg blue increases the effect of tranquility. For the artist Wassily Kandinsky, green brings restfulness to blue's cool depth. Kandinsky linked color to a spirituality that combined the emotional with the transcendent, and he believed blue-green's deeply soothing effect was not just seen but deeply felt through other senses. In different shades of blue, he heard flute, cello, double bass, and organ. Though we are not all synesthetes like Kandinksy, color can still evoke taste or smell or even sound. Blue has the "heavenly" effect of a symphony.

Such experiences of color make visible what might otherwise remain invisible. And haint blue offers a vivid connection between spirit worlds and material worlds. Haint blue can be traced to the Gullah people of coastal Georgia and South Carolina. According to folklore, evil spirits, or "haints," would not travel across water, and porch ceilings, like doors or window frames painted blue, create the appearance of aqueous thresholds. Other stories say that a blue ceiling represents air rather than water, and sends haints skyward, up and out of the porch before they can reach the interior of the house. One application fools and the other deters. Both protect the house at its key threshold, the porch.

*
**

With these stories and traditions in mind, I set out to paint my porch ceiling blue. Its ceiling was the same gray as the rest of the cabin. The neutral color was fine for watching shadows and reflections, but I wanted to understand the ceiling as another element in the making of the porch. An element that might further temper the porch's response to its climate, like tilt, air, and screen. Choosing a color became its own project. There are as many blues for porch ceilings as there are porches and people who sit and rest there. Curiously, among today's options, not one color is named "robin's egg blue." You can go back to the 1930 edition of *A Dictionary of Color* to find a short description and its color card. There, "robin's egg blue" swims in a sea of names and hues that mix color with shells: bird's egg green, eggshell blue, and eggshell green. Today, commercial paints employ names from aquatic and vegetal sources alike. Sherwin Williams offers coastal aqua, tame teal, geyser mist, blue iris, swimming, refresh, aqueous, cooled blue, watery, tidewater, mariner, Bora Bora shore, and spa. For its "robin egg" colors, Valspar suggests sea air, frosty, sea wave, inspiring hue, aqua glow, nautical, sprinkle, aquatic mist, and fresh mist. With Benjamin Moore, there's waterfall, thunderbird, warm springs, spring sky, and spring rain. Behr adds swan sea and Tahitian sky. Many of these names allude to a mix of sea and air that might not be found in most places but is quite real on the Homosassa porch.

The lack of a single "robin's egg blue" is a reminder that color is subjective, as it is also dependent on context and, in the paint industry, on focus groups. Internet searches for "robin's egg blue" return a deluge of Pinterest sites, lists, and top tens. Colors are freighted in style and fashion, and the afterimage of this one holds a particularly weighty presence in popular culture and trends. Some ally it to Tiffany Blue, which was recently patented and undoubtedly conjures a saleable and precious aura, but its hue seems oversaturated for porch ceilings and lends itself more to boxes, bags, and jewelry store walls.

"Robin's egg blue" does have a historical lineage. Many references, including the *Dictionary of Color*, pin the origins of the name to 1873, but it had already been used in the 1840s to describe a New Hampshire mineralogist's discovery of a blue-green hue that occurs when acid from molybdenum rocks mixes with zinc. The resulting pigment lent itself to fabric dyes. And then in 1873, *Harper's* published Mary Nutting's poem "Robin's-Egg Blue," which tells the story of "a maiden artist" who fashions a bonnet for "the veriest queen of girls." The result of her work is a "recherché shade" that is not "common" blue, but "the very latest." This nod to fashion's modishness echoes Tiffany's influence, which stems from its own shade of blue and its annual blue book, but what comes through most acutely in Nutting's tale is the realization that the bonnet and its color are a function of the girl's labor and her fleeting break from reality. Nutting invokes the "broken reality" of the "dream-land" the hat symbolizes. Blue-green is the color of dreamers.

With elements of design, including color, architects are known for deliberation that can verge on the protracted, even the pathological, and I am not immune to the pitfalls of obstructing action with the weighing of options. Wrestling with my color choice, I found encouragement in the French painter Gustave Moreau's idea that "you must think through color, have imagination in it. Color must be thought, dreamed, imagined." So, after a lot of reflection, many test swaths, and even a little angst, I chose a color Sherwin Williams calls "Pool Blue," readily available, and not too precious. A modest budget played a part in the choice, but there was not a lot of difference in cost for what amounted to less than two gallons of paint. Even though it is ranked number four on *Southern Living*'s website, I ultimately chose this one because it garnered approval from my family, it balances blue and green, and quite simply it's what I have imagined a porch ceiling to be.

"Pool Blue" doesn't exactly resonate with poetry or porches. In fact, it's probably the least emotive designation in a field already challenged with elegiac and treacly prose. Its name calls to mind the generic aquatic and the over-chlorinated, but there is some comfort to be found in the subtle calibration of its RGB mixture: Red 181, Green 227, Blue 226. Like most paints in this group, the green and blue numbers are close, but I am convinced that the slight edge to green is what differentiates Sherwin Williams paint number 6944 from what the company considers to be similar colors, like "Swimming" and "Aqueous." That uptick of green also tempered my aversion to the color's name and the sense that it has been arbitrarily generated. That extra bit of green floods the name's conventions with a tinge of algae, inflecting the suburban pool with a bit of front porch wilderness.

A reporter once asked Eudora Welty to describe what she saw in the Mississippi swamp. She answered: "Oh, sort of blue." This is not a phrase marked by diffidence or indecision. It is a precise observation from a writer's eye—more exacting than any RGB values. Welty wasn't just looking at the swamp, she was seeing its air and its sky. After a pause, four more words completed her thought with an analogy: "Like an ink wash." Wet pigment suspended in space.

Air holds color like it holds water. Like it holds grains of pollen in what Zora Neale Hurston calls "pollinated air." As it is also the medium for the "thought pictures" her characters conjure when they tell a story on the porch. It may not always be visible, but it is there. And you have to feel it. You come to understand the color of air as you also come to understand the air's humidity through your skin. Like breaking a light sweat on a porch in the summer. If there is a breeze, or if there are fans on the ceiling, that sweat will evaporate, cooling your skin. The color of air on a porch cools your mind. On a porch, you wear the air around you. Gottfried Semper theorized that architecture preceded clothing, and even if they don't have screens, porches do dress your body. Your vestments are blue because porches draw in—they make intimate—what poet Richard Savage called the "bright, transparent blue, that robes the sky."

Welty's sight worked like that, a poetic vision that brought all the senses to bear. It casts an ultraviolet light on a scene, probing and then revealing, finding traces of evidence. She uncovers the invisible links that surround us. And a lot of times she does this by describing the color of air. In Welty's story "The Winds" and its dreamlike narrative, a storm is coming and parents pull drowsy children from the sleeping porch and the exposures of night. Welty's description of the atmosphere surrounding the porch as "violet and rose" fills the air with color so that you can see it, but only on the very cusp of its visible spectrum. Breathing deeply, you smell its color, its tremulous sweetness, and your skin feels the pulse of thunder that rides fluid air. Is there a more intimate form of matter? Is there a more intimate place than the porch to experience it?

When I finished painting its ceiling, the porch's air was a mix of blue and green. It was the color of cedar berries after rain. It was a mullet's eyelid, and how the tannin lens of the lagoon water gives its fins their pale blue aura. It was the color of a manatee's skin immersed in the headwater's spring. It might have been the dizzying effects of a day of twisting and craning, but there was a tangible difference. And it wasn't just that the ceiling was a different color, much brighter than the muted gray. It was that the porch had become a room. The blue-green ceiling furnished the porch with its own identity within the cabin. In that sense, painting the ceiling had finished out the porch, domesticated it, drawn it inward.

But at the same time, this act of painting had loosened it from the rest of the house. Painting a porch ceiling blue brings the sky in. It also opens up to a cerulean expanse. I am reminded that, for naturalist John Burroughs, tree limbs became ceilings that linked house to sky. His formulation of the "roof-tree" is another version of the porch held in place, grounded, by the sky. Burroughs wrote that a building's roof "allies it to the open air." Screens admit fresh air, but it is the porch's ceiling that stitches a porch to air, from above and below. Painting the porch ceiling amplified this effect. Planting the roof-tree brings Burroughs joy as it "bears the golden apples of home and hospitality" just as those patches of sky that Rawlings saw from her porch touched her with delight. On a porch, you are sheltered in the sky.

The porch's blue ceiling also lets the ceiling recede. Blue is the color of distance. Canopy beds were sometimes topped with blue fabric, and on the ceiling of Mantegna's bridal chamber in Mantua, a cylinder of sky rises behind winged putti capering around the balustrade. A trompe l'oeil, the depth of that blue circle is almost unfathomable. Kandinsky knew very well how blue recedes, but he also found an intimacy in its process: "blue . . . moves in upon itself, like a snail retreating into its shell," drawing "away from the spectator." It turns in on itself as it expands. It retreats as it flies up. This mix of depth and interiority, for Kandinsky, was the underpinning of the "profound meaning" he found in blue. It is the color of the heavens, and Kandinsky reminds us that the halos of mortals are gold, while spiritual beings have "sky-blue" halos and the breath of repose. And blue's movement, its ascent and its oscillation between expanse and center, slows and pauses when blue limns green for its soothing hue. When I walk onto the porch, it is a hole in the roof but it is also like staring into a well and seeing a piece of sky.

The porch roof doesn't need its posts anymore. The ceiling glows with the last bit of the day's light. Its green is platinum now. It is lifted into place and held aloft on air. In its wake, the blue of a robin's egg swirls in breezes that braid the screens. The smell of fresh paint mixes with hot cedar. It's low tide and salt rime dries on coral rock. The island's skinny loam mulches from the day's warmth. Now I understand what Wallace Stevens had in mind when he wrote of the "brown blues of evening."

Before I painted the ceiling, I traveled to Sweden to see a porch designed by Sigurd Lewerentz. Attached to the Resurrection Chapel, it was one part of the architect's work in the 1920s at the Woodland Cemetery in Stockholm. I have been intrigued by this project since I began studying architecture. Not only is this monumental porch detached—ever so slightly—from the chapel's main building, but this offset is skewed even more subtly—though ever so significantly—from the chapel. The angle hardly registers in floor plans, and it is easy to miss the gap as you move from the porch into the chapel. Initially, whether you recognize the gap or not, you have a sense of passing from one state to another. The angle is a matter of inches—a difference that could be interpreted as mistake rather than intention. It is a lateral slant not unlike a porch floor's horizontal tilt. Once you realize it is there, this skew has the import of life and death. It affected me most deeply when I looked up and saw the gentle taper of sky. It was a sliver of blue.

The Nordic days were lengthening in the middle of May, and my last visit to the cemetery stretched into the evening. Elms planted nearly a century ago held the sun overhead as I sat sketching on the mound that marks Lewerentz's last project at Woodland. From here I could begin to triangulate the architect's overall plan and reflect on my visit and the porches I had seen. In front of me, the Path of the Seven Wells gently pried apart the forest on its way toward the distant porch of the Resurrection Chapel. That narrow wedge of air reminded me of the sliver of sky between porch and chapel. On my left, shadows from the elms reached into Monument Hall's forecourt, completed by Gunnar Asplund after his partnership with Lewerentz had ended.

Monument Hall's porch still holds the ghost of Lewerentz's original idea—a columned forecourt that presses out into the main entrance path to welcome visitors as it also shelters mourners leaving the chapel. The austerity of its simple concrete forms of column and roof provides comforting clarity for both groups. Funeral-goers enter the Hall as individuals, wrapped in anguish, and they leave as a community of mourners into the porch, breathing deeply with light and shadow. This porch is monumental and personal. It reconciles private grief and public solace. This porch is a forest of columns, a stand of trees, where eight decades ago one observer watched Asplund's funeral and witnessed how the "pale red rays of Autumn sun" cloaked the porch with hope.

Up here on the mound, the Resurrection Chapel is straight ahead, down the Path. Even though it is a half mile away and the day's light is slowly dimming, I can still see its copper roof, its pediment, and the deep shadow of its bronze doors. Most clear are the two columns that flank its entry. Tree shadows angle across the distant clearing into the limestone shafts, and the western light that makes it through—there's still a lot at eight o'clock—pierces the depth and races to me like the contours of a familiar face that has just turned, eyes squinting, features raised in high contrast. As night approaches, its columns make the chapel appear closer than it is, as near and present as the cool wind that blows across the crest of this hill that Lewerentz mounded up and planted. The birds are singing in the elms, and the smell of ashes drifts away to the east. That distant porch reminds us why we are living.

The porch rests so deep in the firs, it also reminds us that we will die. Shadows have filled the path, but earlier in the day the evergreen trench held the sun, flaring an axis of light, as if to recall its original purpose as a firebreak in this grove of ten thousand trees. Now, only hollow filaments scratch the dark.

Behind the porch and its chapel, the high tree canopy catches the rest of the setting sun. Deep in the path, a solitary figure runs toward the porch. Another walks away. Halfway along, where they meet, like shades, a wayward pine trunk strung amid the firs catches another shard of sun. It lights with the same intensity of the two porch columns. I feel like I am watching something with the gravity of an eclipse.

How many landscapes of architecture can testify like this? How many works of architecture can be read from a half mile away with this same precision and humane proximity? Lewerentz never said why he skewed the chapel's porch. He didn't want to talk about his intentions because his story might preclude my story, your story, their stories. It might tell every stroller, jogger, tourist, visitor, teenager, tour guide, mourner, priest, curator, groundskeeper, photographer what to see, how to be in this place. This cemetery's architects have guided us to a point, but they don't tell us what to think. In the cemetery's vastness, the porch leaves us room to consider why we're here. To contemplate the barely fathomable, to think the depth of blue. I walked down the slope thinking about an architecture and a landscape as reassuring yet fluid as life and death.

I had spent most of the day in the porch of the Resurrection Chapel. It is about thirty feet wide and twenty-eight feet deep. The porch's interior height is about the same as its depth. On your approach from the north, low walls flank the transition from the Path into the open court, which is a clearing in the woods. The space between the middle two columns widens slightly for you to enter the porch. Morning sun has made the eastern side—four of its ten columns—warm to the touch. From outside, the roof floats across the blue sky despite its heavy entablature. Inside, the ceiling is an illuminated shadow. The ten columns have the caliper and taper of trees, bristling with conifer details. Each Corinthian capital is different; each has the peel of pine bark. This porch is a temple in a grove. Its classical details set it off from the chapel and the austerity of its bare walls. But those details also connect it inextricably to the grain of the forest. When you step into the porch, you haven't left the woodland. The ground under the roof pitches like a domestic porch. Gravel slopes east and west to troughs that carry water back into the forest. The air of the porch swells with pine needle light. It is a shade tree that has grown up close—maybe too close—to the building. The crunch of my step echoes as I reach the stone threshold. Then, soundlessly, under the wedge of blue sky, I cross and step up into the chapel.

I forgot the measuring tape I had packed. Having come all this way, from Florida to Sweden, crossing almost exactly thirty degrees of latitude, all I had was a pen, my sketchbook, and my body. The plan had been to measure the distance between porch and chapel and to figure out the exact dimensions of the angle. A little disheartened, I stood in the wedge of light and started to see how my body fit the space. I spread my arms, hugging the air, but the distance was too narrow. The span of my forearm was too short to reach across and too long to serve as a reliable unit of measure. My limbs hung in the air, slackened, unmoored, imprecise. I tried my hands, but pressing my palms to ground was too awkward and I was too self-conscious, digging and scuffing in the gravel, in the middle of a UNESCO World Heritage site. I soon found that the width of my boot was the measure most consistent with the offset. Starting at the west corner of the porch, where the distance between porch and chapel is narrowest, and stepping sideways foot to foot, I tallied five boots, plus the width of my thumb. On the east corner, six boots plus a thumb separated porch from chapel. I stood and marveled at one boot width of difference across the entirety of the porch, the chapel, the cemetery, the city.

In retrospect, forgetting the measuring tape was fortuitous, a fillip to improvisation but more significantly a lesson in precision, one which Lewerentz certainly valued. That angle is about difference rather than dimension. Its presence, not its absolute measure, which is less than a degree, is a lot like the porch's general offset from the chapel. The porch almost touches but doesn't. It stands freely and it skews slightly. That is enough.

As I improved my measuring techniques, I found differences in the spacing between columns, sometimes as much as a whole boot width—outside of what is tolerated in construction and beyond what could be seen as human error. Though subtle, they also carry a weight far beyond their physical dimension. Like the porch's skew, I think they are about imperfection, about human fallibility (like my forgetting the measuring tape), and ultimately about mortality. And then zooming out to look at the cemetery as a whole, all one hundred hectares of it, puts that mortality in perspective. The skew of the porch—its tilt within the vastness of the world—is a fraction—about one ten-thousandth—of the more than half-mile distance of the Path of the Seven Wells. I am reminded of the tiny no-see'um I watched on the porch screen and the vast distance of her prospective journey across the river.

Yet that small change between porch and chapel is tangible.

Watching the porch from the mound—it is nearly dark now—I can still feel it. Its blue is a splinter I still trace. It grounds me and temporarily roots me to this place, four thousand five hundred ninety-eight miles from the Homosassa porch. Lewerentz's porch is one square in fifteen thousand other squares across the cemetery. This range in the changes of scale speaks to human experience as it also helps guide the cemetery's process of reconciliation. The Woodland Cemetery's family of porches—and I think the Resurrection Chapel's porch is the progenitor—underpin this process.

In Sweden, I visited an architect who had worked with Lewerentz. As we passed through Stockholm's central subway station, he showed me a door that marked the passage between two of the station's zones. Here, he said, is the design Lewerentz was most proud of. The hinges allow the door to swing both ways smoothly between its open and closed positions, without then fluttering back and forth as other swinging doors do. An architect of thresholds, Lewerentz loved such portals, and he lavished the same attention on gates and doors as he did entire buildings. A gate at the cemetery in Malmo was his last project. My friend helped detail its simple latch, and he recalled pinning the drawings to a board suspended over the architect's bed in his final days so that he could draft out further refinements. A student of classical architecture, Lewerentz had looked closely at the Temple of Portunis, dedicated to the god of gates, keys, and ports, and I see that temple in the vertical proportions of the Resurrection Chapel's porch. This porch is a gate that has been left ajar.

Lewerentz's porch is physical evidence of our innate connection with the natural environment. Like a hinge, it affords coming and going, living and dying. The porch's skew acknowledges and anchors our mortality within the world's immensity, within a natural context that supports us but also challenges us. Left ever so slightly ajar, it is not just an invitation to enter but a cue to pause before going in. It is also a reminder that someone has gone out. And so Lewerentz's porch is an exercise in the delicate tuning of what it means to be human and what it means to interact with nature. I encountered the essence of this connection when I discovered the forest in the porch and when I strung my body across the air between chapel and porch. Here, in this place, I could begin to weigh the world.

That wedge of air between porch and chapel, its slice of blue sky, tells us that this process is one of constant adjustment in the ongoing work of reconciling our place in nature, and its place in us. It tells us how human precariousness can anchor stability, in the way that the chapel, and even the whole cemetery, pivots on the smallest turn of this porch. It signals an approach to nature that is deferential, respectful, but also filled with knowledge and imagination and a curiosity to know more and to continue learning. The anomaly of Lewerentz's porch reminds us that reflection is a critical part of any reconciliation. Walking between the porch's columns in the blue-green light of the forest, I think about the fifteen tons of each cylinder of limestone. Each is the weight of a tree. Almost two hundred times my own weight. Pulled from the earth and cast into air. Carried across the Swedish landscape. A heavy body raised in anthropomorphic spirit, at the limit of what humans can do. Such architecture is not about our ability to control, because Woodland shows us our limits. This immense weight is not about strength, but human fragility.

There in the porch, it was calming to reconcile the smallest changes—the width of one human's foot and the restful spirit of the thinnest blue—with the weight of the world.

Why are robin's eggs blue? The sheer joy that finding a nest of blue-green eggs brings is more than enough, but the scientific pursuit of the question deepens that sense of wonder, as it also extends the story of painted porch ceilings. Which is to say that imagination and science meet along that thin membrane of color. I recall Rachel Carson's experience—as a child, the robin's egg was a vehicle of wonderment for her, later serving as a bellwether for environmental degradation. The mystery of a shell's pale blue inspires awe, and the fact of its thinning—caused by man-made chemicals—stirred deep concern. The sheer blue of a robin's egg is a reminder of just how delicate the balance of our environment is. Eggshell fragile, porches also absorb all that is around them.

So, why blue? Why that particular blue? Even Charles Darwin was stumped by the question. About the same time Nutting wrote her poem, he asked colleagues to study this phenomenon more fully. Nearly a century and a half later, scientists are still trying to understand why some eggs are this blue-green color. One recent theory is that the blue-green pigment from biliverdin offers an egg's contents resistance to ultraviolet light. This so-called parasol effect shields the interior from solar radiation. Much like a porch roof. And researchers have uncovered something else. While many eggs blend with their nests, blue-green eggs are highly conspicuous, an extreme contrast with a nest's browns, but their color actually matches the ambient light. Scientists have found that this type of camouflage, known as "crypsis," even tunes color to location. Eggs closer to the ground are deeper blue, and those higher up are lighter. In a certain sense, these eggs occupy an idealized woodland shade on a sunny day, where ambient light is blue-green, half sky and half leaves. It is a color that taps and mixes the green of foliage and the blue of sky, the protective embrace of a nest in a tree and the dizzying expanse of air in the sky. It is the same color that suffuses a porch.

The blue-green color extends daylight, and blue light is a propagator. It has the ambient light of a forest. And so a porch feels like a clearing in the woods, like a loosely fitted room carved into the trees. And out here in Homosassa, the effect of blue-green extends even farther in a porch that has been scooped out of water and humidity. When Louis Kahn wrote about how the porch belongs to the sun and its interior belongs to humans, the architect touched on the logic of eggshells and parasols. Both protect from the white heat and glare of direct sunlight. At the same time, the room of the porch is flooded with the blue ambience of scattered light, twice dispersed by air and water. I imagine this effect as its own kind of crypsis where the porch dweller, swathed in blue, begins to meld with the environment, hiding in plain sight.

*

For the longest time, I couldn't fathom how water moves across the porch ceiling. I read up on specular reflection and studied the angles of incidence when light hits water. But watching those reflections wave, flicker, expand, and contract above my head, I soon learned it's a lot more than simple geometry. For the river to meet the ceiling depends on many factors—seasons, tides, clouds, trees, distances, and angles.

Some change and others don't. The ceiling must wait until early fall, when the sun rises far enough to the south of east, for its rays to shoulder past the cedars at the lagoon's mouth. Ripples of light strike the porch's back wall soon after the sun crests over the tree line across the river. But the porch still seems too far from the river to capture these reflections. And its ceiling's slope seems too steep—how it angles up and away from the water, away from those bounced shards of light. I imagine that those lines of sunlight must curl under the front edge of the porch roof and, once through the screen, bend upward. By April, the reflections are gone.

Even the tides matter in this finely tuned alchemy of light. When the tide is low and the sun is deep into its winter position, the reflections linger through the morning. But if the sun is too low and the tide is too high, the reflections are dammed up against the porch's back wall and never quite reach the ceiling. If the sun has risen high enough and the tide isn't low enough, those reflections miss the porch altogether and float unseen into the sky, catching the undersides of an oak or a cedar along their way. Which is to say that those reflections don't just depend on the presence of sun and water; they also depend on the tides that depend on the moon, and I think there is a little of its radiance in those reflections on the porch ceiling.

This morning in mid-November, the river is molten. Its reflections have oozed from the back wall up to the ceiling, diaphanous along its eggshell finish. And now its surface rolls like wind through a hanging sheet, except the folds ripple with light more than shadow. Reflections blow in on wavelets that the ceiling can't contain, and I love how they continue unseen in the air beyond. Before they leave, I can read winds and wakes, ripples and currents. On mornings like this, the ceiling catches the river's mood. When it's windy, the water is impatient, and waves march with a sprinter's pace. But mornings are often calm. The heat of the day has yet to agitate the air with drafts and convections, and bands of light saunter like flaneurs, crossing the ceiling this way and that, waterlogged with sights and sounds. Sometimes, with a boat's wake or a gust of wind, water discos across the ceiling. Dancers bump into one another, and the ceiling evaporates in chaos. I catch my breath at the collisions. The water loses its mind.

A shrimp boat passes and the ceiling pulses. Fast, slow, fast, slow. The wake rattles around in the lagoon. I hear it under the dock and against the limestone. I see it in the strobe of light above. And then it slowly settles back into a regular pattern, a flow and rhythm with subtle differences as intricate as fish-scale light. This is how waves till water, and how light combs air. When the sun's out, this dance is always there. I just need the porch's ceiling to see it. And to sit back and enjoy it. When I look to the ceiling, I am underwater. I look up through air filled with light, and I look up through water. I know that the porch's future depends on how fast that water rises.

Later, the lava roll of light leaves the porch, as if its slope is shedding light rather than rain. It catches under limbs that arch over the lagoon, as the sun heads toward its low zenith and I head for a swim, the river still warm enough even in late fall. The tide is blowing in, and I am swimming in the blue of a full moon. Indigo. It is the kind of current where you have to fin your arms to stay upright. Afterward, I can read its swiftness in the canopy of limbs over the lagoon. Reflections move like a sweeping gesture, motioning away from something.

Sunlight chandeliers under the cedars. It appears to move the Spanish moss in a breeze I cannot feel. When a boat passes, bubbles of light siphon up and down peeling bark. Then they flash like a thousand watch faces catching the sun, and the chatter of cicadas dopplers from side to side.

When Maurice Merleau-Ponty wrote about reflections from water on the screen of cypress trees, he echoed Monet's fascination with the way air touches things. The philosopher reminds us how air carries light and water: "I must recognize that the water visits it as well, or at least sends out to it its active and living essence. This inner animation, this radiation of the visible, is what the painter seeks beneath the names of depth, space, and color." Watching river light move across the ceiling deepens the links between water and sky, moon and sun, imagination and experience. I float in a vessel filled with air and water. I swim on the porch.

Watching reflections also brings introspection. When I try to figure out how they work, I am also ruminating—how they reach the ceiling connects me to the river, how they mirror the river's mood connects me to nature and atmosphere. The river becomes an intimate companion. That's how John Burroughs characterized small rivers that don't idealize the landscape but reflect what he called the "negative beauty of nature." And in the river's mood, in its animation—whether restless or calm—reflected on the ceiling, I discover what I am feeling. Right there with Burroughs, I can hear John Prine singing "Summer's End"—"You never know what you're feeling until you watch the shadows cross the ceiling." Immersed in the river, I discover an aerial imagination. It began when I painted the ceiling robin's egg blue, but what really sets it in motion are those reflections. They show me how boundless a porch's capacity to inspire really is. How art is sheltered right there on your doorstep.

⁂

On vacation in northern Connecticut, Paul Strand watched shadows on a front porch. The rented cottage on Twin Lakes was likely one of the late nineteenth-century houses built on a rise that looked southwest over the lakes and the wooded hills beyond. More than three hours north of New York City, accessible at the time only by rail and dirt roads, this house was a retreat that Strand knew well. In 1911, at the age of twenty, as the lake camps became cottages and the rail station was completed, he had snapped a painterly photograph of chickens in the cottage's yard. Five years later, on the cusp of the avant-garde, he was back with his handheld Ensign camera. That summer of 1916, the cottage's porch hosted work that deeply influenced the photographer's vision as it also marked a threshold for the history of photography itself.

Strand once said that the "artist's world is limitless. It can be found anywhere, far from where he lives or a few feet away. It is always on his doorstep." Far from New York but close at hand, this porch is a familiar piece of architecture; but it is also extraordinary. This porch, its round columns, squared balustrades and tilted wooden floor, didn't just host a photographer making pictures; it fed the cerulean depth of his imagination.

When the summer sun laid down shadows across the porch, Strand watched light tilt tables, grasp bottles, and even rock chairs. The porch also played host to a chiaroscuro where the photographer found a "range of almost infinite tonal values." In the late morning, he watched as sunlight,

and its shadows, angled through balustrades against the grain of floorboards. Toward midday, a higher sun shortened the shadows, still askew from the porch's southwestern bearing, and made a darker ground for a jar and a lighter ribbon for its own shadow. Nearby, another object—an orange—also bridged light and shadow and, at noontime, stitched shadow and floorboard together. Both jar and orange cast dark shadows that contrasted with the luminescent, light-filled shadows of the porch's balustrade across the floor.

Later, the shadows lengthened again and turned more oblique. Strand helped them along, turning a round table on its side and adding it to the geometries he discovered along the porch's edge, bringing it into this play of light and shadow. In this photograph, the balustrades that cast the shadows are now out of the frame, and their shadows rake the subtle lines of the floor and then turn dramatically upward across the arc of the table, onto its surface. This is the photograph that Alfred Stieglitz, the impresario of modern art, would publish a year later in the final issue of his influential journal, *Camera Work*. He called it a "direct expression of today" and said that Strand had "actually done something from within." In the previous issue, Stieglitz had noted that Strand's photographs were "rooted in the best traditions of photography"; now, Strand had become "the photographer who has added something to what has gone before" with work that is "brutally direct . . . devoid of all flim-flam . . . of trickery and of any 'ism" without "any attempt to mystify an ignorant public, including the photographers themselves." Some say this picture and its porch siblings are the first intentionally abstract photographs. And so, as Albert Einstein presented his Theory of General Relativity (in May of 1916), and as World War I raged, Strand stepped out onto a traditional porch and made pictures that changed the world and how we see it.

The porch work came a year after Strand's famous photograph of Wall Street. And so, when Strand left the frenetic streets of New York to continue sounding the depths of abstraction in the bucolic setting of the Twin Lakes, he was also moving from porch to porch. He made *Wall Street* from the neoclassical porch of Federal Hall. This porch and its steps gave Strand room to compose his shot along the street's narrow canyon. In it, people rush to work against the tide of morning light streaming from the east as if gusting across the East River. The dark figures march along the lines of white marble molding, and their shadows are Giacometti long. This backdrop is the new headquarters of J. P. Morgan and Company, and the recessed rectangles of glasswork are black chasms, giant doors to industry and capitalism.

Strand surely felt the significance of this place. Taking this picture, he knew that porches can expose the political process to a general public. It was a similar porch in Tallahassee where my wife and I received a freshly printed copy of the Florida Supreme Court's ruling in the case of *Bush v. Gore* in 2000. As the late afternoon in November turned chilly, we climbed the portico's steps alongside journalists and reporters, walked between Doric columns, and received a stapled sheaf under a coffered ceiling that echoed with footfalls and protestors' shouts. Back down the steps, bearing the weight of hundreds of pages, we watched cable news anchors speed-reading its contents on the sidewalk, in the long shadow of the porch.

Taking his Wall Street picture, Strand stood under the ghost of another porch that played a significant role in national ceremony and identity. On April 30, 1789, George Washington was sworn in as the nation's first president in an elevated porch on the front of the original City Hall building. After Washington's inauguration, the building became known as Federal Hall and served as the first seat of Congress. Amos Doolittle's 1790 engraving of the Hall depicts a throng of congressional lawmakers pressed out onto its balcony. Where Ramón de Elorriaga's painting shows the interior of a spacious, sunlit porch overlooking Wall Street, Doolittle's exterior view of the Greek Revival façade casts a more modest open-air space in an outsized role for national politics. The former is an expected, formalized use of this ceremonial architecture—in much the same way architect Pierre L'Enfant would later design vistas in Washington, DC's urban fabric. The latter is a much less organized, even chaotic, view to the inner workings of a country's nascent legislative system, which only a liminal space like this porch could reveal and adequately frame. Each captures a monumentality, and to walk up and down Federal Hall's steps, around its Doric columns, under the high ceiling, is to imagine Strand's own deliberation as he looked for the oblique view that captured the raking light and long shadows of the morning procession. Strand's picture demonstrates how a porch can link the personal to the anonymous and an individual to a wider metropolis. As it critiques a nation's arc toward the alienation of capitalism, it also exemplifies the creative genius that same nation can incubate.

This porch and its steps witnessed other events. Three years after Strand was there, Charlie Chaplin stood out front, wielding a megaphone, rallying thousands for Liberty Loans in April 1918. Five years after Strand, New Yorkers on those same steps saw the worst terrorist attack up to that time when a wagon of dynamite exploded in the street. A reporter described the event: "It was a crush out of a blue sky—an unexpected, death-dealing bolt, which in a twinkling turned into a shambles the busiest corner of America's financial center." And in April 2012, Occupy Wall Street protestors assembled on the porch's steps under the statue of George Washington to extend their movement against economic inequality. An official "Temporary Access Change" to Federal Hall by the National Parks Service, which oversees the building, sequestered protestors behind steel barricades in a zone called "The First Amendment Rights Area."

On the porch at Twin Lakes that summer of 1916, Strand took a photograph that is an outlier to the rest of the porch series, but is an equally significant threshold in his body of work. It is a portrait of Harold Greengard, who sits on the porch in a rocking chair, and it tests the edges and possibilities of portraiture. We see him up close, as if we're sitting on the porch, listening. There are really four of us—Strand and his handheld camera, Greengard, and an unseen interlocutor on our right. Greengard is a close friend from New York, where he may have worked in the J. P. Morgan building. He leans back in a white dress shirt, dark tie with a pin in the center. Flecks of light catch in the tie's weave. He carries the city's formality in his tailored clothes. He also bears the weight of *Wall Street* as well as the other photographs Strand will take when he returns to New York in a few months. His presence brings to the porch a feeling of deep friendship and a kind of reckoning with the not-so-distant city.

Back in New York, Strand will photograph street people, including the woman in *Blind*, a picture that has many similarities to the Greengard portrait. From his chest up, Greengard's head is turned, eyes smiling, mouth open in a half smile, white teeth, white eyes, white shirt. Cedar shake siding, the chair's frame, and its wicker weave make a geometric background that turns to stone in the granite blocks and white mortar lines of *Blind*. Those lines tilt unnervingly behind the woman's form, which follows the frame of the picture; she has the vertical stability of the stark white porch column in Greengard's portrait. In *Blind*, Greengard's tie becomes a placard around the woman's neck. The white of the sign offsets the black lettering "BLIND," and the medallion of the peddler's license takes the position of Greengard's pin. The white of the woman's unseeing eye hauntingly follows Greengard's gaze over the left shoulder. The rocking chair where he sits rolls back to match his recline. Its top edge follows a line of cedar shake siding across his line of vision, just as the heavy shadow line between blocks of granite courses behind the blind woman's head.

Strand's portrait fosters a deep kinship with the blind woman. I think he learned to balance form with empathy on the porch in Twin Lakes. He explored it in the oblique—the way that Greengard cuts an angle across the frame. It sets the picture in motion like the rock of the chair, the triangle of conversation, the slope and tilt of the porch floor. Strand listens, and the longer you sit with this picture, the longer you sit on this porch, occupying this picture, you realize he listens to both porch and subject, in the same way he listened to the blind woman and the street. Attentive, he listens and he sees, and the porch talks back in the language of light and shadow.

Porches hold light and shadow, Strand knew. He waited for the morning sun, low enough to cast the balustrade's shadow deep into the porch. In the upper right, we see balustrade and column base, and this picture joins the rest of the porch series. Column, balustrade, and floor. Here, abstraction has a context. An everyday porch yields the extraordinary. The everyday arcing sun yields the epiphenomena of geometry, rhythm, and performance. Light and shadow play on the porch, and the floorboards angle just off from the horizontal ground of the frame. They are a musical stanza for the notes of sun. The deepest shadow is at the most vulnerable place—the middle of each balustrade's projection. At the base and toward the top, its shadow is softer, filled with light from the porch's painted floor. The sun's music continues along the balustrade itself, where a shadow on the back of the pickets matches the sun-filled gaps on the floor. Shards of light along the balustrade's bottom rail erase the material, in small measure, but with enough emphasis that the picture flattens, here where its depth and its construction would be most evident.

The Twin Lakes porch was a laboratory. It had the temporary stability of a field research station. The rhythm of the balustrade, the level horizon of the rail, the overhead roof, even the parallel—though sloping—floorboards all provided degrees of precision and control. The porch is also a transitional space where environmental effects change and where they can be tested, and under Strand's watch, this porch lab was further unmoored so that it could explore transitory forms. Strand tested light and shadow along the porch's smooth and dimpled surfaces, where he discovered layered shadows.

The porch is an everyday space marked by surprise and expedience. It was familiar to Strand because his family often vacationed there. The porch was a place where common objects became less predictable, where daily events—like the sun raking over whitewashed flooring—might become extraordinary. The directness of Strand's vision and the porch's capacity for the chiaroscuro range of tonal values mean that the porch could hold the entire photographic process. It was subject, studio, and darkroom. In Strand's mind, the photographs were already being processed as they were taken. Strand printed these shots not on Platinum paper but on Statista paper, a wartime substitute that degrades with age. As a result, the printed images were themselves fleeting and unstable from the outset—evanescent like the experience of sitting on a porch on a hot summer day in the bluing ozone of a rainstorm's approach.

⁎⁎

I open the can of paint, and the sheets of plastic fill with the breezes that tail behind a weak cold front. I have hung these plastic sheets as vertical drop cloths to protect the porch's screens and posts from the roller's spatter of paint. But now the sheets billow and dance into the porch. The material is clear and the view out is a blur of color, a stained glass skin of azures, jades, and golds that now lifts and twists. I should have known that plastic only one mil thick, draped in a place built to capture the slightest breath of wind, would do just that. Even the heavy shells and chunks of coral at each sheet's corners roll off and mock me. I am wrestling with the wind. I abandon the comical attempt to keep the sheets in place, and simply stand and watch. It's beautiful. Polyethylene wraiths reach across the porch to the door. Are they haints on their way into the cabin? Or carefree spirits under a ceiling not yet blue? Out of the east, the wind is all the same, but each sheet fashions its own performance. The sheets form a line dance of nonconformists. When the breeze rests, the sheets hold their poses. They are casts of air and water.

The paint rollers on the ceiling didn't really cause that much mess, so I let go of the utility of the sheets, but they taught me about the performative nature of the porch. It is a rich experimental ground for testing and learning. Painting the ceiling continued the intimate dance the wind-filled membranes had set up. Painting on the porch inscribed my body into its air, across its length and width. I was measuring air, as I was also probing the depths of blue. I found that I could reach the ceiling from the floor up to the last few feet where it touches the cabin. Even though it was so close, the ceiling seemed to lift after that first coat of blue, making room for aerial imagination.

Strand discovered the phantasmagoric in the porch. When he tested abstraction, his goal was not to defamiliarize. He reintroduced us to the common objects and places around us. It was the discovery of another way of seeing. Strand rejected the "tricks of process or manipulation" he saw in some modern photography at the outset of the twentieth century. The porch brought direct contact with things, which then allowed for abstraction. He probed materials, but he also delved into less tangible systems of projection and illumination. The Twin Lakes porch was a place where he could immerse himself in the effects he was documenting. It was a very personal yet very rigorous place. When Strand entered the porch each day with his camera, he climbed inside a magic lantern.

Clouds touch the corner of the porch. Air currents bear this fragment of architecture aloft; they push it along like a kite launched on a clear summer day that will soon host an afternoon thunderstorm. Strand took this photograph outside the Twin Lakes porch, looking sharply upward, from below the floor where he made the better-known interior shots. The corner of the porch occupies the upper right. Above an unseen horizon, lines of clouds careen from the lower left to the up-

per right. The balustrade is a ladder of gray and black rungs hanging from the sky. It drops vertically along the right edge. Behind its rounded column, under its deeply shaded roof, the porch catches the streaming air. Under those billowing clouds, looking at this photograph is like waiting for lightning to strike.

This photograph catches an environmental vision. How

weather and climate and sky anchor the boundless depth of artistic vision. This picture is both frontispiece and coda for the porch series. It is the equivalent of a front stoop that invites us on to the porch, where Strand tests light and shadow, only a "few feet away" from home. It is also the invitation to find our own porch to that "limitless" world. It is an invitation to daydream. Staring at this picture fosters vertigo, like you've been swinging in a porch hammock too long. Or you have been lying on the ground, hands behind your head, reading the clouds. You drift off, until someone blocks the sun and its warm rays. The porch leans over, waking you up. It speaks to you, even though it is backlit and its details are lost in deep shadow, even though the print now suffers from age and the flaws of wartime photo-paper.

Strand flies the porch like Benjamin Franklin's kite. In black and white, he demonstrates how the porch, along with the artistic vision it enables, is a function of climate and its changing effects. He casts the porch and all that he has learned with it into the sky. Its cool grays and billowing whites support the warmer, deeper tones of the porch's shadows. And it holds blue without color. There is the blue of imagination in each wisp of moisture, each swell of cumulus, each sun-filled nimbus. Strand studies atmosphere's artistic potential in and along the margins of porch architecture, and he connects these phenomena to the edges of our psyche. He finds in the oblique the tilt of empathy. Along the way, Strand tethers us to Alexander von Humboldt's definition of climate, which includes not only the atmospheric but also the emotional.

Later that year, when Strand writes about the photographic medium as a means to "an ever fuller and more intense self-realization," he is talking about an artistic epiphany, but he is also talking about art's capacity to deepen our collective bond with the environment. When Strand writes about the "necessity of evolving a new form," he is talking about creating when there is no precedent, but he is also talking about how "actual living" can bear those creative experiments. Which is how a porch delivers abstraction, and how it also points toward an environmental vision as deep and wide as the grayscale blue in that summer sky.

The last coat of blue-green paint has dried, and robins are milling all around the porch. Their short flights seem indecisive, like they're not sure where to go. It's late January, and the clusters of berries on the Brazil pepper trees wave in the northeasterly breeze. Unable to resist the lurid red peppercorns, they are unwitting agents in the trees' northward invasion.

Robins are the birds of migration. Covering the whole of a continent across the seasons, their arrival marks winter in the south and spring in the north. Bearing the Latin *migratorius* of its species, they are the birds of thresholds and crossings. Known for tracking the seasons, robins also follow the food, whether north or south, east or west, and the red peppercorns have brought them here. And so they don't just follow the seasons—they work across and between them. Along the way, their eggs are emblems of wonder, like small pieces of sky resting comfortably in soft beds of straw and twigs. Robins and their eggs carry the mysteries of adaptation, and science can't explain them fully. They demonstrate our limits to understand nature. But we must continue to try, and in that attempt, like Strand learning about light and shadow, we need places like porches.

Eudora Welty photographed her blind mother's garden from her sleeping porch. Welty called her photographs "snapshots" for the way they captured fleeting moments, and one of them—a black-and-white shot above Chestina Welty's garden—wheels and turns vertiginously, as if taken from a nest or a high perch. Welty's sleeping porch was filled with books—not just any books, but childhood books, fairy tales, and books of myth. Welty indexed them in her autobiography: "Grimm, Anderson, the English, the French, 'Ali Baba and the Forty Thieves'; and there was Aesop and Reynard the Fox; there were the myths and legends, Robin Hood, King Arthur, and St. George and the Dragon. . . . I could go straight to the stories and pictures I loved; very often 'The Yellow Dwarf' was first choice . . . making his terrifying entrance flanked by turkeys."

Welty also shelved her own books here, particularly the editions in twenty-nine languages. That sleeping porch at 1119 Pinehurst Street in Jackson, Mississippi, built as a part of its Tudor Revival house in 1925 by Christian Welty, housed myth and translation as it also housed Welty's vision as a writer, photographer, and seer. Welty once wrote that the "fictional eye sees in, through, and around what is really there." That's what myth does, and that's what the best translations have to do. The fictional eye sees the air—whether it's the blue of a swamp, the violet and rose of a storm, or the brown blue of evening. And the fictional eye finds a home on the porch— whether it's Welty's storied sleeping porch or Strand's laboratory of abstraction. On a porch, that fictional eye might see—we might see—the full implications of the most subtle and, at times, invisible phenomena around us. But we have to practice seeing *in*, *through*, and *around* what we're looking at. And a porch, immersed in the blue of its imagination, helps us do that.

6

ACCLIMATE

Our first trips back and forth to the cabin felt like a camping expedition. We could bring only what the pontoon would carry. And even though the cabin had more amenities than a campsite, it still drew together past excursions to the coast where we had pitched tents on dredged coral, slept under driftwood trees, listened to lapping water at midnight, and tasted brine in grilled fish. Out on the Homosassa, the Milky Way coated the sky, our bonfires charred coral rock thousands of years old, and the water in the back creek brimmed with phosphorescence caught up in our nets. When storms came, thunder avalanched around us, and the air smelled of salt, cedar, algae, and distance.

We felt like this was an edge of the world. As we grew more accustomed to the place, it was the porch that still felt like camping, still kept us on that edge. The porch flickered with paradise. Teetering between retreat and escape, it stayed vivid with the pleasures of camping. On a porch, sunrise warms your hands like a driftwood fire that sends coffee bubbling into the percolator's glass top. River mist spirals like the curl of smoke from a cast iron pan. Sunlight breezes across the screen as if passing through a tent flap. Fresh air meshes with dreams, and sleep comes in its wakeful depth. On the porch, we go camping without leaving home.

The porch also shudders with crisis. Now, when those storms light the sky, their ethereal glow and distant thunder remind me that being on the coast, on a wild edge of land, is like being on a porch. And it holds two frontiers. One is at the house's edge where it probes nature. The other is on nature's cusp where it witnesses climate's crisis. Both are vulnerable and both are changing. The porch, where they overlap, is a climate frontier.

In one sense, the porch where I sit is moving. When I began this project a decade ago, the porch was seventy miles north. In just this past year, it's slipped another seven south. The mangroves have grown up into trees, I have watched another sabal palm next to the porch succumb to saltwater, and in the lagoon, the stained limestone that darkens below the average waterline and never seems to dry out has inched higher. Across the river, a sea ox-eye daisy has sprouted under the rampikes that still make me think of Homer's painting. That daisy bloomed all last month, basking in the salt and the sun and the warmth. It reminds me of a homesteader on some distant plain.

Because in another sense, the porch stays put. It digs in. Anchored to this place, it waits and we are complicit because we wait with it. Camping out, watching, witnessing, learning. We linger, a little too long. I see the same faith in the river's ospreys. Ornithologists call this "nest-site fidelity," and each year we look out for the osprey pair to return to the same makeshift, storm-swept nest on top of the channel marker that lists on one side of the Pearly Gates. It is not easy to give up our perch on the river that runs with the sea. But change comes to us.

Soon after she first decamped to Florida with her family, Harriet Beecher Stowe wrote her friends back home that she and Calvin "have set up our tent." She compares their house to a bivouac in a faraway place where they temporarily reside, destined to return after the northern climate completes its "heroic agony" of freeze and thaw. Her reference is not simply metaphorical. The porch itself, where they spend most of their time in Mandarin, is like a tent. Its canopy stretches from house to tree, and its openness affords the fresh air of a camping trip. Harriet packed her gear for this adventure: "I am going to take my writing desk down to Florida."

Stowe's porch presses out from the house, into the air. Four wide columns, each with three Victorian-era cutouts, flatten along the porch's lip, and it looks as if a storm has just peeled away the wall, opening an interior room to our view, surprising the five seated figures inside. An oak branch hangs overhead, its leaves shining in the afternoon sun, just out of reach. The steamboat whistle soaks through the heat. Sweat glazes your skin as you step off the wooden walk, and the slope of the riverbank puts you at eye level with the family on the porch. A daughter looks up from her card game to meet your gaze; the others look out into the distance, toward the brackish river, through orange blossom air. Frozen by the slowness of the shutter, they pose for the photograph, but they wouldn't move much anyway. It's hot, they are dressed in layers of fabric and wool, and their stiffened bodies wait for the sea breeze.

The Stowes first explored Florida in the spring of 1867, fifteen years after *Uncle Tom's Cabin*. South of Jacksonville's port, they found an enthralling climate and an exotic landscape that readily mixed the actual with the imagined. A year later with her husband, Calvin, Harriet purchased a house in Mandarin along the St. Johns River and, by 1872, completed renovations. Most significantly, she added the porch—she called it her "veranda." This open-air space harbored dreams and visions for writerly inspiration. On the porch, Calvin reads, translates, and hallucinates, while Harriet watches, listens, and writes, spooling the narrative threads she witnesses from her porch and spinning what she called "ideal webs out of bits that he lets fall here and there."

You might have interrupted one of these moments as you draw near the porch in the stereoscopic view widely circulated in the 1870s, arriving like the wayward tourist who has climbed up from the river's landing. The porch fills the middle ground, framed on the right by that magnificent live oak's trunk. Its unseen canopy measures your approach. To the left, Calvin has put down his reading, and Harriet—head tilting pensively—casts an oblique, preoccupied view across the river. The porch's columns frame two other vignettes of domestic life: in the middle bay, their twin daughters are playing cards, and farther to the right another woman quietly sews, her rocking chair turned to face an empty seat. Everyone sits right along the front edge of the porch. The porch's hard tilt follows the slope to the river, and though firmly planted, they seem ready to tumble down onto the lawn where you stand.

"Shangri-La," a friend tells his wife on a shaky cellphone call from our cabin's porch. It is refreshing to hear, even though the idyllic nature of this place is certainly fiction and its reality much more complicated. The porch's sheltered position enhances its mystique. And this porch anchors the sense of harmony and calm that still ties us to this place. My friend's comment reminds me of Harriet Beecher Stowe's letters north to family and friends. She sends word of paradise: how jasmine blooms at one end of the porch, orange blossoms scent the shaded air, and hens cackle "drowsily" around the porch's steps. In the previous century, William Bartram had already identified the paradisiacal qualities of Mandarin, some of which inspired Samuel Taylor Coleridge's Xanadu: "How happily situated in this retired spot of earth! What an elysium it is!" Stowe echoed the naturalist's paean in *Palmetto Leaves*, where she documented her Florida sojourns and porch reveries: "No Dreamland on earth can be more unearthly in its beauty and glory than the St. Johns in April." She found paradise on a Florida porch.

The Stowes' paradise was on a frontier. As nineteenth-century settlers continued across the nation toward the Pacific, Harriet and Calvin went south rather than west, but they still followed the cusp of a slowly expanding population. Only a decade before they sunk the tent pegs of their porch, the official Census line that designated "frontier" lands of two people per square mile lay just south of Jacksonville and just north of their homestead. The Stowes' move to Florida actually probed two frontiers: the latitudinal shift southward and a lateral shift outward. The porch was a veritable covered wagon traipsing across micro- and macro-climates alike. It tracked each frontier, one at the southern limit of the continent's climate zones and its available lands, and the other on the edge of an airless house caught up in the heat and humidity of this subtropical life.

For Stowe, the porch expands both frontiers. Her advocacy of fresh air found a home at the limits of the house. On the porch, she could apply her principles of domestic science, published concurrently with her first trip to Florida. Her prescriptions for health called on all homesteaders, no matter their location, permanent or temporary, to open doors, windows, and flues and to explore the farther-flung, but intimate, territories of porches. And her porch in Florida was effectively an experimental lab where she could continue to test these healthful imperatives in a less forgiving climate. Stowe bore this domestic science of the porch to its limits, to a place of frontier living—whether defined as the edge of a continent or the edge of a house—where, as she wrote to George Eliot, "the veranda is the living room of the house."

Oh, it must have been hot. Imagine spending a summer's day outside in Florida, layered in heavy regalia or bundled up to play in the snow that is really hot sand. They don't just sit on the porch, they perch along its leading edge, positioned ostensibly for the stereoscope portrait but really—on the porch's domestic frontlines at a nation's frontier—to catch the slightest riffle of air. Harriet in crinoline and Calvin in suit, waistcoat, and full beard, they are climate pioneers.

Needless to say, the Stowes did not have air conditioning. A search for comfort led the Stowes onto the porch. Today, comfort, buoyed by twentieth-century advances in mechanical systems, has led us inside the house. That conditioning of air has redoubled the frontier status of the porch. It still hovers on domestic margins, as it did for the Stowes, but it now makes up an even wilder frontier because the artificial conditioning of the interior has effectively increased the distance between inside and outside. We may have forgotten that our bodies can still adapt to the climatic conditions that wrap where we live—and not even fully adapt, but just be comfortable, even for a short duration.

I must confess that our cabin has air conditioning—central air since the late 1990s (until Hurricane Hermine flooded the compressor), and wall units for about three decades. One of those ancient machines still cyclones our bedroom with frigid air, so that most mornings we wake to windows sheeted with condensation. I'm no climate pioneer, but I do seek the porch's frontiers. I retreat there every chance I get. Not heroically, or as a neo-Luddite, or even as some form of domestic activism. I simply prefer to experience the climate that surrounds me. On the porch, I can swim that humidity. I know when a storm approaches, I hear the birds sing the delicate shift of seasons, and I can tell the temperature. Leaving the cabin for the porch, I leave air conditioning for other kinds of conditioned air. This is my acclimation.

Architects differentiate between active and passive systems for heating and cooling buildings. Active systems use energy and mechanics to modify an interior environment. Passive systems rely on what the outside environment provides, such as natural ventilation. Porches epitomize such passive systems. Here in Florida, where cooling is the main goal, they rise above the ground and remain open to catch breezes, and they are shaded from the sun. In architecture, we refer to such areas as "unconditioned" spaces. But there is a two-fold problem of language here, part of a deeper problem of perception. Porches may be unconditioned from the perspective of engineering, but they are intensively conditioned by nature. On the porch, I am regularly stirred by all that is around me: breezes move across porch screens, fresh air fosters dream-filled sleep, and that blue ceiling draws on air's depth as well as its folklore. And "passive" suggests the inert and the dull, rather than the vital and the wondrous atmosphere of a porch. Its connotations weaken the very dynamic engagement that porches foster with the environment and with the idea of climate itself. Porches are entirely active agents on this climate frontier.

Seeing the Stowes on their porch reminded me of a year we spent living in an A-frame in south Florida. The entire cabin was a veritable screened porch. Looking back, that A-frame was a steppingstone toward the porch in Homosassa, as it seeded the idea of this book. It is where I learned about the human body's capacity to tune itself to changes in climate. It is also where I discovered that I could detect changes in temperature down to the degree. I'm not sure I will ever get to that point again—even on this porch—but the potential is there. Some aspects of a frontier must remain as ideas that we aspire to. Their significance is that they exist, and we acknowledge them, even if we don't reach them.

In the context of global warming, the meaning of this capacity to recognize, and attune to, one degree takes on even greater importance. That one Fahrenheit degree is only a fraction—not even a fifth—of the three Celsius degrees of median global warming projected over the next eight decades. The porch offers a place where we can perceive the subtle changes that have such global impact. And living in unconditioned spaces, even part of the time, reduces the need for conditioned air, and by extension, the consumption of energy to fuel those mechanical systems. There is a certain irony that our movement—our de-acclimation—from the immediate environment—its temperatures, its air, its habitats—has helped fuel the climate crisis. Losing the ability to acclimate, we have lost control of energy consumption. On the Homosassa porch, I haven't reached the level of acclimation that the Stowes achieved, but I cling to this threshold for detecting that degree of change, and I know this human capacity to adjust is there, because I once felt it, in a house that was a porch.

✳✳

Shelter in place. The command was clear but the course of action wasn't. It was late spring in south Florida, and afternoon rains from the Everglades had saturated the evening's darkness. The air held the searchlights in an eerie suspension, solid like a bright wall that cut through the jungle. Two helicopters hovered low as we stood blinded on the path between the A-frame and the main house, still boarded and bandaged after the eye of Hurricane Andrew passed over nine months earlier. The surge of the rotors might have been the roar of that storm. And the circling wind might have been a tempest's gale. Banana leaves tore, and golden orb spiders trampolined on their webs, limpid veins across the path, cool veils across our faces as we ran toward the A-frame to make the call, to try to learn what was happening, where we should go, what we should do. The dispatcher said to stay where we were, shut the windows, lock the doors. But how do you secure a place that has latches for locks and screens for windows? Where do you go when you live in a porch without a house?

We had been told that an "old hippie" built the A-frame. He was a carpenter who had milled the wood from local pine, dug the wells for water, and powered the house with solar panels. One side of the A was nearly vertical. With its metal roof as a wall, this steep side held the kitchen, bedroom, and a bathroom—finished out with homemade tiles of mermaids and shells. The other side lifted and opened toward papayas, coconut palms, pineapples, and mangoes. The main entry door split top and bottom, like a Dutch door where the lower part keeps animals out and kids in, while the upper part swings open for light and air. To the right of the door, there was a plate glass panel, as large as a suburban house's picture window, but out of place, as if an afterthought or even a jest. An ironic piece of architecture because the rest of the house was completely open through its screens.

A heart-pine frame held grand swathes of screen mesh, where earlier that day we had watched lizards chase each other: the larger brown anole—its razored back slicing air—lunged at the green one as it supermanned off the screen into the jungle. We had listened to the armadillos scratching underneath the avocado tree planted in the fall, and the morning breeze was light but just strong enough to carry the smell of citrus blossoms through the weave of mesh. During the day, the screen dissolved in the jungle's yellow light and connected us with everything outside. At night, it became a wall of lamplight, feigning solidity. It was a false sense of security easily breached by light and air, readily compromised by warnings of intruders, armed and dangerous. So that when we hung up with the police hotline and looked around at our shelter afire with the swinging searchlights, we realized there was no inside.

In that A-frame, we felt the weather. More than that, we lived the weather. Extreme shifts and delicate changes alike coursed through the shelter. The winter before, we woke to a thin film of ice in the cup of water by the bed. It was record cold for that part of Florida, but we didn't pay attention to the statistics or forecasts. What we were attuned to was the cold that humid air can hold, like wearing a towel dipped in an ice bucket. That spring, subtropical weather took hold and there wasn't a lot of variation between night and day. In the summer, the humidity would temper that diurnal shift, bleeding the sun's warmth into moonlit swelter. That's when we learned to identify changes in temperature to the degree. We didn't need thermometers or weather reports. We knew if it was going to rain. Humidity, barometric pressure, thunder came to us through the screen like the truth of rain itself.

Panels with plywood and corrugated plastic provided a deep overhang to protect the screened rooms from sun and rain. These panels hinged at the top and were fixed in place by braces, near-permanent extensions of the lower-slung side of the roof. When it rained, cascading water formed a second screen, a fluid curtain that noisily splashed down eight feet away on the jungle's limestone ground. When a storm threatened, the panels pivoted down between the screened frames and latched to the pine posts, a system that proved just right for Hurricane Andrew. While most every other house in the area was destroyed, this A-frame survived. Damp, but intact. It was handmade and solid, built with dry joints and wooden dowels, by a committed craftsman. But what really saved this house from destruction was its openness. Its porosity let shards of wind move through, allowed pressures to equalize, and generally tuned itself to the churned air. The panels shed most of the storm's rain, and they shielded its interior from wind-blown debris. But overall, they were more like baffles than total barriers, tricking the storm, damping its intensity with a loose-fitting shirt of enclosure, small gaps and seams breathing air in and out. A house without walls is essentially a porch, and a porch might be the most resilient part of a house.

A porch's strength is its indecisiveness. It's neither inside nor outside. Porches thrive in this condition, a kind of architectural limbo, a place between other spaces. Porches don't want to be relegated to any kind of closure, and this porch-house was no different. Work led us to California for the summer, and the hurricane season began on the day we left. We earnestly lowered and latched the panels in place, and set off. We returned in August to find everything covered in mildew. Hell in south Florida is a sealed-up unconditioned A-frame. No hurricanes that summer, just an internal cyclone of fungus. Not just wipe-away flecks, but a complete blight. Our books were the biggest casualties, some furry beyond recognition, others chewed by palmetto bugs—Florida's version of cockroaches, larger and hungrier, who couldn't get enough of the sweet glue in the book spines, particularly the older editions. Riven with gnawing, these books had to be opened to decipher their titles. Most had to be thrown out.

We aired out the A-frame and stayed in the porch-house for another year, vowing never to close the panels again. We sweated and survived. We also felt attuned to the environment like never before and wouldn't feel again until we climbed out onto the Homosassa cabin's porch decades later. We were adjusting to a post-disaster environment. Whether we liked it or not, we had acclimated.

A porch is a comfortable place that can test the limits of comfort. But the porch is also a place to think. It is a reflective place that offers frontiers of imagination. Is a porch a poem? Is a poem a porch? Born of paradox? Framed out of imagination and words as much as built of wood and air? I would like to ask Wendell Berry these questions, sitting here during one of those glistening fall days when the setting moon rides a blue sky. His poems are laced with porches, both visible and unseen. This summer day, watching the tide press up the river, I pulled out *A Timbered Choir*. Reading slowly, I lingered on the porches:

Phoebe birds return to build their nests under a "stilted porch," a place altered by water and now propped up after the spring floods. Father and son reflect on how consequences of life's choices remain unseen, cast across time's silence like the porch where they sit, wrapped in the comfort of its darkness. A "windy porch" suspended between sky and sea welcomes travelers from moonlit darkness where time and hospitality slip between the present and a Homeric past. A west-facing porch affords the simple pleasure of watching clouds that recall love: "Finally will it not be enough, . . . to sit on the porch near sundown / with your eyes simply open, / watching the wind shape the clouds / into the shapes of clouds?"

On a porch, is imagination also a form of acclimation? I think about how Calvin Stowe talked to Goethe on his Florida porch. You might attribute the professor's hallucinations to the heat or the phantasmal shimmer of the river, but he had them all his life. Calvin was quite forthcoming about his conversations with six-inch fairies, someone named Harvey, the devil (from whom he had many visits), and in particular his favorite figure, Goethe. The porch's openness to the air, its freshness, and the relaxed setting likely assisted the frequency and lucidity of these visions, and I wonder if Calvin ever had a vision of Goethe relaxing on his own veranda in Weimar. Calvin's hero also practiced porch sitting, not just for fresh air and comfort, but for inspiration and reverie. There on his *Gartenhaus* porch, Goethe tuned himself to the world: "Wrapped up in my blue cloak, I laid myself on a dry corner of the veranda terrace and slept amid thunder, lightning and rain so gloriously that my bed was afterwards quite disagreeable."

I think about how Calvin limns worlds between the physical and the spiritual, as Harriet finds room for her imagination to take hold. The porch stimulates her advocacy of fresh air, which in turn inspires writing and further encourages her to write nature and climate into her narratives, just as Goethe's *Gartenhaus* experiences write climate into his thoughts and his personal theology. Harriet grows a foundational myth around the porch's construction. After steadily improving "the hut by lath and plaster," she oversees the addition of the "wide veranda all round." This return to shelter's origins is not merely about creating an outdoor living area suitable for the climate. The porch must also be "built around the trunk of a tree," which holds great significance for the family, certainly as a metaphor for the home's refurbishment—"we added on parts . . . as a tree throws out new branches"—but also as the symbol of vertically defined, mystical frontiers. I think the Stowes must have heard what Berry called the "timbered choir" under the porch and its tree, gathering sun and offering shade.

On my porch many times before, particularly when a weak light turns the screens dark and I see the outside mostly in its sounds, I have wondered about the porch as a kind of bardo, an interval space between life and death. In Berry's collection, I turn to the fifth poem in the series from 1996. Berry is careful to point out that these poems are a series and not a sequence, but here near the end of the collection, the poet grows older, the porches become more apparent, and the words and porches fathom, more and more, the air between earth and heaven. In the poem, from its porch, under its roof, we watch raindrops send rings across water in a river seen through the trees. A porch is where you can recall the happiness of rain on a river. Drops of rain, circles carried along, growing, fading, growing, fading. Evanescent. A porch bridges memories of time and space because it truly straddles both. On a porch—as Berry writes, bridging lines of poetry—"sometimes here / we are there." And when a couple sits on their porch in the series of poems two years earlier, they wait in a stillness between life and death as tangible as Lewerentz's chapel porch. Their "one mind" creates an architecture of waiting, prepared for who might go first and who "sits on a while alone."

Thirty years earlier, Berry wrote a poem that I have read

again and again. The porch over the river. The poet looks into the river to find the mood of the world. Its atmosphere plays out in the strong bond between porch and river. The day is ending, the wind has lifted, and the world pauses. It might be a few seconds or it might be an hour. Stillness. Where lightness meets heaviness. When Berry writes "the beautiful poise of lightness, the heavy world pushing toward it," I am there on the farmhouse porch over the Kentucky River, a witness. Its brown water, slack but taut, reddens with the air. I am there, suspended, like the leaves. That stillness is wildness.

It's raining now. I hear it on the porch roof. Not loud, a low sizzle. I see it between the porch posts. Not everywhere, only when it etches the darkening green on the far bank. White scratches across thin earth between sky and river. Both patina silver. Wind slicks fallen rain across the river's surface. The tide has made its gentle but insistent turn. It runs inland to my left. Low clouds glide to my right. The shower moves on, and tree shadows return as if on the wind, rolling like a shrimp boat's wake. Another squall, a lull, and then another. Its brackish scent tastes of seaweed. A lull, and the cormorant flies toward the gulf, webbed feet and oily wings tapping the water, making puddles on the burnished surface. Here on the porch, serenity idles in saturated air. Laden with moisture and anxiety. The anhinga's beak pierces the lagoon and dives again. I have never felt so calm, yet so watchful. On a porch, nothing happens and everything happens.

I am thinking about how nature supports and imperils us, and how a porch puts us at risk, while it also sustains us. On a porch, control is relinquished just as shelter is provided. For

Berry, this is the idea that "the natural forces that so threaten us are the same forces that preserve and renew us." A farmer himself, Berry draws on the cultivation of land to illustrate how a farm must embrace wildness, because wilderness enfolds the agriculture of the farm. In a broader sense, he is saying that the ordered world humans have made must sustain natural processes in everything it does. But Berry's idea carries a warning, a call for respect and humility. Human activity also occurs within the wider, ineffable, all-encompassing natural context—a setting we can't control and about which we don't know everything.

Berry argues that nature and humanity are different yet indivisible. As it turns out, wildness and domesticity share this paradox. And that is why the margins are so important. Differences meet along edges, and overlaps occur in what Berry calls a "landscape of harmony." And that is another reason why porches are so important. They are where difference and indivisibility coincide along the frontiers of home. On the porch, human domesticity is hospitable to wildness, and nature can also claim this lens of air where wind, rain, sun, shadows, murmurs, calls, even spiders and errant no-see'ums, all reside.

Wildness resides on the porch. Stowe called it the "quaint rude wild wilderness." Her Florida porch hosted a necessary wildness, a place where she limns the freedoms between wildness and domestication, as she also extols a writer's necessary distance. When I clumsily drag the bedframe out onto the porch to toss and turn and impossibly sleep in brackish air, I also seek that residual frontier. It is also quaint, rude, and wild. It embraces the seemingly antiquated in the immediate present. It hosts the messy vulgarity of what cannot be controlled. Frederick Jackson Turner tapped into this spirit when he pitched his tent on his back porch in Cambridge.

Sleep on a porch is fitful but deep. Here is Goethe writing about a night on the *Gartenhaus'* veranda, and I have to wonder if Calvin let this bit fall for Harriet while on the Mandarin porch: "Last night I slept on the terrace, wrapped in my blue cloak, awoke three times, at 12, 2, and 4, and each time there was a new splendor in the heavens." I know the feeling—I go to sleep sweating and wake up shivering, but each interlude is rewarded with a sliver of wildness: a night heron's call, moons riding filigreed wavelets, a river otter's musk. Wet fur and broken crabshell. A gnawing sense of calm and a comforting logic of restiveness.

Berry has called this predicament an "essential paradox," which I think the porch redoubles. The porch reminds us that we occupy a tenuous but fundamental threshold between stability and precariousness. It embodies the predicament; it is a place where we build the inherently unfinished work of life. It occupies the connection between two orders—natural and human, and so it is the scene where we are constantly tuning for harmony, forever imperfect. Berry casts this predicament not as a problem to be solved but as a problematic situation to be practiced. This tuning has two interconnected parts: reflective and practical, and the porch offers a platform for both. Be still. Do.

Porches preserve wildness, not as a separate, distant place, but as integral to domestic life. Porches are then a foothold for the broader work of humanity to preserve nature. What we think and do on a porch translates to the world as a whole. And so the necessity of wildness bears additional weight in today's climate crisis, and the porch is a vehicle for experiencing and, at the same time, reflecting on its significance. It provides direct access to a wildness that we ourselves have wrought. The conditions we have wrought—elevated temperatures, sea level rise, habitat degradation—threaten us and deepen the challenges we face. I am thinking about how a porch is like a poem. Both are havens of wildness. Each of his poems is a hymn that Berry asks us to read outside, where they were composed—if not on a porch, then along another margin shared by humanity and nature. Making things like poems and building things like porches are what make us human. The porch that Stowe fashioned was indispensable in Florida's climate, but it also harbored the eccentricities of the writer and the dreamer. Even as a necessity, the porch is always a joyful leap into uncertainty. It is a place to acclimate and imagine. Today, porches may seem more like an amenity, but they are actually a new kind of necessity. Because porches reconnect to the wildness found not just in nature but in the newly wrought relation between humans and nature. Like a poem, a porch can harness imagination to help us come to terms with—to acclimate to—this new world. What Nabokov called the "porch of the past" is the porch to the future.

When I sit on the porch, I am sometimes the stoic, and other times I am a sensualist. I am a little like Calvin and a bit like Harriet. I might also play the philosopher, the artist, the botanist, the geologist, the anthropologist, the environmental scientist, and the architect. The porch is my field lab. I watch the world, absorbing the phenomena around me like a cotton shirt takes on moisture on a humid day. Here, I can immerse myself in what my senses are telling me. It is a place where I can simply feel. Then my mind wanders, and forces of imagination take over. My reflections extend beyond what I am experiencing. I become lost in thought. How else could I sit here long after the breeze has stopped and the no-see'ums have found their way through the screen, and sweat cellophanes my skin?

A long time ago I had a summer job in Athens on the excavation site of the agora, the ancient marketplace below the Acropolis. We were drawing the stones of the ancient Stoa of Attalos. In the morning, we clambered around the blocks of limestone and Pentelic marble that remained from the reconstruction a few decades earlier. In the heat of the afternoon, we retreated to the coolness of the stoa's colonnade. At a small folding desk, I translated pencil field sketches into ink drawings. Block by block, those drawings made their own reconstruction of the stoa. It was uncanny to look up from drawing the actual stone to see its recreated form lit up in the glare of the Greek sun. Here, among forty-five columns, crowds brushed up against stone, moved in and out, crossed between sun and shadow, stepped between rain and shelter.

The stoa was a porch for the city. Forty feet deep and more than the length of a football field, the Stoa of Attalos was the main shopping center for the agora's market. King Attalos II of Pergamon gifted the building to the city in appreciation of the education he received there, primarily under the tutelage of the philosopher Karneades. It is a prototypical stoa, which by definition is a free-standing portico. Unique to Greek architecture, the building type emerged in the seventh century

BC and endured for about six hundred years. Stoas are porticoes without temples, porches without buildings. Put another
way, the portico is the building itself. Its architecture is relatively simple—a long wall at the back and a line of columns,
sometimes multiple colonnades, along the front. Simple, but
perhaps no other architectural type has accommodated such
a diversity of programs: art gallery, shelter for homeless, philosopher's haunt, outdoor gym, marketplace, memorial altars,
public meals. The stoa was also a place to come in out of the
sun, wait, and watch. When it rained, crowds would pack into
stoas from theaters, agoras, and stadia.

But these urban porches writ large offered much more
than shelter. Among the throngs, stoas hosted philosophers.
Zeno followed the methods of Socrates and laid the ground-
work for stoicism in the colonnade of the Stoa Poikile at the
other end of the agora. Walking to and fro, thinking, talking,
teaching, he outlined a philosophy that opposed relying on
sense-impressions. On break from drawing stones, I would
leave the cool breezes of the reconstructed Stoa of Attalos'
colonnade to visit my future wife, who was excavating in the
agora around the Stoa Poikile's corner that had just emerged
twenty feet below the streets, where Athenians continued the
public life of the marketplace. Standing in the agora's vivid-
ness, I relished the ironies of a philosophy that distances the
senses having been born in the stoa's open-air space, filled
with dust-laden winds, heated stones, strident calls of vendors
echoing along marble walls, and smells of baking flatbread and
sun-warmed olives.

Stoas didn't harbor only stoics. Attalos, the patron of the
stoa where I drew, had learned from Karneades, a skeptic who
countered Zeno's line of thought. We do know some things

from our senses, Karneades argued. The link between a stoa and its occupant is the link between philosophy and place. The stoa's combination of shelter and openness within the civic realm linked inside and outside as it made room for conversations, debates, chance meetings. The stoa would have also inspired dialogues about its own meaning and function. The stoic Zeno may have understood the stoa as a kind of model for escaping rain's wetness and sun's burn; for Karneades, the stoa may have instead served as a vehicle of the senses. The stoa, like the porch, stirs that mix of thought and experience. Here on the porch in Homosassa, I channel Zeno as well as Karneades.

I didn't know it at the time but drawing the stones tracked a method outlined by John Ruskin: "To have drawn with attention a porch of Amiens will teach [a student] more of architecture than to have made plans of every big heap of brick or stone." Ruskin's own watercolor of the north porch at the cathedral's west entrance puts this inductive method into practice. His porch is a cloud of water and graphite, stone and air, light and shadow. It encompasses the church's atmosphere. Ruskin advocated focusing intensely on specific pieces to understand larger issues, and, one by one, the stoa's stones did teach me about the proportions and textures and modules of that open colonnade—lessons that extended to ancient Greek architecture as a whole. Though more vernacular than classical, the elements of the porch in Homosassa have also been my subject. I have studied, and sometimes sketched, those details next to nature's details—some very small and subtle—to understand the larger environmental picture.

When I play the scientist, the porch is an active agent to explore the edges of knowledge. It is as if the porch is an occupiable version of a Stevenson screen, one of those meteorological boxes that record temperature, humidity, and other weather-related data. I think of anthropologists Margaret Mead and Gregory Bateson typing up field notes in what they called the "mosquito room"—a screened chamber nested under the roof of their house in Tambunum, Papua New Guinea. When she described the many activities within their hut, Mead was also summarizing the general utility of the screened room, necessitated by the mosquitoes: "the house has to be primarily considered as a combination laboratory, observation post, fort, outpost, dispensary, and gathering place." Bateson's iconic 1938 photograph of the room shows the pair facing each other across a small wooden table, engrossed in typing up field notes as morning sun glares through the screen. This porch self-portrait (Bateson discretely hid the remote in his right hand behind the typewriter) illustrates the couple's dialogues, and the extended conversations they had with the Balinese people.

Through the mosquito room, I also see the porous nature of research—and living itself—where circumstances influence perception. When they weren't out in the field they were still *in* the field, and across that flimsy screen, a necessary but agile filter, the cultural anthropologists could still hear, see, and feel their surroundings. In my more modest outpost, as I sweat through the afternoon's heat, notepaper like wet parchment, I imagine the tropical climate and Bateson's rolled-up sleeves and long pants and the ghosts of that mesh room washed away long ago in the Sepik River's annual floods, which now rise higher and threaten the livelihoods of those Mead and Bateson learned so much from.

I also think of Rachel Carson sitting out on the porches of

her houses and cabins. Soon after *Silent Spring* was published in 1962, Alfred Eisenstaedt photographed Carson on her back porch in Silver Spring, Maryland. She looks up from a specimen under the microscope, a needle pen deftly poised in her hand. Visible beyond the porch's light frame are tree limbs, leaves, a wide trunk, and dappled light. Though staged for *Life* magazine, here is the scientist and writer at work in the place where she wrote much of her seminal book. Here is the portrait of a woman who could mix science with innate wonder, and then communicate her ideas through the lyrical writing that made up her lifework.

As she suffered from cancer and as her work turned inward toward the data and reports that underpinned *Silent Spring*, Carson had decamped from her other porches, particularly the ones overlooking the Sheepscot River on the coast of Maine. For her first visit there in 1941, she had rented a cottage with a screened porch built right on the seawall, where she could watch the spruces and the birds of Indiantown Island and the herring runs into the cove. With the success of *The Sea Around Us*, Carson built her own cottage on Southport Island. From its high porch, she could examine the trees up close, studying their intricate botany and resting in their "cathedral of stillness and peace." At the same time, she could watch distant wave patterns and tides along the watermarked shoreline, that "granite threshold of the sea." She could look westward across the wide river that connected her to the sea she so loved.

A well-known CBS News report begins on Carson's Southport porch, with a vignette of Carson sitting at her desk, jotting notes, gazing across the river. It feels as though the report's ensuing debate between Carson and male scientists plays out here as well. Dressed in lab coats, the men remain inside; Carson is in and out, walking through the woods, working in her study, out in nature on her porch. After a majority of the time inside with the earnest talk of the men, Carson is back for two minutes to conclude the program. Her commentary on the theme of the balance of nature is as incisive as it is lyrical. We should focus on "mastery of ourselves, not nature," she says. Those brief porch scenes complement what Carson found—the facts of her research—with what she imagined. And the porch harbors the sense of wonder that is so fundamental to her work.

We all need a porch for field research. Philosophical questions may float between its columns like Zeno's stoa. Its makeshift screens might wrap cultural insights that resonate with Mead's work. Or it may mix wonder with science like Carson's porches. Ideally, it combines all of these. Possibly, it hosts them in a structure as precarious as it is stable. Your porch might be a nest equally molded by human activity and nature. A nest that extends your home, sometimes tests your limits, and puts your ideas of a porch into practice.

As the Stowes took up residence on their Florida veranda, John Muir climbed out into his own version of a frontier porch in Yosemite. He called it his "hang-nest." This suspended cabin hung off the gable end of Hutching's mill where he worked. Although it was loosely tethered to the mill's already tenuous position, it was firmly bound to the natural features that surrounded it. In a letter to his sister on April 5, 1871, Muir described how its position afforded views through carefully placed windows and skylights. To the south, through a "hole in the roof," he could look up to see the Half Dome's

sheared outcrop. The oceanic thunder of Yosemite Falls—
"the grandest of all the falls"—appeared through a skylight
to the north. Out the west-facing window, Muir watched the
changing seasons across the entire Yosemite valley. The simple sketch he included in the letter shows a fourth aperture
a little farther back in the mill's roof, where he contemplated
the stars.

Muir's hang-nest doubled as bedroom and study. It was
a living archive of sketches, field notes, and collected specimens. Access was difficult. When Ralph Waldo Emerson visited, the elderly poet struggled to negotiate the steep incline
of the ramps, which Muir himself compared to a hen ladder,
with its treacherous boards nailed across sloping planks.
Once inside though, Emerson would have been enthralled
with the hang-nest's cabinet of curiosities. I imagine a room
loaded with books, papers, backpacks, walking sticks, and tin
cups and walls brimming with drawings, feathers, branches,
mosses, pressed leaves, and eggshells. A small intimate space
built from the inside out, as if it were a nest itself, filled with
things from out of doors.

Muir watched how birds build nests. As a child, he ad-
mired Baltimore orioles and marveled at their hanging nests.
In Yosemite, Muir also studied the Bullock's oriole, but his
greatest affinity was for the water ouzels. He described their
nests, built along the cliffs and at the edges of the falls, as the
"most extraordinary piece of bird architecture" he had ever
seen. How their nests "gripped" and "dovetailed" with the vertical faces of the cliffs surely inspired Muir's own perch. What
he saw in the woven nature of this architecture, Yosemite's
Indigenous people had already witnessed in the weave of water in the falls. They referred to Royal Arch Falls as Scho-

ko-ya, or "basket falls," and the cornice of rock above the falls was named Scho-ko-ni, the "movable shade to a cradle basket," which was a common means for transporting babies on their backs. A porch is a weave of light and air and sometimes water. Isn't that what the blue-green of an eggshell tells us? Elemental wickerwork, my porch is a basket for living and sleeping and feeling and thinking. I watch its screens sift afternoon light while winds of a distant storm thread through.

The architect Rudolf Schindler camped where Muir had lived a half century earlier. From his tent along Tenaya Creek, he was immersed in the sounds and spray of Royal Arch Falls. He hiked among the Mariposa, feet pressing into the softness of Muir's pine needle bedding, and he also watched the orioles, the ouzels, and the valley's wildlife. On this trip, inspired by the landscape that stirred Muir and lodged Yosemite's first residents, the architect decided to stay in California rather than return to Vienna. In West Hollywood, then on the undeveloped margins of Los Angeles, Schindler built his own house modeled on the Yosemite camp. Recalling the openings of parted tent flaps, he left seams of light between vertical slabs of concrete poured on the ground and tilted up into position. Along the ceiling, he pulled a gap between wall and ceiling to allow light from the sky to flow. Here, at the crest of walls, he anchored the outdoor rooms he called "sleeping baskets"—wooden trays with red cedar frames wrapped in hanging canvas, floating on air and light. Even today, when you climb into one of these baskets, you might be camping out in Yosemite among the pines, held aloft by an updraft, or suspended from the sun's cascade.

Muir's dwellings before and after the hang-nest also bear the camper's mentality. When he first arrived at Yosemite, he built a cabin on the firmness of the ground, but he suspended his bed from the rafters over a rivulet he directed from the nearby creek. Inside, frogs sang, ferns sprang up between floorboards, moths fluttered, and the stream's "warbling, tinkling" water meshed with the softness of his bed that was lined with feathered cypress branches. I wonder if Muir had read "Epipsychidion," a poem laced with air and suspension, where Shelley writes about the nature of love: "It is an isle 'twixt Heaven, Air, Earth, and Sea, / Cradled, and hung in clear tranquility." For Muir, the hang-nest cradled a love of nature.

After Yosemite, Muir carried the hang-nest with him. His house in Martinez, high above the Sacramento River, had five porches, each with its ceiling painted a deep sky blue. Historical records include the obligatory porch portraits, like the stereoscope views of the Stowe family, on the front porch— Muir, his wife, Louisiana, his daughter, Helen, and his dog, Stickeen. Those official porches were an important part of the house, but Muir still crafted his own perch along its edge. He often slept out on the roof of the western porch, pitching a tent or pulling a cot out from his study. This was the same roof Muir had modified with metal panels to reverberate with the sound of rain. From here, the horizon would have opened across the Alhambra Valley toward the Pacific, in the same way the hang-nest was oriented to the western vista of the Yosemite Valley.

Typical of such ephemeral architecture, few photographs of Muir's porches survive. Only his sketch and the grainy sepia of a single photograph offer visual documentation of the hang-nest. There is one photograph that captures how he occupied the frontier edges of the Martinez house. From below, we look southward up to the house, where a thick stand of trees and palms obscures the entrance. Above the trees, as if held up like a treehouse, a simple tent, its gable end opening toward us, rests comfortably on the roof of the main porch, which is, like the rest of the front, largely hidden. This was his daughter's tent, firmly tethered to the porch roof's balustrade. Here, after Helen had moved out, Muir weathered the heat wave in 1908—seeking relief in a presumably private location along the house's exposed front. As he grew older, the naturalist's life contracted to his second-floor study and its adjacent sleeping platform on the western ledge. It became his final hang-nest. Muir wanted to be as close to nature—as far outside—as possible.

The footings along the front edge of the Homosassa porch are sinking. There is a softness in the floor I had not noticed until today. It must have been the ride out on the pontoon that helped me see this extra tilt. Set against the tide, each islet rested low in the water. Each floated like a stone tub, a shallow planter for cedars, palms, and pepper trees. A king tide carried along on a light storm surge had filled the river with seawater, and it left only inches of freeboard for these island vessels. Wind gusts from the outer bands of a hurricane sloshed small but insistent waves over their darkened, corrugated lips.

The river's islands were floating—just like Lime Key in the sketch Muir made soon after his arrival in Cedar Key, forty miles north of Homosassa. Not only that, but these limestone rafts listed as if some hidden ballast had shifted. They keeled under the weight they carried. Later, when I walked out onto the porch to watch wind and tide, I sensed the new slope. I checked the framing, and the beams, joists, and footings were intact—no cracks or decay, only the patina of brackish air. Since then, each time I board the porch, I walk back and forth, testing, pressing, studying the angles. There is no doubt about the floor's greater incline. Its edge bends toward the water, and its tilt tells me what I might not otherwise see. Our foundations sink on a floating island, and the porch hangs on the side of the house.

*
**

There is a famous quotation from Muir that I have carried along, thinking and writing about porches. It comes as a fragment from his unpublished journals, and I have understood it as a call to go camping, an analog for Zen philosophy, and a beautifully simple yet enigmatic puzzle. It is a manifesto of in and out, and it is a mission statement for the porch: "Not like my taking the veil—no solemn abjuration of the world. I only went out for a walk, and finally concluded to stay out till sundown, for going out, I found, was really going in." Going out to go in is about experiencing nature. It also affirms citizenship in the world and affords contemplation about our place in that world. The porch is where I go out to go in.

Muir retreats to a frontier. That may seem counterintuitive, but the naturalist seeks harmony rather than safety. Such a process mirrors camping: leaving one home for another temporary one. Camping on a frontier means seeking refuge in unknowns, in places where you cede complete control, potentially in locations vulnerable to hardship. When we came out to the cabin and its porch, we found ourselves astride a national refuge's boundary, immersed in an aquatic preserve's assurance of protection and wildlife. We hoped to connect deeply with the river and the coast in a part of Florida—the outpost of land between Highway 98 and the open water—that was for us a mythical and personal landscape. We didn't seek refuge inland as most would advise. We retreated instead to the crisis itself.

For Muir, going out heads into the heart of nature, just as going into his hang-nest is like finding the edge of your house and stepping out onto the porch. A corollary to this movement is Berry's idea that distance from the comforts of home brings us closer to the central meaning of that home's place in the world. To that I would add that a porch's closeness to its house increases the sense of being outside and allows us to take greater risks as we reach out into nature. In another letter to his sister, Muir wrote: "I do not live 'near the Yosemite,' but in it—in the very grandest, *warmest* center of it. I wish you could hear the falls tonight—they speak a most glorious language, and I hear them easily through the thin walls of our cabin." This position brings nature in.

As he wrote to his sister about the hang-nest, rain dripped from the ceiling, and his writing hand shook with vibrations from the mill's machinery. Muir's hang-nest offered a fully immersive experience of the Sierras. On his frequent ventures into Yosemite's fields and forests, he made camp directly on beds of needles under tree canopies, and the hang-nest was as close as architecture could bring him to those experiences. Both the hang-nest and the porch are architectural compromises, like Jack London's double-screened sleeping porch. It anchors that overlap between in and out. In the hang-nest, Muir is at home in nature, and he lives with nature at home.

If you have stretched out on a porch and felt the sun on your face, or if you have sat out in a storm when rain turns horizontal and thunder mantles you with a sound like the "deep waving roar of the falls," which Muir once compared to "breakers on a coast," then you know what he means: "Nature's peace will flow into you as sunshine flows into trees. The winds will blow their own freshness into you and the storms their energy." We need this edge that places us in the middle of things.

And we all need our hang-nest. It may not be a cabin in Yosemite, much less a room slung off the side of a lumber mill. It may not be the "tangible desideratum" of Marjorie Kinnan Rawlings' porch in Cross Creek, or Harriet Beecher Stowe's empyreal veranda. It may not even be what most people would consider a porch. It could start out as a stoop, the grating of a fire escape, a pickup truck's lowered tailgate, a roof accessed through a window, or the opened window itself. It may even be a screened A-frame, where your body learns to tell the temperature. The key attribute of these places is the exchange of in and out. This is not just the movement between inside and outside, but the interactions of humans and nature, thought and experience, reflection and action. These places, like my Homosassa porch, inspire active reflection and attentive experience like nowhere else.

In January 1868, Muir boarded the *Island Belle*, as it left out of Cedar Key, carrying ideas that would serve as the foundations for his hang-nest. Along his thousand-mile walk to the Gulf of Mexico, he had come to the conclusion that the world is not made for humans alone. And during his time in Cedar Key, recuperating from malaria, he added this insight: "It would also be incomplete without the smallest transmicroscopic creature that dwells beyond our conceitful eyes and knowledge." Nature's completeness relies not just on humans but on all living things, even the smallest, like the mosquito that transmitted his disease, even the no-see'ums that I see flashing in the crisp autumn light. I imagine Muir thinking about this as the schooner headed into rough seas. It pitched and rolled, but he disobeyed orders to retreat below deck. Muir wanted to have the full experience of the sea as he passed the nascent mangrove islands near the mouth of the Homosassa River. He had called them "bouquets."

Two nights before writing to his sister about the hang-nest, Muir scaled the ledges behind upper Yosemite Falls to look for the water ouzel's nest. With only a blanket and a piece of bread, he planned to sleep in the space between cascading water and cliff face. Soaked and near death, he was forced back to his hang-nest in the early morning. Undaunted, Muir returned the next day. Through the "rainbow atmosphere" of the falls, in the yellow tinge of moss, Muir sees what he thinks is a nest. To be sure, barefoot, body pressed against the precipice, he moves between cataract and cliff, between water and granite, to get a closer look.

Muir describes how the water ouzel, his favorite bird, is constantly adapting to a "glorious" but overwhelmingly powerful falls, which hovers on the edge of cataclysm. The nest's suspension reinforces the water ouzel's seamless fit with nature—"so completely part and parcel," as Muir wrote. It is how Muir approaches nature as a whole. In the quest to understand the bird's attunement with its context, Muir embarks on our own project of acclimating to a constantly shifting environment. When Muir writes of the ouzel, he might also be writing about the attentive porch-sitter: "While water sings, so must he, in heat or cold, calm or storm, ever attuning his voice in sure accord; low in the drought of summer and the drought of winter, but never silent." A porch is a perch where we just might find our singing pitch.

Going out to go in is not about being inside or outside, but the overlap. A whole series of going outs and ins. It is a place to deliberate—not decide—whether your hat is on or off. Remember Frank Lloyd Wright's famous quip when he entered Philip Johnson's Glass House, asking, "Am I inside? Or am I outside? Do I leave my hat on? Or do I take it off?" The porch is a place to ask that question, not resolve it. It is where we can also debate its implications.

Today's porches are precarious. A porch on a river by the sea is an extreme case of that instability, but any porch anywhere must contend not only with its local weather but also with the broader changing climate. The naming of Muir's cabin in the air, "hang-nest," vividly renders the joys and the challenges and the possibilities of the contemporary porch. The hang-nest puts shelter and comfort at risk. It suspends assumptions of a house's stability. When a dwelling is not supported with traditional foundations on solid ground, it must find its footing in other ways. Another structure may provide the support, like the mill for Muir's hang-nest, or like the cabin for our tilting porch. But a porch, from where it sits on the edge of its building, can also seek buoyancy and lift, if not complete stability, in nature. Like looking to the horizon to find your sea legs, a porch looks to air and water. It may not always afford physical stability, but it helps us get our bearings. Going out brings stabilizing insights.

Our porch waits for the water to rise. Its weathering is nature coming in, and I inventory these changes. In them, I measure time. The gaps between battens and boards are the soaking and drying of wood, filled with humidity but also with floodwater. Sap oozes golden from the fat pine, even through the recent coat of robin's egg blue paint. The listing and hanging of the porch's front edge is the work of a sinking island as well as undermining storm surges. These changes fit. They anchor vulnerability. They mark time and record change in a vessel that is ultimately ephemeral. This is a porch of the present that looks, Janus-like, to the past and the future. The porch can be maintained, and I will do my best, but even if it were to last another seventy years, its survival will evoke the same questions of Theseus' ship. On new floorboards, behind fresh screens held by columns shored up in support of the latest roof layers, under the latest coat of ceiling paint, a future porch-sitter may ask not only whether it is the same porch but also—and it will likely be floating then—when did the porch become a ship?

Acclimation occurs on the cusp of change. It rides the broader sweep of adaptation like a seed on a wave's crest, like a fledgling mangrove that clings to limestone farther and farther up the coast. An embodiment of acclimation on a climate frontier, the porch affords physical space for critical practices: adjusting our bodies to climatic changes in the short term, and adjusting our approach to climate crises in the longer term. Witnessing is the first step. Then renegotiating the natural and social contracts we have with the world. The porch is where I come to be in nature at home, and it is where I try to discern subtle differences between the world we have made and its natural substrate. Coming to the porch, I carry the world with me. Sometimes barefoot, sometimes bundled up like the Stowes, I come here to reconcile the outer bands of a changing climate.

Just last week I sat in the dark and listened to water surge under the porch. It drafted around mangrove roots and concrete foundations. It slipped below floorboards, close under my feet. I heard rusted nails pop from a board as rising water pried it from the front dock. Then another. They will float, and I will retrieve them when the water recedes. Right now the porch is an island. The sun rises and the ground is water. It fills my visual field, carrying seagrass and styrofoam and other people's docks. When rain comes, it has the roar of wind, even though this storm named Nestor has very little. For a moment, at 9:24 in the morning, a wedge of sun points toward the porch. Deep blue sky arches between a skein of white clouds, dangling like Spanish moss, and higher steely clouds, like waves above. A window opens long enough for light and water to dance on the porch ceiling.

·

Acknowledgments

I thank family, friends, and fellow porch travelers for their inspiration, insights, and expertise. I could not have completed this project without the love and support of Melanie, Aidan, and Phoebe, who joined me for many of these adventures, and my parents. I also thank: Jim Adamson, Bahar Aktuna, Jason Alread, Ann Baird, Sheila Barnes, Cynthia Barnett, Stephen Belton, Xhulio Binjaku, Frank Bosworth, Jeletta Brant, Carla Brisotto, Marsha Bryant, Julian Chambliss, Donna Cohen, Amy Creekmur, John Griswold, Nicholas Guardiano, Martin Gundersen, Tom Hambright, Megan Hobson, Nina Hofer, Aaron Hoover, Lisa Huang, Bruce Janz, Jaeyoung Joo, Mary Kramer, Perry Kulper, Eva Larsson, Ann Lindell, Julia Lupton, Geoff Manaugh, Jonathan Martin, Tisha Mauney, Robert McCarter, Wilfred McClay, Mark McGlothlin, Wayne Merrell, Gill Minor, Jesse Minor, Pamela Minor, Rick Mulligan, Susan Murray, Robert Neff, Kim Nofal, Glen Retief, John Riley, Sami Rintala, Nan Russell, Ken Sassaman, Hans Skotte, Stephen Smith, Sue Smith, Paul Steege, Jim Stege, Kenneth Stikkers, Ke Sun, Ed Tarkington, Thomas Thomas, Philip Tidwell, William Tilson, Carrie Todd, Florence Turcotte,

Arnoldo Valle-Levinson, Matt Walker, Bradley Walters, Adam Watson, Pete Wernick, John Westmark, William Whitaker; the White House Historical Association; my late friends Diana Bitz and Per Iwansson; students at the University of Florida School of Architecture; colleagues in the International Association for the Study of Environment, Space and Place; and the river dwellers of the Homosassa.

I am extremely grateful for the vital feedback and editorial expertise of Timothy Mennel at University of Chicago Press; and I thank Mary Corrado for her crucial editing and preparing the manuscript, Kristen Raddatz as well as the Press' production and design team for their integral contributions, Susannah Engstrom for her tireless assistance, and the anonymous reviewers for their invaluable comments.

The John Simon Guggenheim Foundation provided critical support for this work.

Notes

CHAPTER 1

6 Howard T. Odum . . . Odum, "Primary Production Measurements in Eleven Florida Springs and a Marine Turtle-Grass Community," *Limnology and Oceanography* 2, no. 2 (April 1957): 85–97. See also Odum's "Factors Controlling Marine Invasion in Florida Freshwaters," *Bulletin of Marine Science of the Gulf and Caribbean* 3 (1953): 134–56. Odum called Florida a sponge: "The whole peninsula behaves like a sponge in which water is poured on top and flows out the sides through springs and ground water flow into the surface streams."

7 The habitat they saw . . . Robert M. Ingle, "Potential Research Benefits to be Derived from Estuarine Heterogeneity," *Tulane Studies in Geology* 9, no. 5 (April 16, 1962): 295–99. Ingle was the first marine biologist hired by the state of Florida.

16 I remember reading . . . The 2003 *Granta* was number 83, titled "This Overheating World" and published in autumn of that year.

16 Now we regularly talk . . . Among many predictive models, the Climate Action Tracker calculates the median global warming by 2100 as 3.0 degrees Celsius above pre-industrial levels based on current pledges and policies. In its *Climate Change 2014: Synthesis Report*, the Intergovernmental Panel on Climate Change (IPCC) predicts a 4.5 degree Celsius rise in temperature by 2100. See also IPCC's special report *Global Warming of 1.5 °C* (2018).

16 Assessments of the rise . . . Estimates of sea level rise vary whether they are based on relative (local and regional) or global (eustatic) data.

For this estimate, I have worked with two predictions. Early in 2020, the Virginia Institute of Marine Science (VIMS) published its US Sea-Level Report Cards "Trends, Projections, and Processes to Aid Coastal Planning." It lists them by locality, and its "best estimate" for Cedar Key, which is thirty miles to the north of the cabin, was a 0.5 meter sea level rise by 2050. In "Sea-Level Rise in Florida—the Facts and Science," a Florida Sea Grant publication (July 2013), Thomas Ruppert cites the United States Army Corps of Engineers' guidance for incorporating SLR into projects (EN 1165-2-212). Among the three scenarios, "intermediate" predicts 39 inches of rise by 2100—a figure close to VIMS's estimate, which I have adopted for this work. See also USACE's recent documents EP 1100-2-1 (June 30, 2019) and its online Sea Level Tracker, where the "high" scenario for Cedar Key forecasts 59 inches of sea level change. Placed in the context of wide-ranging uncertainties—coastal oceanographers note the unknown contributions of major ice sheets as well as the fluctuation of SLR values, which can add as much as 6 inches to each decade's projection—these numbers portend a porch adrift.

21 "heel-gnawed" . . . William Faulkner, *The Hamlet* (New York: Vintage, 1991), 138.

22 a method for tuning . . . As an architect, one of my favorite photographs shows Alison and Peter Smithson laying out a porch for the German furniture maker Axel Bruchhäuser. Here are architects known for designing cities and housing projects on their hands and knees, measuring for a porch no wider than they are tall. Axel's tiny porch offers a glazed passage out to the wooded slope along the Weser River. Its facets follow the ground's contours and its wooden mullions angle like tree limbs— "branches that move and branches that don't," the Smithsons once said. This is a porch for a man and his cat. There is a seat for Axel to watch the river and a lower perch for Karlchen to watch birds and squirrels. A departure point for this book has been the Smithsons' description of their project: "The porch can be read as an exemplar of a method by which a small physical change—a layering-over of air adhered to an existing fabric—can bring about a delicate tuning of persons with place." See Alison and Peter Smithson, *The Charged Void: Architecture* (New York: Monacelli, 2001), 552.

25 Statistics from the construction industry . . . Since 1992, the "Survey of Construction," published by the US Census, has tabulated statistics for houses in the United States built with "outdoor amenities," which includes porches, decks, and patios. The Census defines a porch as "a floored

area with a roof, enclosed or open, not sitting directly on the ground. This does not include small covered entryways." From 1992 to 2017, the share of single-family houses constructed in the US with porches increased from 42 percent to 65 percent. A housing industry article published in 2013 hyperbolically, if not breathlessly, noted that porches were built on 90 percent of new homes built in four southern states (Alabama, Kentucky, Mississippi, and Tennessee) in 2012. See Paul Emrath, August 23, 2013, eyeonhousing.org. In 2018, Emrath reported that the share in that same region increased to 94 percent.

27 They make room for . . . John Dewey, "Experience and Nature," in *The Later Works, 1925–1953,* vol. 1, ed. Jo Ann Boydston (Carbondale: Southern Illinois University Press, 1981), 55.

28 Here is Dewey writing . . . Dewey, "Experience and Nature," 43–44.

CHAPTER 2

37 "the steadfast tilted deck . . ." . . . On pages 37–43, the quotations are from James Agee, *Let Us Now Praise Famous Men* (New York: Houghton Mifflin, 1980), 187, 224–25, 245, 227–29, 464, and 470.

40 The book's front matter . . . Agee writes: "It was thoroughly as if principals had been set up, enchanted, and left like dim sacks at one side of a stage as enormous as the steadfast tilted deck of the earth" (470).

44 "sleeping under a dead horse" . . . Bill Bryson, *The Life and Times of the Thunderbolt Kid* (New York: Broadway Books, 2006), 182. Bryson describes the process: "For the first minute or so it was unimaginably cold, shockingly cold, but gradually your body heat seeped in and you became warm and happy in a way you would not have believed possible only a minute or two before. It was bliss."

48 Some would say . . . Marjorie Kinnan Rawlings, *The Yearling* (New York: Scribner, 1938/2002), 263.

52 During Taft's term . . . *Washington Post,* December 11, 1912, 6.

53 "intimate immensity" . . . Gaston Bachelard, *The Poetics of Space,* trans. Maria Jolas (Boston: Beacon, 1964), 183–210.

55 "hardy life of the open" . . . Theodore Roosevelt, August 31, 1910, speech in Osawatomie, Kansas.

63 On the porch . . . Agee, *Let Us Now Praise Famous Men,* 248.

63 "warp of the world" . . . Cormac McCarthy, *The Stonemason* (Hopewell, NJ: Ecco, 1994), 9.

63 Agee pointed out . . . Agee, *Let Us Now Praise Famous Men,* 247.

CHAPTER 3

67 I can't forget that . . . Henry David Thoreau, *Walden* (Oxford: Oxford University Press, 1999), 41.

68 Rudolf Geiger called the air . . . See Geiger, *The Climate near the Ground* (Cambridge: Harvard University Press, 1965), 1–3. By the time he wrote his book, Geiger had redrawn the map for climate classification. In 1940, he updated the work of Wladimir Köppen six decades earlier in the Köppen-Geiger map that classifies climate zones by their native vegetation. Further revisions in the last decade account for recent climate change models and show in full color the dramatic nature of the crisis. In this newest map, one of Geiger's legacies, the bright red of the tropical biome and its "equatorial monsoon" climate has risen just past the latitude of the Homosassa porch, and more than half of the Florida peninsula looks like a finger scalded from testing water that is just too hot. Above the red zone is the seeming security of the forest green's warm temperate zone, but its "fully humid" and hot summers have extended further north in the new map. I think if Geiger were alive, he would sit on the porch, immersed in its microclimate just above the ground, and concur.

69 Sloterdijk characterizes air . . . Peter Sloterdijk, "Foreword to the Theory of Spheres," *Cosmograms*, ed. Melik Ohanian and Jean-Christophe Royoux (New York: Lukas and Sternberg, 2005), 237–38. Sloterdijk also points out that "ventilation is the profound secret of existence."

70 With such pathetic fallacy . . . Eudora Welty, "The Winds," *The Collected Stories of Eudora Welty* (New York: Harcourt, 1980), 211, 256.

71 The King welcomes . . . Homer, *Odyssey*, trans. A. T. Murray, Loeb Classical Library 104 (Cambridge, MA: Harvard University Press, 1919), 7.334–336, 7.343–347. Scholars have variously translated these spaces of hospitality as "porch" and "portico."

72 "right of the visit," . . . Immanuel Kant discusses a universal hospitality, while Jacques Derrida proposes a more open invitation with unconditional hospitality.

72 Priam's bedstead . . . Homer, *Iliad*, trans. A. T. Murray, Loeb Classical Library 170 (Cambridge, MA: Harvard University Press, 1924), 24.642–656.

73 Nestor offers his porch . . . Homer, *Odyssey*, 3.348, 3.399.

74 The prefix of the Greek word . . . When Homer uses the Greek word αἴθουσα to identify the porch, he celebrates its opening to the sky. I have wondered at the prefix αἴθω (gleaming) and its connection to fire,

in a similar way that the Latin word *aedis* identifies a place with a hearth. Akin to Homer's text are the images from the Greek poet Theocritus. Here on the river, in one of his idylls that celebrate pastoral songs, I happily read "and sweet is it in summer-time to sleep in the open air (αἴθριο-κοιτέω) beside running water." Theocritus, "Idyll VIII," in *The Idylls of Theocritus, Bion, and Moschus*, trans. J. Banks (London: Bell and Daldy, 1870), 50 (line 78).

75 On the Proustian evocations . . . Robert Roper, "Net Gains," *American Scholar*, June 8, 2015; Vladimir Nabokov, *Speak, Memory* (New York: Vintage, 1951/1989), 43.

76 The Russian writer recalled . . . Vladimir Nabokov, "Father's Butterflies," *Atlantic* 285, no. 4 (April 2000): 59–75.

82 "crack in the door" . . . Flannery O'Connor to Cecil Dawkins, August 4, 1957, in *The Habit of Being: Letters*, ed. Sally Fitzgerald (New York: Farrar, Straus and Giroux, 1979), 233.

83 When I read . . . Carson McCullers, *The Ballad of the Sad Café* (Boston: Houghton Mifflin, 1951), 6.

88 As I walk around . . . Pausanias' account reflects the story of Aglauros and Herse, two of Cecrops' daughters who succumbed to curiosity despite Athena's warning and opened a basket that held Erichthonius, the second king of Athens. See Pausanias, *Description of Greece*, vol. 1, trans. W. H. S. Jones, Loeb Classical Library 93 (Cambridge, MA: Harvard University Press, 1918): 27.3.

91 In the preface . . . John Ruskin, *The Queen of the Air: Being a Study of the Greek Myths of Cloud and Storm*, 7th ed. (London: George Allen, 1898), vii. Earlier, Ruskin talks about the Greeks'"instinctive truth in ancient symbolism" and "accurate mythic expressions of natural phenomena."

91 Tyndall sings . . . John Tyndall, "On Chemical Rays, and the Light of the Sky," a lecture prepared for the Royal Institution, January 10, 1869.

92 Ruskin makes the case . . . Ruskin, *Queen of the Air*, 48–50.

99 From Boo's porch . . . Harper Lee, *To Kill a Mockingbird* (New York: Grand Central, 1960/1982), 39.

99 Pose on a porch . . . More recently, Dwayne Johnson—known as "The Rock"—posted a selfie from his front porch in Florida to commemorate first responders after the 9-11 attacks. Sweat beads on his tattooed skin, and the camera phone angle twists the perspective from the porch over his shoulder, to the white railing, up to the American flag draped behind his head, and out into the blue sky. Captions on social media cast the image as if this type of shot is a trend: "The Rock took a front porch

selfie." As I completed this book, amid the lockdowns that followed the onset of the COVID-19 pandemic, Instagram and other social media platforms were filled with porch portraits, including #porchportraits, #porchtraits, and #frontporchproject.

100 When a wagon . . . Lee, *To Kill a Mockingbird*, 212.

100 In one portrait from 1865 . . . See "Family portrait posed on front porch of house," 1865, Albumen silver print, The J. Paul Getty Museum, 84.XC.873.5633, location and photographer unknown.

101 Albert Einstein wears fuzzy slippers . . . Einstein's portrait on the porch at 112 Mercer Street is in the collection of the Historical Society of Princeton; Grant's portrait is in the Library of Congress; Miller's is in the California Historical Society's Collection; the photograph of Cudjo Lewis is part of the McCall Rare Book and Manuscript Library at the University of South Alabama; Fields' and Cisneros' portraits are in the Smithsonian's National Portrait Gallery. Other porch portraits include novelist William Dean Howells, poet and abolitionist Julia Ward Howe, writer Upton Sinclair, poet Elizabeth Bishop, and Steve Jobs.

102 Their figures are notes . . . There are at least three versions of this photograph. See Tamara Saviano, *Without Getting Killed or Caught: The Life and Music of Guy Clark* (College Station: Texas A&M University Press, 2016).

104 A tempest of hunger . . . See Robert Coles, *Still Hungry in America* (New York: New American Library, 1969).

104 Portraiture tells stories . . . I have derived this idea from what Berger calls the "identity of spirit" in portraits. John Berger, "The Story-teller," *Landscapes: John Berger on Art* (London: Verso, 2016), 63.

105 They gargoyle its roof . . . Helen Levitt, *New York*, 1939, Collection of the Museum of Modern Art.

105 That porch evokes . . . Beyoncé Knowles Carter, *Lemonade* (New York: Parkwood Entertainment, 2016).

106 Now, she occupies her own porch . . . Zora Neale Hurston, *Their Eyes Were Watching God* (New York: Perennial, 1999), 255.

107 "back-porch listener." . . . Lee, *To Kill a Mockingbird*, 111–17.

108 In the 1930s . . . See Colin Asher, *Never a Lovely So Real: The Life and Work of Nelson Algren* (New York: W. W. Norton, 2019).

112 Near the end of the *Odyssey* . . . Homer, *Odyssey*, 20.351–357. Jacques Derrida has written about the connection between hospitality, hosts, guests, and ghosts. The Latin word *hostis*, which means both guest and enemy, is not unlike a porch's paradox—its "undecideability," Derrida might have said. See *Of Hospitality* (Stanford: Stanford University Press, 2000), which records Derrida and Anne Dufourmantelle's dialogue, translated by Rachel Bowlby.

112 John Keats, in his poem . . . "The Eve of St. Mark" (1819/1848); Washington Irving, "Saint Mark's Eve," *Bracebridge Hall* (New York: R. F. Fenno, 1900), 83–88. St. Mark's Eve is April 24.

113 This organization of the church . . . I am drawing from *Epistola Canonica*, ascribed to St. Gregory of Thaumaturgus, who lived between AD 213 and 270. Subsequent canons modified these rules, including the twenty canons of the council of Nice in 318. Numerous commentaries discuss these variations; see, for example, J. E. Riddle, *A Manual of Christian Antiquities* (London: John W. Parker, 1843).

CHAPTER 4

121 "very simple everlasting . . ." . . . Louis Kahn, *Perspecta* 7 (1961): 10.

121 "You say to brick . . ." . . . Louis Kahn, *Perspecta* 19 (1982): 92.

122 Kahn wanted to . . . Louis Kahn, *Perspecta* 7 (1961): 9–10.

123 On one particular walk . . . Rainer Maria Rilke, *The Notebooks of Malte Laurids Brigge* (New York: Vintage, 1990), 45–48.

124 When architect . . . Clarke developed two schemes: one square that fit the porch outline exactly and another semicircular, which is tangential. See Zachary Rutz, *Chatham: A Landscape Introduction* (Richmond: The Garden Club of Virginia, 2006), 19. See also Gerald Karr, *Historic Structure Report—Architectural Data Section*, ed. Harlan D. Unrau (Fredericksburg: Denver Service Center, January 1984).

127 Kahn says . . . John W. Cook and Heinrich Klotz, *Conversations with Architects* (New York: Praeger, 1973), 197, 198.

130 And the porch rails . . . We have been careful not to collect anything below the mean high-water line or on public land.

138 "The much approved *Daton* . . ." . . . "Robert Sinclair," *American Farmer*, ed. John S. Skinner, Baltimore, vol. 5 (1823): 288.

139 Two years earlier . . . Thomas Massey, "The Construction and Management of a Dairy," *American Farmer*, vol. 3 (April 17, 1821): 71. At this time, homeowners were also known to stretch cheesecloth across window openings.

143 Five years later . . . S. S. Block, "Insect Tests of Wire Screening Effectiveness," *American Journal of Public Health* 36 (November 1946): 1279–86.

146 Jack London wrote . . . London, "When the World Was Young," *The Night-Born* (New York: Century, 1913), 65–98.

147 In another passage . . . Thoreau, *Walden*, 78–79.

148 The country's frontier . . . Ray Allen Billington, "Frederick Jackson Turner: The Image and the Man," *Western Historical Quarterly* 3, no. 2 (April 1972): 137–52 (149). The original sources are letters from Turner to Mrs. William Hooper, July 16, 1913, and from Turner to Dorothy Turner, September 20, 1912, at the Huntington Library.

148 Sinclair Lewis' novel . . . James M. Hutchisson, "Introduction," *Babbitt* (New York: Penguin, 1922/1996), vii.

148 Like Babbitt himself . . . On pages 148–51, the quotations are from Sinclair Lewis, *Babbitt* (New York: Penguin, 1922/1996), 2–4, 12, 85, 242.

150 Their light is like . . . William Shakespeare, *Timon of Athens*, Act IV, scene 3. And in the foreword to Nabokov's *Pale Fire*, Kinbote tells the story of watching Shade burn the papers. It is here, from the porch, that we read his first use of "pale fire."

151 At least until . . . Lewis, *Babbitt*, 3.

157 Like Paul Cézanne . . . This photograph is *Cézanne at the Mont Sainte Victoire* by Kerr-Xavier Roussel in January 1906.

157 It asks for a way of seeing . . . Stéphane Mallarmé, "The Impressionists and Edouard Manet," *Art Monthly Review* 1, no. 9 (September 30, 1876): 117–22. This article was reprinted in *The New Painting: Impressionism, 1874–1886*, exh. cat., San Francisco and Washington, DC, 1986. In the essay, Mallarmé has borrowed "Each work should be a new creation of the mind" from Manet.

158 "nature is on the inside." . . . Maurice Merleau-Ponty quotes Paul Cézanne in his essay "Eye and Mind," in *The Merleau-Ponty Aesthetics Reader: Philosophy and Painting*, ed. Galen A. Johnson, trans. Carleton Dallery and Michael Smith (Evanston, IL: Northwestern University Press, 1993), 125.

158 "texture" . . . Merleau-Ponty, "Eye and Mind," 127.

158 And Merleau-Ponty also said . . . See Merleau-Ponty, "Eye and Mind," 142; and Maurice Merleau-Ponty, *The Visible and the Invisible*, trans. Alphonso Lingis (Evanston, IL: Northwestern University Press, 1968) 150.

163 She met their gaze . . . Marjorie Kinnan Rawlings, *Cross Creek* (New York: Simon and Schuster, 1996), 158.

164 I feel certain . . . Rawlings, *Cross Creek*, 266.

165 "The humming-birds come in . . ." . . . Rawlings, *Cross Creek*, 280.

CHAPTER 5

170 Such views . . . Rawlings, *Cross Creek*, 317–18.

172 "heavenly" . . . Wassily Kandinsky, *Concerning the Spiritual in Art*, trans. M. T. H. Sadler (New York: Dover, 1977), 38.

173 You can go back . . . Aloys John Maerz, *A Dictionary of Color* (New York: McGraw-Hill, 1930), 177.

174 And then in 1873 . . . Mary E. Nutting, "Robin's-Egg Blue," *Harper's New Monthly Magazine* (February 1873): 336.

174 Wrestling with my color choice . . . Gustave Moreau, quoted in Roger Benjamin, *Matisse's "Notes of a Painter": Criticism, Theory, and Context, 1891–1908* (Ann Arbor: UMI Research Press, 1987), 29.

175 A reporter once asked . . . Eudora Welty, *More Conversations with Eudora Welty*, ed. Peggy Whitman Prenshaw (Jackson: University Press of Mississippi, 1996), 86.

176 Like it holds grains . . . Hurston, *Their Eyes Were Watching God*, 15, 51.

176 "bright, transparent blue . . ." . . . Richard Savage, "The Wanderer," *The Poetical Works of Richard Savage* (New York: William A. Davis, 1805), 57. The previous line in Savage's poem prepares for a mix of blue and green: "All-cheering-green, that gives the spring its dye."

176 Welty's description . . . Welty, "The Winds," 211.

177 I am reminded that . . . John Burroughs, *Signs and Seasons* (New York: Houghton Mifflin, 1895), 247, 252.

178 Kandinsky knew very well . . . Kandinsky, *Concerning the Spiritual in Art*, 37–38.

178 "brown blues of evening." . . . Wallace Stevens, "Mrs. Alfred Uruguay," *The Collected Poems of Wallace Stevens* (New York: Vintage, 1990), 248.

179 Woodland Cemetery . . . The Swedish name for the cemetery located in Stockholm's southern district is Skogskyrkogården. I am using its English translation, "Woodland Cemetery," throughout. In 1994, the cemetery was named as a United Nations Educational, Scientific and Cultural Organization (UNESCO) World Heritage site. For its broader history, see Caroline Constant, *The Woodland Cemetery* (Stockholm: Byggförlaget, 1994).

180 one observer watched . . . Carl-Axel Acking, *Asplund*, ed. Claes Caldenby and Olof Hultin (New York: Rizzoli, 1986), 21. The scene describes the funeral on October 26, 1940.

186 One recent theory . . . David C. Lahti and Daniel R. Ardia, "Shedding Light on Bird Egg Color: Pigment as Parasol and the Dark Car Effect," *American Naturalist* 187, no. 5 (May 2016).

190 The philosopher reminds us . . . Merleau-Ponty, "Eye and Mind," 36.

191 Strand once said . . . Paul Strand, *Paul Strand: The World on My Doorstep, an Intimate Portrait*, ed. Catherine Duncan and Ute E. Skildsen (New York: Aperture, 1994), i.

191 "range of almost infinite tonal values." . . . Paul Strand, "Photography," *Camera Work* (June 1917): 3.

193 He called it . . . Alfred Stieglitz, "Our Illustrations," *Camera Work*, nos. 49/50 (June 1917): 36. In the series of photographs, it is the second-to-last plate, before another image from the porch—a closely cropped and widely shadowed assembly of bowls.

195 A reporter described . . . George Weston, September 16, 1920, report for Associated Press. On May 14, 1884, the street and the Federal Hall porch also hosted the panic of the failure of Grant and Ward brokerage firm.

200 "tricks of process . . ." . . . Strand, "Photography," 3.

202 definition of climate . . . Alexander von Humboldt defined climate as that which "indicates all the changes in the atmosphere which sensibly affect our organs, as temperature, humidity, variations in the barometrical pressure, the calm state of the air or the action of opposite winds, the amount of electric tension, the purity of the atmosphere or its admixture with more or less noxious gaseous exhalations, and, finally, the degree of ordinary transparency and clearness of the sky, which is not only important with respect to the increased radiation from the Earth, the organic development of plants, and the ripening of fruits, but also with reference to its influence on the feelings and mental condition of men" (*Cosmos: A Sketch of the Physical Description of the Universe*, vol. 1, trans. E. C. Otté [New York, 1877], 317–18).

202 Later that year . . . Strand, "Photography," 4.

204 That sleeping porch . . . Eudora Welty, *One Writer's Beginnings* (Cambridge, MA: Harvard University Press, 1984), 8.

CHAPTER 6

209 Soon after she first decamped . . . Harriet Beecher Stowe, *Life and Letters of Harriet Beecher Stowe*, ed. Annie Fields (Cambridge: Riverside Press, 1897), 336, 314.

210 "ideal webs . . ." . . . Harriet Beecher Stowe to George Eliot, February 8, 1872, in *The Life of Harriet Beecher Stowe* (New York: Houghton, Mifflin, 1890), 464. See also my article "Florida Porch Reverie" in *Florida Historical Quarterly* 90, no. 3 (2012): 324–30.

211 "How happily situated . . ." . . . William Bartram, *Travels through North and South Carolina, Georgia, East and West Florida* (Philadelphia: James and Johnson, 1791), 105.

211 Stowe echoed . . . Harriet Beecher Stowe, *Palmetto Leaves* (Gainesville: University of Florida Press, 1968), 155.

212 "the veranda is . . ." . . . Stowe, *The Life of Harriet Beecher Stowe*, 469.

219 Reading slowly . . . Wendell Berry, *A Timbered Choir* (Washington, DC: Counterpoint, 1998), 129, 168, 171, 177.

220 There on his *Gartenhaus* porch . . . Goethe, writing on May 3, 1776, quoted in George Henry Lewes, *The Life and Works of Goethe* (Boston: Ticknor and Fields, 1856), 378–79.

221 After steadily improving . . . Stowe, *Life and Letters*, 339.

221 gathering sun and offering shade . . . Berry, *A Timbered Choir*, 83. I have derived this phrasing from Berry's line: "Receiving sun and giving shade."

221 On a porch . . . Berry, *A Timbered Choir*, 201, 179.

221 Thirty years earlier . . . Wendell Berry, "The Porch over the River," *The Collected Poems* (San Francisco: North Point Press, 1985), 62–63.

223 "the natural forces . . ." . . . Wendell Berry, *The Unsettling of America* (San Francisco: Sierra Club Books, 1976), 130.

223 "landscape of harmony." . . . Wendell Berry, "Preserving Wildness," *Home Economics* (San Francisco: North Point Press, 1987), 151.

224 "Last night I slept . . ." . . . Goethe, writing again from the terrace on May 19, 1776, quoted in Lewes, *The Life and Works of Goethe*, 379.

224 "essential paradox," . . . Berry, *The Unsettling of America*, 130.

228 a method outlined . . . John Ruskin, *The Works of John Ruskin* (London: George Allen, 1904), 501.

229 When she described . . . Margaret Mead, *Letters from the Field* (New York: Harper and Row, 1977), 241.

229 This porch self-portrait . . . Gregory Bateson, photographer, *Margaret Mead and Gregory Bateson Working among the Iatmul*, Tambunam, 1938. Gelatin silver print, in the Manuscript Division of the Library of Congress (211a).

230 Here is the portrait . . . Alfred Eisenstaedt, *Rachel Carson in 1962*, National Portrait Gallery, Smithsonian Institution.

230 From its high porch . . . Rachel Carson, *Lost Woods: The Discovered Writing of Rachel Carson*, ed. Linda Lear (Boston: Beacon, 1998), 174, 115. In her book *Silent Spring* (New York: Houghton Mifflin), Carson included the reports of granules of aldrin being swept from the porches in Detroit (90).

231 In a letter to his sister . . . John Muir, Letter to Sarah Galloway, April 5, 1871, in *The Life and Letters of John Muir*, vol. 1, ed. William Frederic Badè (Boston: Houghton Mifflin, 1924), 246–49.

232 He described their nests . . . John Muir, *The Mountains of California* (New York: Century, 1894), 289.

232 They referred to . . . Ansel F. Hall, *Guide to Yosemite* (San Francisco: Sunset, 1920), 22.

234 "warbling, tinkling" . . . Muir, *The Life and Letters of John Muir*, 208.

236 There is a famous quotation . . . John Muir, *John of the Mountains: The Unpublished Journals of John Muir*, ed. Linnie Marsh Wolfe (Madison: University of Wisconsin Press, 1938/1979), 439.

237 In another letter to his sister . . . John Muir, Letter to Sarah Muir Galloway, March 24, 1870, *The Life and Letters of John Muir*, ed. William Frederic Badè (New York: Houghton Mifflin, 1924), 212.

237 If you have stretched . . . John Muir, Letter to David Gilrye Muir, March 20, 1870, *The Writings of John Muir*, ed. William Frederic Badè (New York: Houghton Mifflin, 1923), 210.

238 Along his thousand-mile walk . . . John Muir, *A Thousand-Mile Walk to the Gulf* (Boston: Houghton Mifflin, 1916), 139.

239 Undaunted, Muir returned . . . Muir, *The Mountains of California*, 278, 291.

Illustration Credits

All images provided by author, unless noted.

Page 51: Sleeping porch on the roof of the White House, Library of Congress, Prints and Photographs Division, LOT 12359–1C

Page 192: Paul Strand, *Porch Shadows*, Twin Lakes, Connecticut, 1916, silver platinum print, 32.8 × 24.4 cm, The Metropolitan Museum of Art / © Aperture Foundation, Inc., Paul Strand Archive

Page 201: Paul Strand, *Twin Lakes, Connecticut*, 1916, silver platinum print, 31.3 × 23.7 cm, The J. Paul Getty Museum, Los Angeles / © Aperture Foundation, Inc., Paul Strand Archive

Page 212: *Florida residents, Prof. and Mrs. H. B. Stowe*, 1875, The Miriam and Ira D. Wallach Division of Art, Prints and Photographs, The New York Public Library

Index

Page numbers in italics refer to figures.

abstraction, 145, 148, 155; climate and, 33; on porches, 200, 203, 254n; porch as laboratory for, 204–5; in Strand's porch photographs, 193–94, 197
acclimation, 4, 20, 31–34, 213, 239–42; minute, 154; penance and, 114; on porch, 24, 29, 32, 63, 215, 225; post-disaster, 219; risk and, 29. *See also* adaptation
Achilles, 72
acqua alta, 8
Acropolis, 85–91, 93, 226
Adams, John Quincy, 54–55
adaptation, 144, 213; architecture and, 26, 62; of mangroves, 17; mysteries of, 203
Aedes (mosquito), 142
aedis, 249n
Agee, James, 38, 39–42, 50, 55, 63
agora, 86, 90, 226–27
Alabama, 39, 55, 101, 246–47n
Alcinous (king), 71–72, 113

Algren, Nelson, 108–9
Allman Brothers, 102
All Saints' Eve, 112
Amazon (company), 25
American Farmer, 139
Amiens Cathedral, 228
anachronism, 4, 109
Angola, 122, 126
Anthropocene, 16
Antopolsky, Daniel, 102, 103
Aphrodite, 89
Arete (queen), 71–72
Aristotle, 12, 29
Arrephoroi, 88–90
Asplund, Gunnar, 179, 180
Astor, John Jacob, 6
Athena, 85, 87–88, 90, 91–93, 249n
Athens (Greece), 86–91, 93, 226, 249n
Attalos II (king), 226, 227
Auden, W. H., 68
aule, 113

Cohen, John, 95, 96–97
Coleridge, Samuel Taylor, 211
comfort, 29, 33, 213; of home, 59,
    237; limits of, 26, 219; on porch,
    33, 49–50, 72, 84, 97, 219–20; of
    porch light, 117, 122; risk and, 27,
    62, 240
compromise, architectural, 237;
    of porch screen, 121, 145–46,
    148, 151
Coolidge, Calvin, 55
Crosby, Stills and Nash, 102
Cross Creek (Florida), 50, 159, 164,
    170. See also Rawlings, Marjorie
    Kinnan
crypsis, 187
curiosity, 44, 185

Darwin, Charles, 186
daydream, 202. See also reverie
Derrida, Jacques, 248n, 250–51n
Destrehan Plantation, 105
Dewey, John, 27–29, 38
Dictionary of Color, A (Maerz),
    173, 174
Dione, 89
Disney World, 7
domesticity, 223
Doolittle, Amos, 194–95
Doonesbury (Trudeau), 56
drowned karst, 10, 48

eavesdropping, 26, 32, 84, 106–7
echo, 9, 72, 85, 182, 194, 227
ecliptic, 47, 63
ecology, 6, 92
edge, 4, 27, 54–55, 223, 238; of
    buildings, 24, 39, 52, 85–86,
    240; of catastrophe, 61; of
    house, 64, 67–68, 127–29,

208, 237; of knowledge, 147,
    223, 228–29; of mystery, 41; of
    porch, 5, 48, 126, 170, 212–13,
    240
Edison, Thomas, 6
Einstein, Albert, 101, 193, 250n
Eisenhower, Dwight, 56
Eisenstaedt, Alfred, 230
Eliot, George, 212
El Lissitzky, 135–36
Elorriaga, Ramón de, 195
Emerson, Ralph Waldo, 232
Eminem, 102
empathy, 197, 202
Enelysia, 87
entropy, 10, 152
"Epipsychidion" (Shelley), 234
Erechtheum, 85–93, 89, 105, 117
Evans, Walker, 39–42, 55, 63
Everglades, 215
experience, 4–5, 25–29, 33, 38–39,
    43; ephemeral, 54; reflection
    on, 158; thought and, 228, 238.
    See also Dewey, John

Fair Wind, A (Homer), 20
fall line, 124, 147
Faulkner, William, 21
Federal Hall (New York City),
    194–96, 254n
Fields, W. C., 101, 250n
Fisher, Irving, 52
Florida Supreme Court, 194
Fredericksburg (Virginia), 123, 124
frontier, 124, 138, 146, 211–12;
    climate, 208, 214, 241; of home,
    212, 223; of imagination, 219,
    221; porch, 27, 147–50, 212–13,
    231; retreat to, 236; screen as,
    119–20, 165

Gainesville (Florida), 131, 145
Gamble House, 60
Gartenhaus, 220, 224
Gedney, William, 104
Geiger, Rudolf, 68–69, 248n
ghost, 111–12, 117, 250n
ghost note, 103
Glass House, 240
global warming, 215, 245n
Goethe, Johann Wolfgang von, 220, 224
golden hour, 47, 115–17
Grant, Ulysses S., 101
Granta, 16
Greene and Greene, 60
Greengard, Harold, 196–97
Gulf of Mexico, 3, 6, 16–18, 136, 238
Gullah, 172

habitat, 7; degradation, 225; of screen, 154, 163
"habitat climate," 69
Halcomb, Mary Jane, 96
Halcomb, Roscoe, 96–97
Half Dome, 231–32
Halloween, 23, 112
Harper's (magazine), 174
Hector, 72–73
Hell Gate (Homosassa River), 8, 17, 46, 95
Heraclitus, 29
Hermes, 73
Highway 98 (Florida), 131, 237
historic preservation, 124, 125
Hoban, James, 54
home, 4, 54–55, 75, 107, 236–37. *See also* frontier; hospitality; nature

Homer, 72, 74–75, 85, 107, 248–49n
Homer, Winslow, 6, 15, 19–20, 95, 208
Homosassa River, 3, 6–8, 19, 239
hospitality, 72–73, 117, 219, 248n; as acclimation, 101, 111; guests on porch, 70–71; home and, 177; of porch light, 75; and porch's paradox, 250–51n
hostis, 250n
How to Live (Fisher), 52
Humboldt, Alexander von, 202, 254n
Hurricane Andrew, 61, 215, 218
Hurricane Easy, 13
Hurricane Hermine, 3, 13, 213
Hurston, Zora Neale, 50, 97–98, 101, 105–6, 176

Iliad (Homer), 72
imagination, 127, 191, 225–26; as acclimation, 220, 225; aerial, 190, 200; color and, 174, 186. *See also* blue, for porch ceiling; frontier impressionism, 157. *See also* Monet, Claude
Insect Wire Screening Bureau, 142–43, 144
introspection, 149, 164, 190
Irving, Washington, 112
Island Belle, 238

Jacksonville (Florida), 209, 211
Johnson, Dwayne, 249n
Johnson, Philip, 240
Joy of Cooking (band), 102
J. P. Morgan and Company, 194, 196

Stone, Edward Durrell, 126
Storm of the Century, 93. *See also*
   No Name Storm
storytelling, 5, 84–101, 108–9, 134.
   See also portraiture
Stowe, Calvin, 210, 213, 220, 224,
   225. *See also* Stowe, Harriet
   Beecher
Stowe, Harriet Beecher, 209–15,
   212, 220, 223–25, 238, 242
Strand, Paul, 191–99, 192, 200–
   203, 201, 204–5
Sweden, 178, 182, 184
synesthesia, 172

Taft, William, 51–52, 54
Tallahassee (Florida), 194
Tambunum (Papua New Guinea),
   229
Tampa (Florida), 16, 47, 106
Telemachus, 73, 74
Temple of Portunis, 184
That High Lonesome Sound (Co-
   hen), 97
Their Eyes Were Watching God
   (Hurston), 105–6, 176
Theoclymenus, 111–12
Theocritus, 249n
Theory of General Relativity, 193
Theseus' ship, 11–12, 241
Thoreau, Henry David, 4, 67–68,
   146–47, 148
threshold, 29, 42, 158, 184, 203;
   aqueous, 172; of comfort, 49;
   porch as, 24, 75, 131, 215, 224,
   230
Tiffany Blue, 174
Tiger Tail (Seminole Chief), 95
Tiger Tail Bay (Florida), 46
Timbered Choir, A (Berry), 219

time, 152; frozen, 63, 98, 102; marking, 79, 103, 241; measuring, 19,
   24, 57; narrative, 99; real-, 25,
   43, 142; slow, 166; stretched, 77;
   telling, 154
timelessness, 19, 122
To Kill a Mockingbird (Lee), 98–
   99, 100, 107
Tower of the Winds, 91, 92
traces, of porches, 123–24
Trees and Houses (Cézanne), 158
trompe l'oeil, 178
Trudeau, Gary, 56
Truman, Harry, 55, 56
tuning, 29, 32–33, 185, 218, 224;
   to changes in climate, 5, 214;
   person and place, 22, 103,
   246n
Turner, Frederick Jackson, 147–48,
   224
tympanon, 9
tympanum, 9, 169
Tyndall, John, 91

Uncle Tom's Cabin (Stowe), 209

Van Zandt, Townes, 102–3
veiling reflection, 154–55, 161–62
Venice (Florida), 16
Venice (Italy), 8
Vladivostok (Russia), 128, 135

Walden, 146. *See also* Thoreau,
   Henry David
Wall Street (Strand), 194, 196
wandering line, 21, 26, 117
Washington, DC, 52, 55, 195
Washington, George, 194, 196
weathering, 37–38, 57, 120, 124,
   240. *See also* patina

266 INDEX

weaving, 140; air and light, 91, 233. *See also* screen mesh

Welty, Christian, 204

Welty, Eudora, 69–70, 117, 175–77, 204–5

West Hollywood (California), 102, 233

White House, porches of, 54–55, 138; roof, 50, 51, 56; Sky Parlor, 55; Solarium, 56; Truman Balcony, 55

wilderness, 28, 175, 223

wildness, 146, 222–25

Wilson, Woodrow, 50, 53

witnessing, 2, 117, 208, 241

wonder, 5, 27, 186, 231

Woodland Cemetery, 179–84, 253n; Path of the Seven Wells, 179–80, 181, 183; porch of Monument Hall, 179–80; porch of Resurrection Chapel, 178–86

Works Progress Administration, 98

World War I, 193

World War II, 25, 28

Wright, Frank Lloyd, 240

Xanadu (Coleridge), 211

xenia, 72, 111, 117. *See also* hospitality

Yearling, The (Rawlings), 49, 60

Yosemite, 231–34, 237–39

Zeno, 227, 228, 231

Zeus, 87